Praise for *Coins in the Fountain*

"You don't need Audrey Hepburn and Gregory Peck to enjoy this delightful Roman holiday…Armchair-travel books are rarely as good as this one."

—*Kirkus Reviews*

"Wide-eyed with wonder, Judith Works takes us on an extended Roman holiday, learning to laugh and love la vita bella. Tag along as she's introduced to grappa and guanciale, puntarelle and priest stranglers. A delicious life, indeed."

—Nancy Leson, Seattle's voice of food and fun

"Coins in the Fountain celebrates the traveler in all of us. It's a beautifully descriptive memoir, a snapshot of life in Rome that tantalizes the senses and makes one long for another visit to The Eternal City."

—Jennifer Criswell, author of *At Least You're in Tuscany*

"Wry, witty, wonderfully evocative. A must-read if you're moving to Rome, or just dreaming about it."

—K.S.R. Burns, author of *The Paris Effect*

"Judith Works so humbly captures the discomfiting realities of culture immersion that as a reader I wanted to jump inside the pages and explore for myself what it means to be an expatriate in Italy. *Coins in the Fountain* is for dreamers and explorers, food lovers and art aficionados. Recommend!"

—Sarah Kishpaugh, author of *The Shame of Losing*

"*Coins in the Fountain* gives us all the details—positive and negative—of living in Rome as an expat: the neighborhoods, the majestic monuments, the chaotic traffic, the difficulties of coping with cultural differences. Judith Works' memoir is a must-read for all who dream of a season in the Eternal City and a delightful déjà vu for those who are living the dream."

—Mary Jane Cryan: historian, author, cruise lecturer,
and 50-year resident of Italy

"Judith Works lands a dream job in Rome, and suddenly, she and her husband's casual conversations about someday living in Europe turn into reality. Almost nothing goes as expected, from the office politics to life inside their postwar apartment building with its elevator barely big enough for two. Works deftly uses food, history, and travel to describe the expat life. The "real" Rome, she discovers, is chaotic, energizing, frustrating, and romantic in ways most tourists never get to experience."

—Carol Pucci, travel writer/photographer/blogger

"In the captivating memoir, *Coins in the Fountain*, a bored government worker and mom from Portland, Oregon becomes a United Nations attorney based in Rome, Italy. Judith Works offers insight into life in Rome during her two sojourns, beginning in the late eighties. Readers will be enthralled with fascinating history and stories of magnificent food, fashion, and friends. Judith's travel stories within Italy, to other European countries, and to Africa are intriguing, but I was most riveted by her work with the UN World Food Programme which conveyed Judith from the ruins of Cambodia to a refugee camp in Kenya, bordering Sudan. Readers will be charmed by Works' countless adventures and misadventures in this lovely memoir of a world far from home."

—E. C. Murray, author of *A Long Way from Paris*

COINS
IN THE
FOUNTAIN

A MIDLIFE ESCAPE
TO ROME

Judith

JUDITH WORKS

Published by Gemelli Press
9600 Stone Avenue North
Seattle, Washington 98103

Cover design and typesetting by Enterline Design Services LLC

ISBN: 978-0-9864390-9-4
Library of Congress Control Number: 2016900045
Originally Published in 2011

To Glenn, who continues to give me a *dolce vita*

"All these things without the assistance of the gods
and fortune could not have been."
—Marcus Aurelius, *Meditations*

PART ONE

RUNNING AWAY TO THE CIRCUS MAXIMUS

I

The celebrations to mark the new millennium were over and it was time to leave Rome.

My husband, Glenn, and I sat on the sofa while the movers carefully packed our last purchases and remaining clothes in layer upon layer of white paper. It was the final act at the end of our second tour in Italy, one that lasted six short years. The rest of our material goods were already in a shipping container waiting to be transported "home," a concept that after so many years in Italy had taken on a somewhat uncertain meaning. Geographically it was to be a small town near Seattle, but in my heart I knew home would always remain Rome. We now favored pasta over potatoes, stylish clothes and strappy sandals (for me, anyway) instead of gray fleece and tennis shoes, and Vino Nobile di Montepulciano rather than beer. Our conversation was peppered with Italian words when we couldn't recall the English equivalent, and visits to our once and future Pacific Northwest home were remembered for the dreary weather and excruciatingly slow drivers.

My contract as a human resource manager for the United Nations World Food Programme was completed and family beckoned. Glenn was content to give up the charms and challenges of Italy for a more settled life, but I was anxious. Losing my friends, work, and country, however temporary it had all been, was a large dose of change to manage at one time. Already starting the transition, we moved out of our home for the last six years when the rental contract expired a month earlier. We were now perched in an apartment on the Aventine Hill, house-sitting while the regular renters were on leave in Quebec.

When the movers departed they presented us with a bottle of prosecco in thanks for the business. While we sipped we tried to look into a cloudy crystal ball (in reality our smudged wine glasses) in a vain attempt to see the future. We soon gave up, turning back instead to thoughts of the events that had shaped our lives. Immediately coming to mind were those of the first months in the Eternal City on our initial Italian sojourn. It began on the same Aventine Hill.

"Do you remember?" Glenn asked.

"How could I forget?" I answered.

• • •

"Hey! What are you doing? STOP that!!"

I sprang up from the floor where I was lounging on a deflated air mattress and rushed into what was supposed to be our dining room in the echoing, still-empty apartment. Why was Glenn shouting? I found the answer when I saw my normally mild-mannered husband hanging out the window yelling at a group of nuns in their crisp black-and-white habits as they dumped wheelbarrows filled with garbage into the open space behind our building. They looked up briefly. Then, paying no further attention to the outraged foreigner, they finished their work and swished off toward an unseen convent.

It was Saturday morning, a month after I'd started with the UN on a four-year contract. We stayed in a hotel on the Aventine Hill for the first two weeks after our arrival in Rome and then in a new colleague's apartment for another two weeks while he was back in California. Now, at the unsettled beginning of our second month, we were tired and cranky. We'd been sleeping on the living room floor on a bed of flattened cardboard cartons that originally held an air mattress, a few dishes, pots and pans, two folding chairs, an old card table, and some clothes. These items comprised our air shipment, meant to tide us over until the shipping container arrived by sea a couple of months later. The air mattress we hoped to use over the cardboard had slowly and irreparably deflated, paralleling our naïve enthusiasm for the whole adventure of a move to romantic Italy.

We had been anxious to find a home. The hotel was expensive and my settlement allowance was running out. The American Embassy located apartments for its staff, but my new office offered no assistance. The rental agents we contacted from newspaper ads had nothing satisfactory to offer, nor did the few ads on an office bulletin board. Word of mouth eventually led us to another agent, a disagreeable American who made her living finding apartments for greenhorns like us with minimum effort on her part. She insisted that we take the bus to the apartments she suggested, leaving us scrambling to find buildings in unfamiliar locations and waiting until she drove up at her leisure and parked her car on the sidewalk. Worse, after she signed us up we began to hear stories circulating in the gossipy expatriate community that was welcoming us. One story in particular made us especially cautious about the woman: several years before our arrival, Marge invited a client for lunch at her own apartment, which was filled with cats and their untended litter boxes. After a microwaved meal of fettuccine Alfredo, she announced that she had an appointment and left, locking the man inside. He was trapped with the cats. After waiting an hour, he managed to signal a neighbor on an adjoining balcony who reluctantly let him climb over the railings to escape an unknown fate.

We weren't subjected to such dramatic events, but then again, Marge hadn't shown us anything livable either with her numerous dark and dilapidated suggestions. At the point when we were getting agitated she finally produced an attractive solution that we later heard was yet another apartment where she had resided. Our proposed new home had large windows on both sides of one end of a small family-owned building. It also came with a telephone—a bonus, as it often took a year to have one installed (this was just before cell phones became widely available). Best of all, there were two balconies on one side and a sunny terrace opening off the master bedroom and living room on the other. The outdoor spaces were the real attraction for migrants from a cloudy home near Portland, Oregon.

We nodded to Marge in agreement. The next day she and the owner came to my office after work to present two contracts, both in Italian. The only part Glenn and I could read was the rental rate. The first document showed the low, legally allowable amount. The second was for the remaining exorbitant amount that we paid. Needless to say, the first document would be used for tax purposes. I signed as the breadwinner, and handed over a pile of cash to our new landlord and another to our agent. After we shook hands, we were given a bunch of huge keys, the type one would expect to be used in an old monastery or castle dungeon. The place was ours. Before Marge walked off fondling her commission, she offered some advice: "Always buy De Cecco pasta."

Early fall, and it was still hot. I tried to focus on a remark by the ancient Roman orator Seneca: "Travel and change of place impart new vigor to the mind." Well, I always wanted to have a change of place, and now my wish had come true. But sometimes mental exhaustion was a more common sensation than new vigor as my brain tried to get organized to meet the dramatic changes in my life.

Our nights were spent lying awake on the floor contemplating my job, the antics of the nuns, and the difficulties of getting settled. Packs of incessantly barking dogs left behind when their owners went on vacation provided a background to our thoughts. Adding to the noise, eerie sirens like those in World War II movies split the night air. We squirmed on the flat, sweaty air mattress while considering our decision-making skills—deciding to leave secure jobs for a flight into fantasy. *Mamma mia!* What had we done to ourselves?

II

Why exactly were we sweating in an empty Roman apartment? As I roamed around our new home in the middle of the night, perspiring and worrying about the decision to come to Italy, I paused to look out the window of what was to be our dining room if our furniture ever arrived. In the distance I could see a glowing green sign advertising the national airline, Alitalia. Like a statue of Mercury that fired my travel dreams as a child, the airline promised travel, the answer to my question, "Why are we in Rome?"

Interest in Alitalia came late but Mercury figured early on when I met his statue in the library of my parents' social club. The Roman protector of travelers I looked at as a child wore winged sandals on one end and a traveler's hat on the other with nothing in between to protect him from Portland's dreary elements. Balancing one delicate foot on the breath of the wind while carrying a snake-entwined winged staff for protection, his lithe body appeared to fly through the ether as he went about his rounds. When not circling the statue to inspect his interesting anatomy, I looked at travel magazines and the latest issue of *National Geographic* while I waited for my parents to finish their drinks at the club's bar before collecting me on their way to the dining room.

I dreamed that maybe someday I would have an interesting life like the people pictured in the magazines riding in Venetian gondolas, digging up lost treasures in the Egyptian desert, or studying bare-breasted black women sporting a few strategically placed beads. But since it was Oregon in the 1950s, my only other contact with Mercury and his duties was looking at his logo on the doors of florist shops where he symbolized speedy delivery of flowers. I dutifully ate meat, potatoes, and overcooked brussel sprouts while wearing midcentury modern: pointy bras, tight sweaters, circle skirts, and white buck shoes. Later, as expected in those pre–Betty Friedan days, I married my high school sweetheart and temporarily dropped out of college. Daughter Kathryn arrived in due course.

Portland wasn't an exciting place to live. Despite occasional travel to Canada and Mexico, I was never satisfied, although what I was looking for was undefined other than wanting to travel ever farther. Suffering from the traveler's curse, where there is always another place to see, I tried to talk my husband into a round-the-world freighter trip. It didn't work. Next, it was a move to Washington, DC. No dice. Finally I nagged him into a three-week grand tour of European capitals. But the long-awaited trip turned out not to be so grand at all. By the time we arrived in Rome I finally realized that my increasingly distant and grouchy husband kept slipping into phone booths to call his office at times that it was unlikely to be open.

"Why are you calling your office?"

"Don't bother me. It's none of your business anyway. You're annoying me with your questions."

The net result was a divorce as soon as we returned. He rapidly married his phone companion, a non-traveler. I popped off on a cruise to Mexico to assuage my hurt feelings.

Glenn made his first appearance a year after the breakup, at our mutual workplace, the US Forest Service. "Dave asked me to buy you a drink," he ventured when we were seated at the same table at a boring meeting. I knew Dave but who was this guy? I looked at him: wiry and handsome with one eye green and the other brown. Well, why not give it a chance, I thought. What's one drink anyway? It was a gimlet, and it changed my life.

We clicked together like magnets. Kathryn also took to him and that clinched the deal. It wasn't long before we married and he adopted her. Soon after, we set off on regular escapes whenever we had vacation time. Our European visits were especially appealing, although when planning the itinerary I avoided Rome, always remembering that it was the culmination of a dream trip that turned out to be a nightmare presaging the acrimonious split. Besides that, it was dusty and noisy. I never wanted to see Rome again.

Glenn and I were sitting on the terrace of a café in Normandy on our second European venture. Over a glass of Sancerre we looked at each other and simultaneously remarked that it would be interesting to actually live in Europe. Our departure after two weeks of museums, food, and wine was bittersweet as usual—we were unable to imagine that we could ever experience the good life for more than a few weeks at a time. Meanwhile, back at work, where I was being insufficiently entertained troubleshooting endless staff problems, I looked around for something to keep my brain in gear. I settled on evening law school at Lewis and Clark College in Portland without any overt goal other than getting a JD and avoiding the onset of midlife ennui.

Starting each day with a mugful of espresso, I'd charge out the door at 6:00 a.m. for work, rush to the law library at 5:00, then to class. Three years later I had my degree with honors. I spent the summer evenings studying for the bar exam. I passed. Now what? Eighty-hour weeks grinding away in a law office wasn't appealing, nor was medical school: blood put me off. But boredom began to loom again. Something else needed to happen.

Not long after, a former coworker showed up at a party. When I asked where he had been for so long, he grinned as he answered, "Rome." He'd been on a program the American government established to allow its employees to work for international organizations. My ears pricked up when he regaled guests with stories about working for the Food and Agriculture Organization of the United Nations. Located in Rome? The home of fabulous food that I never tasted when I was there for three days? This was interesting news. I thought that the United Nations was only in New York. When he recounted stories about travel, opera, great meals, and fascinating people, my mind cycled back to my only visit—the one with husband number one. Could what I was now hearing possibly be true?

Despite being enchanted as a teenager by the romantic film *Three Coins in a Fountain*, set in a Rome replete with fountains, mellow-colored buildings, happy natives, and no traffic, the city I encountered on that dreadful trip was hot and dirty, the dust of ages settling over everything, including me and the phone booths. I retained only one lovely sight in my memory: the gilded bronze equestrian statue of Emperor Marcus Aurelius, which my guidebook said was cast in AD 175. The emperor had overlooked the center of Rome from his pedestal set in Michelangelo's Piazza del Campidoglio since 1538. When I visited he was enduring the indignity of small cars and motorcycles driving around him at furious speeds while blowing exhaust fumes in his face. Despite this affront, he continued to stretch out his hand, blessing the passing scene. I hoped to be included in this gesture of goodwill, but evidence of my husband's distaste for me and the whole trip, argued to the contrary. After three days of a Roman circus I didn't throw any coins into the Trevi Fountain in the hope of romance. I had no intention of returning to the city, as had the happy stars in the movie.

Now my former colleague was describing a different city. He didn't say anything about dirt and disorder, a third-rate hotel, or the stale, limp food-truck pizza smeared with a tablespoon of tomato sauce—pizza I ate while watching others digging into bowls of pasta on vine-draped restaurant terraces. Was the old movie accurate, after all?

After hearing my tale of boredom, he said that he was still in touch with Rome and knew about a vacancy in human resources requiring a law degree. He suggested that I apply. After some brief family discussions, I sent in an application in one of those "what the hell, why not" moments.

Several weeks later the telephone rang at four in the morning. Worried that an elderly relative had died, I jumped up to answer. Rather than bad news, a nice English voice said, "I'm calling from Rome. Would you like to come for an interview?" My eyes snapped open as I whooped, "Yes!" The noise woke Glenn and we sat up for the remainder of the night drinking coffee and considering the possibilities. He didn't want to have wasted years making vats of espresso and vacuuming around me while the cat and I studied, both of us barricaded by law books on the carpet near a sunny window. Kathryn was out of the nest and I had the possibility of achieving a lifelong dream to be somewhere else. It wasn't Paris—but then it wasn't Ouagadougou either.

The interview consisted of a short chat in Seattle, presumably to see that I didn't have two heads and could string a sentence together. I learned that the long title of the agency was abbreviated to FAO or "faouw," as it was pronounced in Italian. I was handed a couple of brochures about FAO's mission, but otherwise it remained a mystery. Shortly after, a second call came—come to Rome for another interview. The transatlantic portion of the flight on Alitalia was filled with Italians. I was worried when they crossed themselves as we sped down the runway for takeoff. Their relief when we landed was also heartfelt as they applauded our safe arrival. I joined in the congratulatory atmosphere. I'd made it this far.

Rome wasn't the dusty city I remembered. Instead, it was pouring, the ground so waterlogged the umbrella pines were falling over. In contrast to the unpleasant weather, the interviews were relaxed and friendly and all seemed to be going in a positive direction. I was rather pleased with myself. Despite the rain but without my first husband, Rome now looked attractive with its ochre-colored buildings and ancient monuments. I might be heading for a more exciting life, a Roman holiday, if we could make arrangements on the US end.

Back home after three days, it should have been time for some hard thinking about our future, but when there was only silence from FAO we put a move out of mind except for the occasional desultory conversation starting with, "I wonder what ever happened . . . ?" Four months passed before another call came—come back to Rome. More managers and directors wanted to interview me. To ensure a stunning impression on the second round, I bought an expensive linen suit from Nordstrom, hoping to present a *bella figura* to sway a new platoon of interrogators.

III

I arrived back in Rome assuming that I was a cosmopolitan traveler, seeing that this was my second business-class excursion to Europe in one year. The *pensione* booked for me this time around, however, was shabby. Neither the aged British ladies who owned it nor the room, slightly less spartan than the convent cell reserved for me on the first interview trip, had been updated since the end of World War II. Dinner was *en famille*, starting with pasta served with half as much sauce as we slopped on at home. Despite the lack of sauce, the meal was seasoned with lively conversation from my tablemates, who all seemed to be either agricultural experts on their way to or from Africa or Asia, or Irish couples planning their weddings. I rapidly realized I was back on Earth with nothing interesting to say to the self-assured fellow eaters.

My rosy view of the stimulating guests vanished when, in the middle of the first night, I woke up to the sound of a key turning the lock on my room door. A man entered. I gasped with fright, unable to scream, while watching him standing in the light of the full moon shining through the open window. He was silent for a minute or two before excusing himself in English and shutting the door. Wide awake with my heart pounding, I got up to visit the shared bathroom at the far end of the hallway. The toilet room floor was covered with water (at least I hoped it was water), and men's dirty underwear hung on the bidet. I walked on my heels in an attempt to avoid the unknown substance lapping at my toes through my flimsy slippers.

The next morning, with little sleep and bags under red eyes, and with my new suit looking as if I'd packed it in an accordion—it fell off the garment-bag hanger during the flight—I shambled off to the breakfast room. I had no idea how to reach the office from this location, so I picked out the best-looking man in the room (not my intruder, I hoped) and asked if he was going to FAO. If so, could he give me directions?

He introduced himself as a climate expert working for a UN organization in Nairobi. He was in town for a meeting and, yes, he would be glad to accompany me. We picked our way over the Caelian Hill, one of the seven, through a park filled with wildflowers and marble chunks from the Roman Empire. From there, we walked past a military hospital and several old churches before we came to the main road, in ancient times the start of the Appia Antica. Instead of chariots, I was confronted with a seething mass of small cars and motorcycles maneuvering in crazed rush-hour traffic separating us from the FAO headquarters. We bobbed and weaved across the cobbles like football players heading for the goal and made it to the entrance unbruised. But the trial by fire had yet to begin.

This second set of Roman interviews took on an entirely different flavor. Instead of my new suit making a stunning impression, I was the one stunned. When I arrived in the office, my potential supervisor was practically wringing his hands while he briefed me on who I was to meet and what, and what not, to say. I found my way from office to office where senior executives grilled me with glee. One interview included table pounding, demanding that I agree that I would offer up what was wanted in the way of legal opinions despite any caution or advice I might have to the contrary. Personal opinions wouldn't be appreciated. The table bounced with the impact of my interlocutor's fist. It was obvious that something was going amiss, but the more my potential betters threw down their gauntlets the more I wanted the job. *I'll show them*, I thought.

Many questions about night law school were posed. It was a concept unheard of in Italy or anywhere else. Simultaneously working and attending class confirmed deep suspicions that something was peculiar about me. One interviewer asked what was my worst fault. (I briefly contemplated saying, "nagging" or "ask my husband.") Another, a French senior executive, informed me that I could not possibly get along in an international environment because I was an American, and even worse, a female. Then he said:

"It was brave of you to apply for this post."

Me: "Why?"

Snotty Frenchman: "Because I see that you are about to be fired for incompetence."

Me: "What? You must be kidding. My outstanding performance has been recognized. Look again at the application!" (NOT said: "Can't you read?")

He backed off and looked at the application again. By this time it was the lunch hour-and-a-half *à la Romana* and I was unceremoniously left alone to find a place to eat in the building complex. No one wanted to be seen with me; another sign of displeasure. I had gathered up more pamphlets about FAO between interviews and propped them up in front of me, trying to remain incognito while I ate the same salad that other people were ordering—lettuce, mozzarella, hardboiled egg, and tuna fish, with lots of olive oil and salt. The salad was good but no one else was eating alone.

The ordeal resumed unabated in the afternoon. By the time eight hours of torture were completed I looked like my suit: tired, limp, and wrinkled. The most important lesson I came away with was not to buy linen for interviews.

As I disconsolately left the building I ran into my morning guide. He took pity on me for a second time, suggesting a drink at a bar facing the Colosseum. We sat outside in mellow late afternoon sunshine watching a postcard view of that eternal symbol of Rome. Despite feeling like one of the Christians who'd been thrown to the lions, the sight of the ancient building still standing after two millennia cheered me up after the day's disaster. The wine helped too. He wouldn't let me pay, but did ask if I had an extra bag he could use for his flight back to Kenya the next day. I offered him the garment bag that failed my suit. At the last minute, while he was standing in my doorway with his hand outstretched for the bag, I made one final check and came across yesterday's panties tucked away in the bottom. Snatching them back, I thought of leaving them on the bidet as a token of esteem for the guests who shared the bath. But, being cheap, I packed them home.

What *un flop*, as the Italians say—I was home so fast I didn't have time to get jet lag and didn't expect to hear anything further, let alone ever see the Colosseum again. Rome seemed to have it in for me.

Time slowly passed once more. Perhaps my assumptions about a new life were wrong and I would be condemned to continue the same well-worn track after all. Then, while I was at a meeting in Atlanta four months later, one of the office staff interrupted the group to say that Rome was calling. I scrambled to the phone. Would I accept a four-year contract and come to work the following week? I was calling Glenn in a nanosecond.

Our friends and relations were aghast. Had we both suffered some sort of brain malfunction? Many believed that the UN was part of the American State Department, confusing UN with US. A few were sure that black helicopters could be sent to ferry foreign troops to take over the US government at any moment. They were all pretty hazy on Rome too. Wasn't that where women didn't shave under their arms or take showers? No, wait, that was France. Or, possibly Spain?

Kathryn, who by this time had finished law school and was clerking for the Oregon Appeals Court while studying for the bar examination, gave us a different opinion. Envisioning unlimited trips to Europe at our expense, she asked how soon we were running away to join the Circus Maximus.

As Dante described in the opening lines of *The Inferno*, we had reached the middle of the journey of our lives and the way ahead wasn't clear. Which road to take? Stay home and whine about boredom or leap into the unknown? Which Rome would we experience? The one of my first visit with dust and chaos, or the one my former colleague so vividly described with art, music, and perfect lunches in hill towns? This was our big chance to find out, and we were sure there would never be another.

When I learned that I would have the same opportunity for leave from my government job as our friend who first told us about working in Rome, the gods smiled again and produced a staff cutback that made Glenn eligible for an early retirement from his Forest Service civil engineering job. While not having obsessive daydreams about living abroad, he was open to adventure and agreed that it would be interesting to move to Europe and try a new lifestyle, far different from the one he had experienced so far. From high steel and tunnel-boring work, he moved into forest road and trail design and construction, often horse-packing into the Northwest high country for long periods of time, and he had spent more time that he ever wished fighting forest fires. So, he cheerfully agreed to hang up his caulk boots and hard hat, the one with the bullet hole—a remnant from some long-ago target practice that made him look pretty tough. He began to picture himself lounging on the Via Veneto wearing trendy sunglasses, a full wine glass in hand.

Fate was propelling us to Italy. I accepted the offer.

After negotiating a more realistic report date, we sold the house. I bought an Italian dictionary, a biography of the Borgias (did I subconsciously expect to be poisoned by the vengeful Frenchman from the second job interview?), and a new Michelin guide to Rome. I couldn't find anyone to give us Italian lessons in such a short period of time, so as a substitute we viewed a large number of Italian neorealist movies that scared us witless with their black-and-white postwar angst. We also watched Federico Fellini's *La Dolce Vita*, his 1960 story of the search for meaning in decadent and materialistic Rome. Like *Three Coins in the Fountain*, the Trevi Fountain scene was nice, but what did it all mean for us? Would we become as jaded as Marcello Mastroianni? Would I luxuriate in the rushing waters of the fountain as had Anita Ekberg? The answers to these questions would be revealed later. Meanwhile, we watched the movers pack our furniture into a shipping container. They were extremely careless, but we were too distracted to do anything about it.

As the plane took off, we clinked our champagne glasses together in a toast to our new life. Hours later, when we awoke from a nap on the second leg, we pulled up the window shades to see red-tiled roofs, a sparkling blue sea, and the vestiges of Ostia Antica, the ancient Roman port, as we descended into Leonardo da Vinci airport. A new life was beginning.

FAO arranged for us to stay in a small hotel located on the Aventine Hill, another of the storied seven. The hotel was set in umbrella pines, oleanders, cypresses, and orange and palm trees. Nearby embassies and villas were painted ochre and Pompeian red with green shutters. Roman ruins were scattered about and ancient churches with their melodious bells called to us. Up the street was a piazza designed by Piranesi in 1765. On one side was a view of St. Peter's through the keyhole of a garden gate, an entrance to the headquarters of the Knights of Malta. The beautiful neighborhood was an ideal welcome to Rome.

The hotel's courtyard had an outdoor breakfast area that turned into a bar in the evenings. After dinner we sat outside listening to the visiting agricultural experts talk about their work and trying to learn some Italian from the barman. He rapidly decided that we needed help—a decision that didn't take much effort on his part. After the basics like *buongiorno*, he moved on to a word that he was certain all Americans would want to know: *ghiaccio*, ice, which only Americans put in drinks. I didn't care about ice. The words I really wanted to know were, "How much does it cost?" and, "Do you have these shoes in my size?" It was only much later that I achieved such an elevated level of discourse.

The evenings also brought back thoughts of Marcus Aurelius, whom I briefly met in a college philosophy class. The emperor's *Meditations*, in which he lays out his Stoic philosophy, reflect his belief in fate, reason, logic, and the concept of doing one's duty with fortitude and patience. The first thing we'd done on arriving at the hotel was to march off to the Campidoglio so that I could show Glenn his statue, the one pleasant memory of my first visit to Rome. It was gone, the pedestal empty.

IV

Marcus Aurelius had disappeared, taking with him what I hoped would be a blessing on our new endeavor. Real life was at hand and it was immediately clear that boredom would not be one of our problems. Two days after our arrival, I began bringing home the bacon, or since it was Italy, *pancetta*. Glenn began his retirement by trying to get our life organized, exploring the residential areas of Rome to look for an apartment, and learning how to shop and use the transit system. It was a toss-up as to who was working harder.

Facing the unknown, I felt a frisson of anxiety as I walked in the entrance to the complex of five FAO buildings just across the street from the Circus Maximus. A clerk was sent to collect me. She escorted me to a room where I signed the oath of office requiring that my loyalties would be to the United Nations, not to the United States. That gave me pause but I was committed, having signed the contract. When I found my new office, a glamorous Italian woman, long of hair and short of skirt, paused in her personal telephone conversation to say hello. Then she hung up and said, "Tell me, what was the date and time of day when you were born?"

"Why?" I asked.

"So I can cast your horoscope."

She was visibly disappointed when I mumbled that I didn't know the time. But after a brief pause, she brightened up and firmly informed me that she and my new supervisor were going to celebrate his birthday with a long lunch at the Sheraton Hotel, which was miles away, and that I should not expect her back that afternoon. And she didn't come back until the following day. Round One went to her.

I was dumbfounded by this inauspicious start. With no work to do and my supervisor, Jean-Jacques, and office assistant, Paola, living it up, I spent the remainder of the first day worrying again about what I had gotten myself into, shuffling some papers, and idly watching a huge demonstration outside the window. The thousands of stylishly dressed protestors marched along a wide tree-lined avenue. They chanted and waved red flags and banners of solidarity against some government action. Communists! I felt like joining their party.

At the start of the second day work life picked up. Paola showed up (late). Jean-Jacques invited me for coffee, neither of us bringing up the previous day's events. Managers stopped by. What was my opinion on a new manual section on one arcane subject after another, would I start a disciplinary action against some presumed wrongdoer, or did this person's problems make him eligible to receive a disability pension? How they expected any advice from me after one day on the job was either an unwarranted vote of confidence or an attempt to demonstrate that I didn't know anything, which was obviously the case. I met my legal assistant, Johann, who, contrary to Paola, was very quiet and reticent. Meetings were arranged. I rummaged through the office safe, which held files on disciplinary cases and appeals. Someone asked me to lunch.

I slowly became organized and started looking around. Nothing looked anything like a Forest Service ranger station with its rustic architecture and rustic staff. FAO's main building was a product of Mussolini's grandiose ambitions. Begun in 1938 as the Ministry of Italian Africa, it was built of brilliant white marble and travertine to house the administrators of *Il Duce*'s conquests. The beautiful garden was filled with umbrella pines, oleanders, and other flowering shrubs, along with acanthus plants, whose graceful leaves the Romans sculpted on so many Corinthian capitals, topping the columns of their temples and civic buildings. On one corner of the property was a seventy-eight-foot-tall obelisk carved with false doors and windows dating from the fourth century AD. The Italians looted it from the holy city of Axum in Ethiopia in 1937. The Ethiopian government was carrying on a furious campaign to get it repatriated while the Italians dreamed up excuse after excuse why they could not move it. (It was eventually returned after being damaged by lightning and no more excuses about protecting it were credible.)

Inside the entrance to the main building was a room hung with flags of member nations; this was where visitors congregated to wait for appointments with staff or to meet family members. Some of the flags were emblazoned with various intimidating combinations of automatic weapons, upraised arms, and hammers and sickles. Statues and other artwork donated by member governments filled other public areas and meeting rooms. One was sculpted by sexy actress Gina Lollobrigida, proving she had more talents than I thought. The grandiose main staircase was gray-streaked white marble and tricky to navigate when the British kept to the left and others kept to the right, ensuring collisions when "ups" met "downs." Bathrooms were tiled bright blue and had bidets along with the usual fixtures. Perhaps more was going on at noontime than I typically associated with office work.

The huge plenary hall reminded me of the hopefulness of the United Nations' mission of peace and prosperity. With booths for simultaneous translators working in English, French, Spanish, Chinese, and Arabic, flags of the member states, brilliant stained glass windows, and a sky-blue and golden yellow tile ceiling installed in the 1950s in a pattern of stars, futuristic cities, and spaceships, the hall promised a better future, one that seems perpetually just out of reach.

But it was the terrace adjoining the eighth-floor cafeteria that captured my imagination with the city's most beautiful and evocative view of Roman history. Facing leftward, I looked at the dome of St. Peter's, the synagogue in the old ghetto area, and the grassy oblong of the Circus Maximus, presided over by the skeletons of the emperors' palaces on the Palatine Hill. Straight ahead, beyond the remains of an aqueduct, the glorious Arch of Constantine and the ravaged Colosseum came into sight. To the right, the umbrella pines and churches of the Caelian Hill overlooked the traffic I had crossed on the way to the second interview in Rome. Farther on, I could see the statues on top of San Giovanni (the Lateran) peeking over the treetops. To my far right, the Baths of Caracalla, stripped to red bricks, sat in its decayed glory next to a sports complex full of joggers. Finally, a *casa di riposo*—a home for ancient people who stared vacantly out the open windows of their ancient building—

completed the panorama. No matter how many times I leaned over the parapet to view the scenery as I sipped espresso, I could still hardly believe that Rome was now our home.

Inconspicuous among the eye-catching sights, a modest building rested on a paved area next to the honking horns and exhaust fumes of the cars and motorcycles navigating the Porta Capena. It looked lonely with discarded papers and other trash scattered near its gated portico. I tried to learn its history but few guidebooks bothered to put it on maps or mention it in narratives. Eventually, a historian told me that it was a little Renaissance *casino*, a bachelor's lair or summer house, called La Vignola. It was moved to the site in the early twentieth century although it was originally built in 1538 in a more salubrious location. While on a walk one day I took a closer look. Affixed to one side of the building was a plaque marking the ancient site of the Fountain of Mercury. Not only was he the protector of travelers, Mercury also protected merchants. This was the spot where they collected water for libations on the god's feast day, May 15, hoping for a prosperous year. A minor god, who presided over my travel dreams as a child, had fortuitously appeared again—a hopeful sign that all my many intended travels would be safely completed.

More reflective of modern Rome, up the road by the baths and the old folks' home were some small lanes and wooded areas—the haunt of the "campfire girls", middle-aged prostitutes whose name came from the small fires they lit during the winter to keep warm in their skimpy outfits. Most of the women looked like grandmothers. When we drove up the road toward our apartment we often saw one knitting baby clothes, presumably for her grandchildren, in between assignments. Another always wore pink leggings and owlish glasses as she sat on an orange crate, doing crossword puzzles while waiting for customers.

Prostitution was such a common line of work that a pasta sauce was named after the workers, who found it was quick and easy to make in between shifts. We frequently enjoyed it for dinner when Chef Glenn learned to cook. He threw some halved kalamata olives, 2 teaspoons capers, 6 ounces chopped anchovy fillets, and some hot pepper flakes and peperoncino into a garlicky tomato sauce while the spaghetti was cooking. He poured the sauce over the drained pasta and we dug into *pasta alla puttanesca*—*puttana* being Italian for whore or harlot.

V

At the same time the area in front of my office allowed glimpses into Rome's complex history, we were beginning to develop our own complicated, although abbreviated, history trying to get adjusted to our new life. Our former home was a typical ranch style with two fireplaces, wall-to-wall carpeting, a garden all around, an efficient furnace, and a large water heater. Our new home was in a typical Roman apartment building from the postwar period, partly faced with reddish Roman brick and partly with white stucco. It contained twelve apartments on four floors. The elevator, with its inward-opening doors, was barely big enough for two. We sucked in our stomachs as we squeezed in a corner to close the doors. Although common in many other apartment buildings, we didn't have a *portiere* to greet us from a small, dimly lit entrance office where he or she watched the *portone*, the front door, snooped, and ran errands for tips. Instead, we had a *donna di servizio* in her blue housecoat and clogs. She came once a week to sweep the umbrella pine needles and cones off the walkway inside the gate and mop the marble entrance and wide interior stairs.

With Paola's help, we bought a washing machine that took two hours to do a quarter-size load, a small stove with an oven so poorly made the light from the little bulb leaked out the back along with the heat, and a miniature refrigerator barely powerful enough to keep a fresh chicken from spoiling overnight. We soon learned why housewives shopped every day.

The kitchen came with a freestanding sink and drain board along with a cabinet hung on the wall. That was it. Glenn wasn't daunted, accustomed as he was to camping for long periods. I was dispirited at the sight of the nearly empty room, especially when I saw that other people had perfectly appointed kitchens like those in design magazines. But we wanted to spend the money on travel instead of fancy cabinets and appliances, so there was no point in moaning.

The two baths ensured a change in our bathing habits from long, hot showers to a less watery style. The smaller room, christened the "Guest Bath," had a half-size tub where if I sat on the higher end only my shins and feet got clean. If I reversed, my bottom ended up with a design matching the screen over the drain and my back an indentation from leaning against the faucet. No matter which way I sat, the hot water from the undersized heater ran out before I was finished. Whatever our guests thought about the arrangement, they were polite enough not to verbalize it, at least within our earshot. The main bathroom had a long coffin-shaped tub not wide enough even for my narrow shoulders, but it did have a handheld shower wand. Unfortunately its slightly larger water heater hung directly above the head end. I warily eyed this sword of Damocles, willing it not to fall as I scrubbed up in a hurry.

The living room floor where we tried to sleep for eight long weeks was wood parquet, but the rest of the apartment floors were made of rock-hard tile, or terrazzo. The windows and the windowed doors to the balconies and terrace each came with a *serrande*, brown-colored wood slats that we rolled down at night and when we were away from home for security. When it was hot we lowered them during the day to keep out the heat. Then the dappled sunlight danced on the floors while the curtains wafted in the little breeze that seeped through the interstices into the darkened apartment.

A biblical plague of locusts and fine red sand landed onto our terrace and the cars in the street when the sirocco wind out of North Africa blew over Rome. The curtains whipped around and the *serrande* rattled noisily for days without ceasing. It felt like no air came into the apartment, though the hot and dry gusts furiously lashed the trees, and the windows on both sides were wide open. It was stiflingly hot. Sleepless nights resulted and everyone in Rome, including us, got short tempered.

The season changed, bringing another weather surprise: cold, damp winters. We had been sure that Rome was eternally warm and sunny, with a toga sufficient for clothing, but the onset of winter brought wind from the faraway Russian steppes, while the rain, somewhat warmer, came from the nearby

Tyrrhenian Sea. To our amazement it even snowed a little. Traffic became even more of a nightmare but the sight of snow falling on the Colosseum more than made up for the inconvenience. How the palm trees and the bougainvillea thrived, we never figured out.

Our floors, so cool and delightful in summer, were like ice as I ran for the bathroom on winter mornings. We bought a portable propane heater to help with the central heating that by law was only on for eight hours a day from November to March. There was still not enough heat and it got tiresome huddling around the *bombola* in the winter while we watched the laundry dry inside instead of flapping shamelessly on the terrace where it normally hung. So we bought an electric heater to supplement the supplemental *bombola*. Later we heard that some old Roman apartments had no heat at all, their inhabitants clearly tougher than we were.

The weather also brought new sleeping arrangements. When we first arrived, the apartment was so warm at night that we remained as far apart as possible with only our bare toes touching while we dripped with sweat. None of our windows or doors had screens. As I lay awake in the heat I watched our night-light, the tip of the slowly burning mosquito coil, glowing in the dark. Then winter arrived, along with our bed, and we clung together as close as possible, turning over at the same time while wishing we had brought the cat to help warm us up.

• • •

Glenn went into a "Works in progress" phase as he hung up newly purchased chandeliers (no light fixtures came with the apartment) and put together *armadi*, our freestanding closets. This was a real challenge because the instructions were in some Scandinavian language that he couldn't read. When he succeeded in constructing them it was a pleasure to pick our clothes off the floor since the apartment had no built-in storage either. We also needed all sorts of odds and ends like towel stands (no racks on the walls), electrical plugs to match the different outlet sizes, extension cords (one electrical outlet in most rooms), and transformers to run our U.S. toaster and iron. Glenn took the bus to a *ferramenta*, a hardware store where almost everything he really needed was put away in drawers and needed to be specifically requested. To get what he wanted he researched the dictionary, which was seldom helpful for specific items like drill bits, then in desperation, thought up sign language as in a game of Charades. His vocabulary of swear words in several languages also increased rapidly as he struggled to get us organized.

Furnishing the terrace was next on our homemaking agenda. We found a nearby *vivaio* where we bought herbs: basil, rosemary, oregano, thyme, parsley, and salvia, essential ingredients for Italian cooking. We added sticky blue plumbago, magenta and orange bougainvillea, geraniums, sedums, and cymbidium orchids. Like other Roman vegetation they all went into overdrive, cheerfully growing and blooming whether it was hot or cold, summer or winter.

The Romans were careless or indifferent to the plants that filled their own balconies and terraces between laundry racks and other unused items stored outside. Abandoned plants, terra-cotta pots, and huge hand-blown olive oil containers were often dumped next to garbage bins on the street. Glenn had a long-established reputation as a scrounger. While driving back roads for the Forest Service he retrieved orphaned rope, buckets, frisbees for Kathryn, a new apron for me, and most infamously, a watch with no hands. This shameless skill was now put to good use at siesta time when he thought no one was looking. As a result of this match made in heaven, many plants and pots were liberated from certain death.

Life on our terrace was always pleasant. Small, iridescent green lizards occasionally stopped by to rest on the hot tiles. European robins and blackbirds sang, along with lovely cooing turtledoves. Hooded crows, looking like executioners, surveyed the scene. Tiny bats slept during the day between sections of the façade. When the sun began to set, they took to the sky to look for their dinner. In the spring, migratory swifts returned to our neighborhood, swooping until sundown when they suddenly dived into chimneys to sleep. As the season changed to winter, we were astonished to see millions of starlings turning endlessly in the evening sky in ever-changing shapes, looking like early computer screen savers with their continually morphing designs. At sunset they, too, settled in for the night.

Aircraft were also in the sky. The Carabinieri, Italy's military police, somewhat equivalent to the FBI (though far better dressed), regularly flew overhead, although we couldn't see a dangling Christ like the opening scene of *La Dolce Vita* where the statue is being ferried by helicopter over miles of new apartments not far from ours. (I recognized a friend's apartment building from the opening scene.) On summer Sunday afternoons we often watched a white helicopter passing above through the heavens. We heard it was *il papa* visiting his retreat at Castel Gandolfo in the nearby Castelli Romani, skipping the traffic and the summer heat in his popecopter.

Beyond the cypresses and umbrella pines, our view sometimes included little children in their pink-and-blue smocks from the nearby *asilo nido*, nursery school, lined up in a crocodile as their minders took them for a walk. Or maybe a Sunday procession from the nearby church passed by with banners held high and smoke from incense mixing with the sound of hymns. One time the sight was microscopic. A dozen or so minuscule ants who shared the terrace with us came upon a dead bee. As if their leader had shouted, "All together now," they surrounded the corpse, hoisted it onto their shoulders, and marched off with their prize.

• • •

Our furniture finally showed up. Small men with typical Roman sun hats made of the previous day's newspaper folded origami-like into toy boats staggered up two flights of stairs to our apartment. Each had a packing case tied with a rope to his back, making them look like pack animals. We were ecstatic. That is, until we set to work. As we opened each box our hearts sank ever further. We had been doubtful about the quality of the moving company in Portland, and now our concerns were realized with bed pillows showing boot prints all over them, a trashed vacuum cleaner, missing antiques, broken china, the sofa back ripped off, and golf clubs and parts of outdoor furniture nowhere to be seen. It was a small-sized disaster and for the first time we felt totally defeated.

I always thought that missing socks from the dryer circled the earth along with asteroids, but there is also a place for objects vanishing in transport. Who would want a chaise longue without its pad or the frame of an antique fire screen, leaving the stained glass for us? Worse, we purchased a pricey dining room table with a glass top and Italian marble base a month before I applied for the job. The glass came through unscathed but the base was smashed into a million pieces.

There was also another problem: before we left Portland we were sent a pile of information, including Italian customs forms and regulations. We were required to declare all electronics, artworks, jewelry, and guns. Glenn stored an old gun with Kathryn but a BB gun was somehow missed in the rush to move. Gun laws in Italy were strict, and we were concerned about having an unregistered one in case we were robbed and it turned up in the hands of someone else, even though it wasn't really dangerous. Glenn went to the local police station to make a declaration. With little Italian and a clerk with no English ability he struggled to get the meaning of "BB gun" across the linguistic divide. Apparently they weren't well known in Italy but she had an inspiration: "*Ah, una pistola per bambini.*" She waved him off, but being in a foreign country we didn't want to violate the law. So, piece by piece and day by day, the *pistola* was slowly taken apart and deposited in the garbage container on the street—at siesta time, of course.

Our unhappy furniture-delivery day was a time for serious rethinking of our decision to come to Italy. We heard of other Americans leaving after a week or a month because they couldn't adjust, and of wives cowering in their apartments while their husbands were at their offices because they were overwhelmed or bored.

I hadn't paid much attention to a college philosophy class and its survey of the Stoics, being busy with wedding plans. As my newer and much-improved husband and I found ourselves in Rome actually trying to live there, the musings of Marcus Aurelius became ever more relevant. In addition to his writings on fate and reason, he remarked that the universe delights in change and that it is ridiculous to be surprised at anything that happens; in other words, pull up your socks and get on with it. So, after much "Why did we come here?" and boo-hooing, and with comfort administered by Glenn, I slowly wiped the tears. Not much *dolce* was visible in our *vita* at that point but we had a bottle of wine and a bowl of pasta before deciding to pull up our (remaining) socks as advised by Marcus.

None of the missing goods ever turned up. We received an offer of partial reimbursement from the insurance company. But we still had only a rickety card table from our air shipment for a dining table. The claims agent suggested that we contact local marble workers, many of whom were located near the main Rome cemetery, to get a replacement. The gigantic graveyard, Campo Verano, is built on land once owned by Emperor Lucias Verus, Marcus Aurelius's brother. Last resting place of St. Lawrence, buried there in AD 258, the cemetery also hosts such luminaries as Mussolini's mistress, who rests alongside many others—famous, infamous, and obscure.

But Glenn wasn't interested in the dead. He found an artisan who spoke a little English who was willing to come to our apartment to look at the pieces of the base before making a new one to measure. He delivered a white Carrara marble piece a month later. But while he may have sculpted some heartrending tombstones, Michelangelo he wasn't. The base was so poorly aligned that the top sat on a significant tilt, making it unusable as our wine glasses tipped and pasta bowls slid. Nevertheless, our *artista* had enough nerve to try to charge us an additional amount for the wooden crate surrounding his handiwork. By this time, however, our ability to communicate with various tradespeople was growing. Despite our fractured Italian, he got the message that we weren't going to pay for his crate. He left holding it, along with a check for the amount we originally agreed on: a reduction of his basic price was still beyond our bargaining skills. We found pieces of the crate near the garbage containers the next day.

Alas, that didn't improve our table. We jimmied the crosspieces supporting the glass and threw a tablecloth over the mess. We had already sewed up the sofa back, used duct tape to put the vacuum cleaner back together, and washed the pillows. The reimbursement check was cashed and life went on.

VI

While I was struggling along at work, trying to understand the culture of FAO and what I was supposed to be doing, Glenn set about learning to cook along with all his other chores. His prior culinary accomplishments were confined to spaghetti (a ton of sauce and a dab of pasta), bacon and eggs, hamburgers, and toasted cheese sandwiches. But he quickly proved to be a whiz and we were soon dining on fresh salads, grilled vegetables, *pasta alla puttanesca*, and pasta sauces he invented as he went along. I thought this was pretty good for a man who once swore that zucchini would never cross his lips and who had never heard of radicchio (neither had I), let alone the other vegetables that were waiting his ministrations. Like Italians, we ate on our terrace whenever possible. Dirty pots and pans ended up on the floor before cleanup due to the scarcity of drain boards and countertops in our miserable kitchen. We didn't care—dining outside was like a permanent picnic.

Glenn's other perpetual, and in this case largely futile, effort was devoted to trying to keep our apartment clean. It was on a bus route, ideal for me, but the resulting diesel exhaust settled on everything. The new white curtains soon turned dark gray. Grime from crumbling ancient walls, temples, and statues mixed with wind-borne Libyan sand and dead locusts, seasoned with pollution from the heating system, presented Glenn with a Sisyphean challenge. Also, the water was as hard as rocks. It was easy to see where travertine came from when we peered at the crust in our sinks and toilets.

We considered hiring someone to clean but didn't want anyone we didn't know in the apartment or the hassle of following Italian rules for domestic workers. We'd heard tales of workers suing their employers, with ensuing years of legal wrangling in the slow and erratic Italian justice system. My good-natured spouse never did corners and windows well, and I did get a little upset when he washed and dried the champagne glasses so vigorously he twisted their stems off.

After Glenn managed to get our household in operation he liberated himself, throwing down his mop and broom to begin enjoying retirement life beyond our weekend adventures. He joined a bowling league, which consisted of Paola and several Indonesians from their embassy. Then he joined a new golf club south of Rome. The club had a lovely name, Eucalyptus, after all the trees in the area, but it was located in a town with an all-too-apt name, Campo di Carni, literally Field of Flesh, home to several slaughterhouses at one time. The name was appropriate for another reason too: it was the scene of heavy fighting in World War II after the Allies landed at Anzio, not far away. While other fancy golf clubs patronized by princes of industry and the Church contained vestiges of Roman aqueducts, Eucalyptus had unexploded ordnance. Looking for balls in the rough was unadvisable due to the likelihood of leftover munitions as well as poisonous snakes.

Glenn soon became acquainted with a group of retired military officers, Italian and British, a retired FAO staffer, and an elderly Italian count. The *circolo del golf* granted Glenn the ideal Italian relief from dealing with the apartment and daily living. Serious golf took second place to leisurely lunches. Hiring a new chef was more important to the membership than hiring a new golf pro. The lunches were long and convivial and avoided all talk of the past, although it was clear from casual remarks that his Italian partners missed Mussolini's governing methods and that they suspected Glenn was really a CIA plant.

Always on the alert for new recipes, Glenn befriended the club's chef, asking him to share some of his creations so he could surprise me at dinner in the evening. One recipe was *farfalle al'Eucalypto*, made with butterfly pasta. While the pasta was cooking, *il cuoco* sautéed a chopped onion in a little olive oil until soft. Then he added sliced young zucchini and a chopped clove of garlic to the onions along with a few ounces of diced *speck* (a type of cured ham from northern Italy) to the sauté pan, along with salt and pepper to taste. He drained the pasta and added it into the zucchini mixture to combine for a minute or so. It was then poured into a bowl preheated with the drained pasta water and served with freshly grated Parmesan cheese. Sometimes he substituted pieces of peeled and lightly steamed asparagus; either variety was welcome.

The middle-aged golfers called each other *ragazzo*, kid, but when Glenn started eating too much of his own cooking they began calling him *cicciobomba*, plump one.

• • •

Our new neighbors remained a blank slate for some time. Finally, after a few months of passing each other on the stairs, a blonde woman introduced herself in English. She was Jana, a Czech who had previously been married to an American, thus her language ability. She told us that she was a singer and that her current husband was a French horn player and impresario. They lived one floor below. She introduced us to her husband's aunt, a well-known composer of atonal music, who lived in the penthouse, one floor up. The other occupants were unknowns, our interactions limited to an occasional polite nod or *buongiorno*.

It seemed clear to us that we would remain aliens. However, they were all keeping a close eye on us, as we were to find out. When we arrived home one evening I could hear the telephone ringing inside the apartment. Kathryn had recently taken the bar examination. I *knew* it was good news. "She's calling to say she passed!" I fumbled with the three sets of locks as we hurried to enter. The door opened and I rushed to the telephone as I slammed the door shut behind us. It *was* good news. A celebration to honor this happy event was definitely in order. Glenn broke out the champagne before dinner.

In the middle of the night I woke up, startled when someone turned on the hall light. "Wake up, wake up, there's someone in the apartment," I croaked as I poked Glenn awake. He leapt out of bed. Dressed only in his briefs and armed with his bare fists, he envisioned rape and murder as he advanced along our long hallway to defend my honor. He came to a sudden halt when a voice in

English said: "Don't worry! We're your neighbors. We found your keys on your doormat and were alarmed!" It was Jana stepping out from behind her husband and another man.

All the building's other occupants stood in their doorways snickering and staring at Glenn in his briefs, confronting them with his fists up. After hearing the conversation, I pulled the bedcovers over my head with a combination of relief and humiliation while hoping never to meet any neighbor again. What a horrible embarrassment, a *brutta figura*.

The next day, Glenn distributed flowers to the ladies and brandy to the men for showing such concern for our well-being. We hung our heads in shame for a few weeks whenever we encountered anyone. In reality, they all probably enjoyed telling everyone they knew about the crazy *stranieri* in their building. Later, we found a suitable Italian weapon in case we were actually invaded—a two-foot-long rolling pin used for making pasta. It was placed by the bed, in case of further nighttime visitors.

VII

All the housing in our neighborhood was similar to ours: standard Italian-issue 1960s and '70s apartment blocks filled with affluent families and their ample supply of barking dogs. Besides the cypress and umbrella pines, thick-stemmed wisteria vines bloomed purple against ochre walls in the spring, contrasting with the bright yellow flowers of mimosa trees. Hot pink, purple, and orange bougainvillea flourished everywhere in all seasons. In the fall, the scene was brightened when small red pomegranates hung from their bushes and yellow-leaved persimmon trees brought forth Day-Glo orange fruit looking like Japanese lanterns. During the winter, the open space used by the nuns for garbage disposal was taken over by grazing sheep. Their tinkling bells made a rural sound, a contrast to those of the nearby church. Where the sheep and their shepherds came from we never knew. Perhaps they were descendants of the animals and herders who occupied the Roman Forum after it fell into the ruin so frequently depicted in romantic eighteenth-century paintings. A mile or two farther out a different scene presented itself with huge and dismal graffiti-covered public housing projects and a military base. Sometimes when the wind came from the west we could hear artillery booming in the night. We assumed it was for training exercises. Beyond, near the Grande Raccordo Anulare, the ring road surrounding Rome, were Gypsy camps of appalling squalor.

We rapidly learned that in Rome one's home is one's castle. Unlike neighborhood-proud American suburbia, here the drawbridge was up and little outside the apartment grounds was considered worthy of interest or attention. Although the curbs were beautiful white travertine, the sidewalks were broken asphalt littered with dog poop, glass from car break-ins, and garbage that somehow missed the containers. Many of the small pink flowering trees planted along the roadside were broken off at the trunk. Cars were parked everywhere, including sidewalks and crosswalks.

On a more picturesque note, water hydrants called *nasoni*, or big noses, gushed in a continuous stream from a curved spout into a drain. If we were thirsty we placed a finger over the mouth of the spout, which turned it into a drinking fountain from the small hole on its top. Like the sewer covers, they were emblazoned with "S.P.Q.R.," the ancient motto: "The Senate and People of Rome." Usually the hydrants were used on Sunday afternoons when men, chased out of their homes while lunch was being cooked, washed their cars while listening to soccer games on their car radios. When the washing was done we saw them sitting in their cars reading the feminine-looking pink newspaper, *La Gazzetta dello Sport*, for the latest soccer and bicycle-racing news. It appeared that life moved at a slow pace, *con calma*, a state of nirvana we had not yet reached.

• • •

As Glenn perfected his cooking we both needed to perfect the shopping. FAO continued to maintain a commissary on the outlandish principle of inadequate food in Rome, though there probably was a need when the organization moved from Washington, DC to Rome in 1951. Despite its modern irrelevance, it was convenient for frozen meat and fish, excellent French chickens, and cans, boxes, and jars of foreign comfort foods like Vegemite, *foule madame*, peanut butter, and Cheerios for us coddled expatriates. Huge supplies of butter, sugar, canned tuna, and various liquors, cigarettes, perfumes, and cosmetics, all tax-free, filled shelves and coolers. Every home we visited had a large selection of liqueurs displayed on a sideboard or drinks cart. So we too bought a dozen or so bottles filled with violently colored liquids. No one ever drank any. Some staff stocked up on prodigious amounts of sugar or other basic items that commanded higher prices in local shops. It was never clear if they were reselling their purchases or taking care of an extended family. Sometimes liquor, clearly labeled for FAO sale alone, illegally showed up in area bars.

Despite the temptation of the commissary, we wanted to live like our neighbors. But first we needed to learn the rules. Taking a less frantic approach to life, we found Italians didn't believe in shopping at any time of day for a week's supply, all within an hour or less. Many of the stores were closed Monday morning and took a midday siesta in addition to closing early on Saturday and all day Sunday. When August rolled around the following year we found that smaller shops, news vendors, and pharmacies closed in turn, sometimes for the whole month. By law, a shop of each type had to be open in the neighborhood. Little pieces of paper posted on the locked shutters told us where an open store might be found. "Plan ahead" became our watchword.

For ordinary food that, given the size and feebleness of our refrigerator, had to be purchased nearly every day, and for staples, we often used a small supermarket a few blocks away. We slowly pushed our cart around looking at the unfamiliar items, some with labels we couldn't read. All the milk was irradiated and sold in cartons stacked on non-refrigerated shelves. Six-packs of bottled water—fizzy, semi-fizzy, and flat—filled shelves and aisles. The meat section offered unfamiliar cuts that sometimes contained bone slivers. We lingered longest in the pasta department where the shelves were laden with dozens of varieties all lined up first by brand and then alphabetically by type, cooking times prominently displayed on the box. One day we counted the varieties of dried pasta packages available. The top shelf of six displayed the leading brand, Barilla, with twenty-nine different varieties. Multiplied by the number of shelves, we were confronted with about two hundred choices with the many different brands, even more counting the fresh packages in the refrigerated section. Unsure of which was best, we heeded our rental agent's advice and bought De Cecco.

Using a plastic glove, we weighed our fruit and vegetables, printing out a sticker with the proper code and price. While we waited to pay, a leisurely process, we listened to one clerk chatting with another at the adjacent cash register. Credit cards were not accepted. We were handed a fistful of small wrapped candies if the clerk didn't have enough change, coins sometimes being in short supply. We paid for the shopping bags and filled them ourselves—no high school kid to help out.

When the weather was hot, a watermelon seller came around at midnight in a small three-wheeled pickup called an *Ape*, bee, crying out his wares over a loudspeaker, "*cocomero, cocomero.*" It was too late in the evening for us to bother to run down to the street but the night-owl neighbors took advantage. For the *casalinga* (housewife), a knife grinder occasionally came by, or sometimes it was a man selling pots and pans who threw in a free trip to some local shrine if the housewife bought a set.

A sturdy peasant woman often walked around the neighborhood. She wore a long black dress with an apron, felt slippers, and a belt tied around her middle, making her look like a walking potato sack. She balanced a large box, labeled Chiquita Bananas, on her head. No matter how far she swayed back and forth, a considerable amount given the size of her haunches, the box somehow stayed in place. This was fortunate because she shouted that she had *uova da bere*, new-laid eggs so fresh you could drink them. By the time we heard her call she was usually well up the street so we only watched her roll along before she turned the corner. Oddly, we never saw anyone sampling her wares.

A small stand up the street sold fresh seasonal vegetables, nothing like the old and limp green beans or broccoli we bought in Portland (or in the *supermercato* if we arrived after the local housewives had creamed off everything fresh). The stall-keeper's wife in her blue smock sat on an old chair off to one side trimming small artichokes with great dexterity before arranging them in tempting displays. They were entirely edible, neither the fuzz in the center nor the stems needing to be removed. Glenn asked the vendor how to cook them. He scribbled his recipe on some scratch paper: "Simmer four artichokes in ¼ glass olive oil, ½ glass water, ½ liter white wine, with some salt, garlic and parsley for 15 to 20 minutes." Romans typically add wild mint, *mentuccia*, although our *fruttivendolo* didn't include it in his ingredients. We were never quite sure what a "glass" of something was in these artisan recipes so Glenn just winged it with good results.

In the spring we enjoyed a chive-like but spinach-tasting green called *agretti*, steamed and served with a slice of lemon, and a variety of chicory leaf, *puntarelle*, which was trimmed to the stem and served with anchovy sauce. We learned to appreciate the biting flavor of many types of greens after Glenn lightly steamed and then quickly sautéed them in olive oil seasoned with peperoncino. A bitter version of arugula, *rughetta*, good for salads, and two varieties of radicchio, round for salad and long for grilling, awaited our shopping bag. Fennel, smelling of anise, also grilled as a side dish or raw in salads, was a new experience. A kilo or two of tomatoes were always added to our selection, with the variety differing according to the season and use: Cerignola or Pachino for snacks or decoration on a salad, others for slicing, and San Marzano for fresh sauce destined to marry its life partner, pasta. No more of the cardboard taste of the mushy ones available off-season in Portland.

Sometimes the vendor would hand over a bunch of celery tops, rosemary, and other odds and ends. I thought that he was getting rid of leftovers, but in reality these little gifts were *odori*, meant to be chopped up, sautéed, and thrown into the soup or sauce to add flavor.

The only food we missed was corn on the cob. The Italian version was so tough it must have been grown as animal feed. It was never on any restaurant menu and after one try, not on ours either.

At first we had to point to get what we wanted. If we wanted two of something we copied the Italians by using thumb and forefinger instead of the first and second, making it appear as if we were holding a gun although we didn't aim at the shopkeeper. One day I pointed at some parsley, not knowing the Italian word. The shopper next to me, a well-dressed matron, glared and enunciated with great clarity, "pret-SSSem-olo, signora." I never forgot the word. A friend had a similar experience when he asked in his halting Italian what the long green vegetables were. The shopkeeper looked at him in amazement and slowly said, "zuu-KEY-ne."

In season, *fichi di india*, prickly pear fruit, and *nespole*, medlar, were available. We also eagerly awaited the heavenly black and green figs and the ambrosial *uve d'Italia*, plum-size green-gold grapes available for a few weeks each fall. One variety of melon came with raffia tied around it for easy carrying.

Oranges of many varieties, including those with blood-red juice from Sicily, and lemons from the Amalfi Coast were piled up along with a large citrus called *cedro*, which turned out to be citron, always associated with my mother's underappreciated fruitcake. Almost nothing was imported—if it wasn't in season it wasn't there, although we once saw a sign for "erotic fruits" in a fancy store, presumably meaning imported tropical fruit. Maybe they worked as advertised.

Along with the fruit and vegetable stands, flower stalls sold an enormous variety of *fiori* at low prices. In spring there were fragrant freesias and dozens of varieties of tulips to tempt us. The vendor always asked if our selection was for our *casa* or for a *regalo*, a gift. A production number ensued if we said "*regalo.*" The vendor took our selection, trimmed, arranged, and then wrapped it in garishly colored crepe paper. He'd then crimp the edges and affix a sticker with the shop's name before handing it over with a flourish. We made sure we didn't pick out any chrysanthemums for our hostess. They were reserved for funerals and cemeteries, perhaps because they naturally bloom around All Souls' Day when Italians visit their families' graves. Aggressive-looking two-foot-tall gladiola stems were most popular as hostess gifts. We were advised to buy an odd number of stalks, even considered to be unlucky.

The main neighborhood shopping street four blocks from home had a *norcineria* named after the town of Norcia, originally known as the birthplace of St. Benedict but later for lentils, pork, and pig butchering. Along with sausage and chops, it carried many varieties of *prosciutto*, which we bought by the *etto*, 100 grams or about three ounces, to be served with figs or melon. The butcher shop was in a row of other small stores on a busy street. A shop for pizza to go displayed in large trays was first, followed by a store for beauty supplies and costume jewelry. Next was a *farmacia* with its flashing green neon cross, the *parrucchiere* where the hairdresser chain-smoked when I went for a haircut, the *merceria* for sewing and knitting supplies, a *pasticceria* for pastries, and a shop with buckets, mops, laundry drying racks, and other odds and ends useful for setting up our domestic life. In slow times proprietors in their smocks and clogs lounged in the entryways smoking while they awaited customers.

Our local bar on another corner was typical of the thousands in Rome and elsewhere in Italy. It was a combination of coffee shop with sandwiches and pastries, drinking establishment, a place to play the *Totalcalcio* football pool, and a gift shop. At Eastertime, large brightly wrapped chocolate eggs were hung from the bar's ceiling while boxed cakes in the shape of a dove were stacked in the windows. During the Christmas holidays, windows and shelves were piled with different varieties of *panettone*, the fruit-studded bread, all in boxes with convenient handles for us to carry home or to guests.

The espresso cups slapped on the counter in front of us advertised the name of the bar's coffee brand. Most logos were simply colorful lettering, sometimes with an additional design like a coffee bean, although one company's cups had as its attraction a black woman with exaggerated inner-tube lips. The design was just one example of the lack of what we called political correctness, like American Indians invariably being called *pelle rossi*, redskins.

Coffee at the bar on our Saturday mornings followed a ritual: First, if we arrived really early, we made sure that we were not in line to get the first cup after the machine had been cleaned because it needed to mellow. When the machine was deemed ready, we went to the cash register to tell the clerk what we wanted, paid, took our receipt, and squeezed between other patrons to place it on the bar with a small tip while giving the barista our order. It was time to watch, smell, and listen as he worked his magic at great speed, grinding coffee and banging out used grounds to make a fresh cup. This was followed by the hissing sound of steamed milk foaming along with the rattling of thick cups and saucers. Morning never really started for us or the Italians until after our first coffee cup was drained, the cup clattering back into the saucer, with life speeding up as caffeine took hold.

The regulars hung out sipping, talking, and reading the paper or slugged a shot laced with grappa before they rushed off. We felt terribly Italian as we drank our cappuccino, trying to look like natives despite our American shoes and clothes—as if anyone was fooled.

VIII

The nucleus of our area of the city had its own history, less extensive than that of the historic center but still with reminders of the past. Seneca said, "Believe me, that was a happy age, before the days of architects, before the days of builders." That quip was made in the first century AD but might have been written about the heart of the *quartiere*, or neighborhood where we rented, called EUR, short for *Esposizione Universale di Roma*. We originally pictured Rome as nothing but ancient, medieval, and Baroque structures fleshed out with nineteenth-century apartment buildings. Instead, we were living in an area surrounding a government complex begun in the 1930s. Ignored by most tourists, the center of EUR was fascinating to us with our newly developed interest in modern architecture and the fascist era.

The district was Mussolini's brainchild. His great building enterprise began in the 1930s as a new center for his imperial capital and for a universal exhibition to be held in 1942 to celebrate the twentieth anniversary of his ascendance to power. Like FAO, it was built of white travertine and marble. The swaggering buildings with their overbearing porticos and gigantic pseudo-pharaonic columns were often set on platforms to emphasize their grandeur and to humble the onlooker with the power of the state. Enormous mosaic panels glorified the regime's agricultural and scientific accomplishments. Flattened eagles looking to us like the pressed ducks that hung in the windows of Chinese restaurants were carved over entrances set at the end of long, dark columned passages. The German writer, Goethe, called architecture frozen music. The music that came to our minds in EUR was drums and trumpets.

Postwar commentators often described the area as "cold, soulless, and inhuman," or "the dead heart of fascist planning." We could easily picture fascist functionaries in their snappy uniforms walking around self-importantly while sharing straight-armed salutes like their ancient Roman counterparts whom they were vainly trying to emulate. During the week, the modern-day bureaucrats populating the buildings stood around outside smoking and talking. But on Sundays when the ministries were closed, the words that came quickly to our minds were "desolate and surreal," reminding me of Di Chirico's bleak early paintings, with their dark shadows lengthening over the sunbaked empty piazzas peopled only with lonely broken mannequins. We felt insignificant as we unconsciously hunched up in the face of the ultimately useless architectural braggadocio as we took an afternoon stroll.

The most architecturally interesting building is the Palazzo della Civiltà del Lavoro, more commonly known as the Square Colosseum. Its six stories with arcades on all sides at all levels cast deep shadows, giving the sensation of loneliness. Due to neglect and deterioration it was indeed a lonely sight, the interior being unsafe for occupancy except for occasional art exhibits. Inscriptions around the top glorify the many Italian achievements in the arts and sciences. Life-sized statues representing the arts sit underneath the arches on the ground level. Monumental statues of naked men and rearing horses stand at each corner of the platform on which the building was erected. The fascists loved to depict naked men sculpted in white marble as heavy as all their other architectural offerings in an effort to make them look tough and manly instead of the stereotypical dark little peasant using his hands to eat spaghetti. The statues were originally sculpted to give the straight-armed fascist salute but after the War they were altered to plain bent arms, welcoming eager music lovers like us to summer jazz concerts on the steps. Sometimes an enterprising prankster drew massive boxer shorts on the statues or added additional graphic detail to their chunky male attributes, the artwork amusing us while we enjoyed Wynton Marsalis and other jazz greats who came to Rome to play for appreciative crowds.

EUR's most prominent church, Saints Peter and Paul, was the location of a funeral for a colleague who was murdered in Africa during a robbery. Built in the shape of a Greek cross, the church's massive walls are surmounted by a heavy dome covered with dragon-like scales. It squats at the top of a long flight of steps dominating an elegant shopping street. The interior has '30s-style mosaic panels, one intended to show God blessing the Roman wolf, but it looked to me more like disembodied hands grabbing a snarling dog. Harsh interior neon lighting gave no comfort at all to those of us at the unhappy memorial event.

The international exhibition planned for 1942 was never held. By that time Italy was already on the losing end of the war. Mussolini's indelible mark was left on the architecture of Italy, but in 1945 he was murdered by partisans while trying to escape to Switzerland. He then hung upside down alongside his mistress at an architecturally uninteresting gas station in Milan.

We tried to learn more about EUR but couldn't find books on the subject. When we asked, we were told it was "*difficile*" to find anything because the architecture reflected the *anni facisti*, the fascist times, best forgotten by all but a few die hards. Then an exhibition of the architectural drawings and artwork went on display in one of the monumental buildings, the State Archives (weirdly interesting because it has an enormous hairdressing shop on one end). The exhibit was so jammed with the curious that we could hardly manage to get in the door. To our disappointment all the posters and books were already sold out.

EUR sprang back to life with new buildings and sports facilities for the 1960 Olympic Games. Towering over an artificial lake used for the rowing competitions is a *fungo*, mushroom, actually the water tower erected for the new neighboring gardens and offices. Topped by a large sign advertising a bank, the phallic symbol is a concrete monument to ugliness, or maybe sex.

Counteracting all the heaviness, the beautiful shopping area yielded a chance to enjoy what Pliny the Younger called "The indolent but agreeable condition of doing nothing." We took his remark to heart, enjoying the *dolce far niente*—the sweetness of doing nothing—as we sat in a café to watch shoppers strolling along the tree-lined streets filled with stylish jewelry, clothing, and shoe shops. Spooning gelato, sipping espresso, or lingering over an aperitif was a perfect vision of our expectations of Italian life.

IX

In between learning to shop, eat, make a fool of myself with the neighbors, and find out what our area of Rome had to offer, I gradually learned my duties and got to know my colleagues.

Just as in the Forest Service, I was still only one cog out of many in a bureaucracy. Rather than logging and firefighting, this one was full of specialists and support staff working on food-related issues. Experts in fisheries management, control of cattle diseases, land tenure, food standards, reforestation, locust control, and agricultural production worked long hours alongside statisticians and those who tried to predict droughts and food shortages. Instead of contributing directly to reducing world hunger I spent time drafting or reviewing personnel manuals for legality and clarity. (As Cicero said long ago, "Even if you have nothing to write, write and say so.") More interesting and challenging duties included offering advice on personnel problems, sitting on the credit union and pension boards, writing legal briefs, and defending what I perceived as managers' sometimes arbitrary personnel decisions due to culture clashes.

Along with figuring out what to do with misfits, my former work life in the Forest Service sometimes involved confronting the unpleasant reality of shocking events that arise in any large workforce, however homogenous. There were occasional suicides, love triangle murders, child molesters, and all manner of incompetence. But the situations now before me in FAO presented new problems complicated by the mix of nationalities, cultures, work locations, and legal arrangements. Adding to the tangle, the United Nations has its own laws as well as individual agreements governing its presence in all member states. With different employment contracts and benefits depending on work and family situations, and local laws applicable to lower-level staff employed in their home countries such as India or Uganda, finding the just or correct answer to an issue was never easy.

Employees converged on FAO from nearly every country only to be scattered again to Asia, Africa, and Latin America, far from home and in difficult circumstances. As a result, strange problems sometimes landed on my desk: What to do about divorces that occurred without informing the stay-at-home spouse, or fake adoptions undertaken to secure benefits for poor friends' children? What was the validity of disability claims for contracting AIDS on the job or cancer from sun exposure? What were the arrangements for payment to families after murders by bandits or during kidnappings? How does one authorize payment for emergency medical evacuations for sick children or women having miscarriages in godforsaken spots? Idyllic as it sounded to the uninitiated, expatriate life in some locations could be more of a nightmare than a pleasant reverie.

• • •

Jean-Jacques, my Belgian supervisor so fond of Paola, was subtle, urbane, funny, and erudite. He had published several books, including one in Latin. He was also interested in astrology and the paranormal. I was concerned that he might peruse my horoscope cast by Paola and find something amiss. His English required close listening to get the drift and his handwriting was as convoluted as his English, so beautiful that it was practically calligraphy and nearly impossible to read. When he was in a talkative mood he told stories about watching the Germans invade his hometown in Belgium when he was a child, and later about living in the former Belgian Congo as a colonial officer. The tales brought to mind our profound differences in background and life experiences, his as the representative of European history and mine as that of middle-class America. Like all good Europeans he was a wine connoisseur. During a trip back to Oregon I dared to buy him a bottle of Willamette Valley pinot noir. He accepted reluctantly, never having heard of such a novel item. After analyzing his expression I thought he'd pour it down the drain, but sometime later he admitted that he was surprised to find that it stood the test against some good French and Italian vintages. Or at least that was what he said.

He was generally relaxed about life, but when a crisis arose he and the director of personnel began, in Jean-Jacques' words, "running around like ants." I followed their actions and did the same.

The director was Tunisian. He had a fondness for cigars. While I was in a meeting in Geneva, a woman rushed in with an urgent message to call the boss. Expecting some disaster, I called with trepidation. He only wanted me to bring him a box of his preferred brand. One day when the weather turned cool I put on a new wool pinstriped suit, only to meet him in the hall wearing a suit of the same material. Because we were about the same height, we could have been mistaken for Tweedledum and Tweedledee. After a quick glance to assess this sartorial mischance, we each looked the other way. I subsequently refrained from wearing the suit unless I knew that he would be out of the office.

Paola turned out to have total command of the arcana of moving documents up and down the food chain while meeting all deadlines, although we continued to butt heads over her Latin approach to work and my rigid American style. Johann, the legal assistant, was a well-intentioned and charming young lawyer, eager to please and reluctant to express an opinion. Like that with Paola, our relationship got off to a rocky start when he took Glenn and me to a town in Umbria for lunch one Saturday shortly after we arrived. The espresso after lunch failed to overcome the wine and he fell asleep at the wheel. I screamed at the last minute when we hit the gravel on the roadside, and he managed to rouse himself an instant before we hit the ditch. The conversation lapsed on the remainder of the journey while I thought of Mercury and reconsidered the amount of my life insurance.

While working for the Forest Service I dealt with a few odd souls, like the clerk who ran around her boss's desk shouting, "Now I know how Christ felt on the cross." Another woman forgot that she left pantyhose in her slacks the previous evening until one nylon toe drooped out and became tethered to a nail in a baseboard as she vainly tried to enter her office. There was a man who said he couldn't come to work because his canary had diarrhea and another who used the office machine to photocopy his private parts. But I need not have worried about leaving these misfits behind because a generous selection of interesting people soon appeared. This time around they washed up from all corners of the world, expatriate life having not much appeal to the more settled and predictable types.

Among the new crowd was a British man rumored to be a former Russian spy allegedly parked in FAO by his government rather than being prosecuted with attendant unsavory publicity. An Indian man handed me an engraved business card that announced "B. Science (failed)" below his name. One colleague, when he didn't want to deal with someone, said, "My psychiatrist says that I don't have to talk to you." Another wore battle fatigues and, rumor had it, drove a midget-sized *Cinquecento* (500 cc Fiat) with a mattress on top to lure attractive young women on camping expeditions. Given the size of the car, I imagined arms and legs dangling everywhere on moonlit nights. A tall, thin man wore an itchy pink mohair suit every day no matter what the weather. I unconsciously started scratching whenever I saw him.

One clerk was so frightened of her boss that every time she made a mistake she ran around worrying that he would "have my guts for garters." When an American executive became annoyed with someone (male) he often threatened to "cut off his goolies." A Japanese man stood and bowed into the telephone, shouting "*hai*" whenever a compatriot called. Then there was a minor nobleman who showed me the hot watches he bought in the flea market. He wore what he called "correspondent" shoes, flashy and two-toned. I asked where the term originated. He replied that such shoes were often favored by sleazy private eyes in England in the prewar era when they were creeping around looking for the "other" man or woman, the required "co-respondent" needed to prove adultery in divorce trials. Who knew? But then who was I to sniff at other people's shoe styles when Glenn once had to rescue me from embarrassment after I slipped on one brown and one blue shoe early one morning when I was in too big a hurry to get to the office to meet a deadline?

• • •

After a considerable time and with great anxiety, I dared to give a Sunday lunch party for some of my coworkers, bosses, and their spouses/lovers. The food was an embarrassment. The tough chicken bought at a local store when the FAO commissary ran out was so impervious to knife and fork that no one could even cut it after knives dulled and tines bent. Fortunately there was a lot of wine available to drown out everyone's memory. All the guests made the usual effort to at least pretend that they were friends as they made polite conversation, when in reality many would have never had anything to do with one another outside the office. To complete the humiliating experience, our gathering took place just after the Berlin Wall crumbled. The several Germans present turned on the television to watch as sledgehammers continued to be taken to the Wall and ever more young men frantically poured over the rubble to rush to the nearest porno store or enjoy other delights unavailable in the East. All the other European guests, harboring unkind thoughts about their former enemy, took one look at this chaotic scene and headed for our terrace. Fortunately it was a sunny day and the terrace accommodated the Germanophobes until the program was over. I stuck to people who I knew were friends after that.

Counterbalancing some of the new colleagues with their competing interests and quirks were many who became friends. These Europeans, Canadians, and fellow Americans became our entrée into the joys of Italian life. They had been in Rome for extended periods. Having already experienced the same overwhelming sensations, they provided us useful advice and moral support. Ever helpful, they invited us to their homes, shared meals, made recommendations for restaurants, and generally smoothed our way. Some maintained homes in the countryside to which we were invited; others lent us an apartment in Aix-en-Provence or recommended a hotel they found in the south of France or in Tuscany. They invited us to share their travels to Florence, Venice, and beyond. I shudder to think how we would have managed without them, small-town souls that we were.

X

The office culture opened the door to abundant learning experiences and cultural adjustments. I found my office, the bathrooms, the plenary hall, the cafeterias, and the terrace easily. But the rest of the complex was a maze of obscure corridors, dead ends, offices with closed doors, meeting rooms, coffee bars, mail rooms, and shops, in addition to the commissary, a large printing facility, and the FAO's medical office. For a while I felt like I needed a ball of string with one end tied to my desk in case I got lost.

The businesses on the ground floor made up a virtual small town with shops selling radios, irons, and clocks along with clothing, flowers, books, and newspapers. The other spaces were filled by insurance agencies and a multilingual lending library, credit union, photo shop, and bank. The auditorium was the venue for Gilbert and Sullivan and Neil Simon, along with productions presented by the various cultural associations. The ground-floor cafeteria walls always had an exhibition of staff members' surprisingly good paintings and drawings, some of which ended up on our apartment walls. The bookstore became a frequent lunchtime diversion, not just for its delightful name, "Food for Thought," but because it was run by English ladies with an unerring eye for expatriate literary tastes in fiction as well as history and art. There was also an enormous selection of dictionaries. All these distractions ensured that the truly timid never needed to leave the building complex unless they went home to sleep.

In those golden days before security was an issue, peddlers occasionally held court in one of the lunchrooms selling me and others beautiful calendars, jewelry, or Gucci scarves that had "fallen off the truck." It was impossible to tell if the scarves were outright fakes, made after-hours at the factory by workers looking for some extra off-the-books money, or stolen originals. Wherever they came from, Gucci could be proud of the design and quality, which was much appreciated by various family members. Less doubtfully, an enterprising American who made bagels and brownies delivered them once a week, always a welcome taste of home.

My office was roomy. I put up a poster of an angel with dirty fingernails playing a lute and brought in a few plants. Others were more creative, with the choice of furnishings reflecting their backgrounds or particular interests. Tribal rugs and other textiles, posters from art exhibitions, original paintings, and prayer mats for the more devout Muslims decorated the walls and floors. If the occupant was Italian, a picture of the ubiquitous Capuchin Friar, Padre Pio, in his brown robe often watched from a wall. He appeared to be a modern-day version of Mercury protecting his charges as his hypnotic dark eyes followed me around the room.

• • •

Being an average, nearly monolingual American, I couldn't read adequately or write in French, the most common language besides English used for communications to or from the staff. The translation service leapt into action, providing me help, although I found out even they made the occasional mistake fortunately corrected by Jean-Jacques. No surprise management was reluctant to hire me.

My maternal grandfather was fluent in six languages but little of that ability was handed down to me. I felt humiliated by my narrow education, which included only a smattering of high school Spanish and French, not good enough. Jean-Jacques had a suggestion to improve my French in the traditional way: take a lover. Surely he wasn't suggesting a *ménage à trois*, with either Paola or his wife, was he? Deciding not to find out (I liked him but he really wasn't *that* attractive) I opted for a duller method and started regular French lessons with a remarkably patient teacher.

The buildings were filled with a true Babel, from Arabic to Urdu. All the non-Americans I worked with spoke at least three languages (often in addition to their native language), generally English, French, and Italian, making day-to-day conversation a real mash-up. If someone was deemed uncooperative they might be dubbed "a bit of a Bolshevik" or a "Bolshie." "*Buon weekend*" meant "have a good weekend," an always-welcome courtesy. When people met in the hallways they sometimes greeted another with "*salve,*" sounding like Imperial Romans to me although no one raised their arm in salutation like the ancients (or the fascists). When they wanted another coffee they said "*bis,*" meaning "again," as in *biscotti*, twice cooked. "I'll revert" equaled "I'll get back to you later"; "I'm going to take a quick coffee" translated to "I'll be gone for at least thirty minutes."

As I struggled along with French and Italian, I also had to learn formal FAO language. Writing style was always in the passive voice and in a stilted diplomatic style. No more, "I recommend . . ." Instead, sentences often began with, "You may wish to consider . . ." "No one" was spelled "noone." Connection became "connexion" as did other English words that I spelled with a "tion." "While" became "whilst," and meetings did not adjourn; instead they "rose" as if everyone levitated from the meeting room. When making a request in writing the word "kindly" was used, as in "will you kindly sign this document." Decisions were not made but "taken," as if snatched from somewhere in the ether.

One of the most puzzling expressions was "at your disposal," which turned out to mean some document was available for pickup or someone was available to meet. This phrase always made me think of the much-missed garbage disposal in my sink in Portland. The word "strictly," meaning "really" or "only," cropped up regularly. I learned that "scheme" was defined as a plan such as the pension or health plan, not something devious at all. Particularly favored (or favoured) by writers from the Indian subcontinent was "your good self." It was an especially useful expression when the writer was pleading for a job. The terms on the application form could also cause problems. Some applicants filled the space asking about "length of residence" by measuring their home.

• • •

Another learning experience was that bringing one's lunch to work was unheard of, in stark contrast to the Forest Service where I grabbed a bite from a brown paper bag. The lunch hour (and a half) was a sacred time. After a bowl of pasta and a salad there were many exercise classes to work off the calories, including yoga, Pilates, and most descriptively, *claquettes*, tap dancing. For the sedentary, an abundance of venues awaited outside the office if workers didn't want to use one of the cafeterias, the formal restaurant, or the several bars that served snacks. A group of American men dined at the same trattoria about four blocks from the office every Tuesday since they were hired, decades earlier for some. Being the wrong sex I was not invited, equality being slow to seep into the corners and crevices of the United Nations. After a year a friend broke the barriers and arranged for my attendance. I accepted occasionally, always feeling out of place (and unwanted by some). The male waiters, with their lifetime jobs, never changed. My co-diners invariably engaged in the same conversations about baseball and football or how much better life in Rome was in the old days.

One day, however, the static situation was disturbed. A small, wizened white man showed up and was introduced as an agricultural expert, in Rome for a few days from somewhere in the African bush. After introductions, he squeezed into the seat next to me. Moving the chair as close as possible, he leaned over and leered, "I haven't seen a white woman in six months." I didn't fall into his scrawny arms, but the nearby campfire girls were surely ready and waiting.

The most spectacular Roman remains from the Imperial period were in front of FAO, but the walk to the trattoria in the opposite direction was an immersion in ever more layers of the complexities comprising Italian history from Rome's earliest days until the present. On the way I passed a monumental equestrian statue in fascist style dedicated by Mussolini to a semi-legendary Albanian named Scanderbeg who united Albania for a time in a fight against the

Turks in the 1400s. The dedication in 1940 was meant to compare Scanderbeg to Mussolini, who annexed the poor and helpless country the previous year. Next were the moldering ruins of the Servian Walls, begun in the sixth century BC when Rome was still relatively small and at the mercy of nearby tribes. One day a modern attraction stood near the wall's remains. A statuesque dark-haired woman with a plunging neckline and a miniskirt was surrounded by four admiring businessmen in sober, perfectly cut suits, briefcases in hand, all eager to gain her attention as she held court on the sidewalk—her jewelry glinting in the sun against her tan body. I sighed in envy.

Rome's only pyramid came next in the historical parade. It was built in 12 BC by Caius Cestius, a Roman government bureaucrat (an occupation that has never waned in Italy) who served at the time of Antony and Cleopatra and was fascinated by all things Egyptian. The pyramid sits many feet below the street level with wild fig trees pushing out between the marble blocks. It always reminded me of a Piranesi etching.

Near our destination restaurant, named after the pyramid's builder, I could see the monumental Ostiense train station and a post office. The train station was built to welcome Hitler. The post office was decorated with X-shaped lattice designs on the two wings, said to celebrate Mussolini's tenth year in power, his gigantic ego never fully assuaged. Separating the two buildings, the Porta San Paolo stood alone in the middle of a traffic circle. It was originally a gate in the Aurelian walls on the road leading to the great church of St. Paul Outside the Walls. It was once the entrance to Rome from the port at Ostia. The walls were fortifications begun around AD 271 at a time when the *Pax Romana* was beginning to crumble. Now it suffered from a different sort of assault, traffic from six roads coming together in a bumper car scenario as frustrated drivers tried to get around the gate. A plaque on the part of the wall broken to let the traffic through commemorates the liberation of Rome by American and Canadian soldiers on June 4, 1944. Other plaques commemorating the Italian Resistance are on the wall surrounding the Protestant Cemetery where Keats's bones and Shelley's heart rest among the feral cats, along with monuments to eighteenth-century travelers who died on their Grand Tour, Italian communists, and others who were non-Catholics who never made it home. A fascinating place to wander if you don't mind the quiet.

Such was the jumble of the city that made every block engrossing, with its mix of eras and styles all piled up together, overwhelming for someone coming from an area where a building from 1850 was a landmark. Merely walking to lunch made me realize the hopelessness of seeing everything in Rome or Italy during our four-year stay, let alone comprehending it.

XI

Marcus Aurelius reflected that it was easy to put away troublesome or valueless impressions to gain perfect rest and tranquility. He also advised that we should give ourselves time to learn something new. Glenn and I were learning something new every day, but not through rest and tranquility.

Sipping coffee in our neighborhood bar was simple, but everything else about Italy looked complicated, *molto complicato*. We observed political Rome from a distance. The unstable governments changed on an annual basis. Over fifty political parties competed for power at any given time, offering a buffet of choices between the far, far left (anarchists), far left (various communist groups), middle left, middle, right, or far right (fascists and monarchists). One of the more diverting short-lived parties was the Love Party, headed by the porn star Cicciolina, a stage name meaning "little fleshy one" or "cuddles." She was reputed to do titillating things with snakes. On entering parliament after her election to represent an area near Rome, she promptly stripped to the waist, something I couldn't quite picture Bella Abzug doing in honor of female power. Cicciolina's other claim to fame was her marriage to modern art superstar Jeff Koons.

Patriotism, as we knew it, didn't seem to exist. While we were accustomed to see flags flying everywhere, sports games beginning with the national anthem, drivers pasting "God Bless America" on their bumpers, and pledges of allegiance recited before civic meetings, we observed nothing like that in Italy. The most important public buildings had the green, white, and red flag undulating in the breeze; otherwise we seldom saw it. Far more common were flags of the local soccer team like the one draped on the front of my morning bus showing the red and gold of the Roma team. Italy has a national anthem, a stirring march, but we never heard it sung, maybe because the chorus includes, "We are ready to die" after each stanza. Even now after 150 years of unification, Italy sometimes seems on the verge of dividing into north and south again.

One of the benefits of being a foreigner was that all these observations only lent more flavor to our life, a background to our own merry-go-round. The carousel ponies of daily living rose and fell according to what provocations or delights confronted us.

I found a dog-eared copy of the first English-language Michelin Guide to Italy, published in 1959. It enthuses about how Italians live and move with perfect ease amid the beauty of the country, a quality called *sprezzatura*—the art of making the difficult look effortless. We hoped to achieve that level of grace but it was easy to see that it was going to take some time, maybe more than our allotted four years.

The old saying, "When in Rome do as the Romans do," was still apt. Like most children, I read various books about daily life in ancient Rome, but unfortunately hadn't found one about daily life in more modern times. We rapidly learned a few important and ever-useful Italian words: *guasto*, broken; *chiuso*, closed; *fuori servizo*, out of service; and *sciopero*, strike. The American concept of the routine daily grind was not part of our experience; instead it was like living in an opera, with dramatic happenings bursting onto the scene regularly. We were totally unprepared for this idiosyncratic way of living, which always seemed to entail waiting for the next beautifully crafted shoe to drop. We were not alone in this sensation. Everyone, including Italians, used expressions for life in Rome: agony or ecstasy; ridiculous or sublime; an *incubo* or *la dolce vita*. But all in all our ratings tended toward the positive, and it is always easy to complain about other people's countries while ignoring the problems of one's own.

• • •

We had only one real concern about coming to Italy for an extended period: the dismal reputation of the Italian medical system. While Italy had excellent doctors and hospitals for the wealthy, the public hospitals were notorious. At the time, a surplus of doctors and hospital beds in the public sector allowed no incentive to finish treatment. Everyone had access to medical care but stories about dead bodies found in some obscure part of a public hospital, ophthalmologists selling their patients' corneas, fake drugs supplied by the Mafia, or hospital food and real drugs sold off to outsiders were often in the papers. Because of poor conditions in these institutions it was common for relatives to move in with the patient, bearing food, towels, and toilet paper to ensure the loved one's comfort. Rumor was that public hospital jobs, like those in the Rome Opera, were apportioned by political party.

Extended or sometimes endless sick leave was deemed a right by some. There were purportedly doctors willing to offer a medical certificate attesting to a staff member's sickness or their need for indefinite leave. The number of days off corresponded to the amount the "patient" was willing to pay the doctor. On the other hand there was one really delightful benefit of the national system: spa cures. Unfortunately, the UN health plan dropped their corresponding provision shortly before we arrived, ending my vision of a cost-free tune-up at some luxurious fat farm.

Men were told their lab tests showed they were pregnant, confounding the family. One friend (female) wanted to deliver her baby in Rome rather than return to the States. She and her husband looked at several public hospitals before making a decision about where to go for a C-section. One of the most highly regarded had cats pussyfooting through the wards looking for rats or mice. That location was scratched off their list, but the private clinic they selected had attendants standing around smoking in the delivery room and watching the action until her husband threw them out.

My worst fear was having an accident and being hauled off to the *pronto soccorso*, emergency ward, and then to the infamous orthopedic hospital. A friend's son had an accident with his scooter and it took ten days to have an X-ray of his leg. He languished in the hospital for a month with what was a minor fracture. Two coworkers also suffered misfortunes with orthopedic surgeons in this hospital, each being discharged with a permanently damaged leg.

Sure enough, I had a brush with disaster one morning. While stepping off the crowded subway car I slipped and first one foot and then the other dropped between the car and platform as I was struggling to extricate myself. Fellow commuters dragged me out before the train started and I avoided becoming much shorter than I am. My shins were bloody but remained between my knees and ankles as I wobbled into the office shaking with fright and dripping blood on my Gucci shoes. The medical office nurse patched me up, and I luckily didn't need to be turned over to the tender mercies of an orthopedist. Mercury was on guard to save my life.

• • •

I also had an ongoing problem. Even before we left for Italy I hadn't been feeling well. I wrote it off to stress from all the changes we were starting to undertake. The symptoms continued after we arrived, and so did the stress of getting settled and learning a new job. I continued to ignore the problem while turning whiter and whiter. We went with an FAO group on a short holiday to Istanbul about the time I started to feel really sick. Part of the tour included a folkloric show featuring a tattered belly dancer who insisted on shaking her tarnished sequins and moving parts in front of us for an interminable time, hoping for more money in her G-string. "How long are we going to have this woman in our faces?" I said to Glenn. She must have understood English. The next thing I knew she was giving me the evil eye.

When we returned to Rome the curse started to work in earnest and I became acutely miserable. I called the American Embassy to ask for their recommendation for a gynecologist. They gave me the name of a Belgian woman whose office, or studio as it was called, was miles away in the embassy district. I made an appointment. We caught a cab in the pouring rain and dark. When the driver found the address, it turned out to be an apartment building with a few offices on the lower floors. After we were buzzed into the studio we looked around in shock. We thought we might have entered a vet's office by mistake when two German shepherds began running back and forth between the waiting area and the examination rooms, barking madly and shedding hair while their toenails clacked on the tile floor. Exhausted and feeling rotten, I stayed to see the doctor who, without any ado, told me I needed surgery.

By the end of the appointment I was in need of a large glass of wine and a bowl of pasta, Italian-style comfort food. When we got home, I brushed off the dog hair and tried to figure out what to do while curled up on the sofa with my glass and bowl at hand. The thought of surgery in Italy was distinctly unappealing after all I'd heard about Italian hospitals. Our excellent medical coverage would pay for the surgery but not for flights home and back. With Kathryn's small apartment our only American *pied à terre*, I had no place to stay until I went back to work, so it looked like the German shepherds and their owner might be the only option.

The next day I pulled my wits together and made a decision to get another referral before committing myself to the dog-lover. One of the FAO physicians recommended an Italian. This doctor was also located in an apartment building, but I was happy to note his studio didn't have any canine assistants. He confirmed the diagnosis after sending me to different labs for various tests. We frequently saw people on buses or the subway carrying X-rays and test results to the next appointment because Italians kept possession of their own medical records. Soon I was running all over the place like everyone else with results tucked under an arm.

Rome is full of private clinics and several highly regarded hospitals used by expatriates if they didn't go home or to Switzerland. I decided to use the private clinic recommended by the doctor. In the interim, Glenn's mother had a stroke and he rushed home, arriving several hours before she died. Trying to get back to Rome in a hurry to take care of me, he got stuck in Chicago for twenty-four hours when Alitalia went on strike, a frequent occurrence.

Early one morning in December we drove to the *casa di cura* in the suburbs on the far side of Rome. It wasn't modern, but it was clean and quiet with a lovely garden and a mossy fountain plinking softly. The room contained two beds in case Glenn wanted to stay, which he did for two days.

Like in many FAO offices, hotel lobbies, bars, and restaurants there was a photo of Padre Pio to welcome me to the simple room. By this time I had heard about his miracle-working capabilities. Much beloved by legions of Italians who flock to his burial site, he remains controversial due to persistent allegations of immorality and fraud. Although not a favorite of the Vatican, he was eventually canonized after decades of entreaties from his supporters. Whatever his character might be, the good Padre overcame the evil eye I garnered in Istanbul and ensured that surgery was uneventful. The Italian-style aftercare, however, was unexpectedly unpleasant. The older nuns who ran the place spoke no English, did not believe in pain killers, and whiled away their time by hand-cranking the bed up and down whether I wanted them to or not. The food was the same as hospital food everywhere, except I was served bland pasta instead of bland rice or potatoes. Even more dispiriting, the coffee was weak too. While I was lying in bed helpless, friends came to visit, which was cheering until they told jokes that made my incision hurt when I laughed.

Thankfully, my sole Italian medical adventure came to a conclusion with a rapid recovery helped along by a short trip to the Greek temples of Paestum south of Naples where flowers were already blooming in the winter sunshine and ancient columns stood white against the blue sky.

• • •

The other aspect of Italy not for the fainthearted was banking, a game where it seemed impossible for an amateur to win. Although Italians were credited with the invention of the financial system in the 1400s, there appeared to have been no improvements since then except for the addition of computers. Like some burlesque of communism, getting the surly bank clerks to work was nearly impossible. The managers were dressed to the nines but many of the tellers slouched around in shabby clothes or old jeans. So much for *la bella figura*. Their contracts allowed jobs for life, an extra month's pay or two each year, the standard eight weeks' vacation and holidays, plus a certain number of days to strike. They could walk out for several hours whenever they felt like it with no loss of pay, and the bank would frequently be closed for a union meeting lasting half a day. To make monetary life more annoying, Italians must have also invented the term "bankers' hours." The offices were open for about three hours in the morning and two in the afternoon after a long lunch break. This schedule meant unfortunate customers spent hours standing in line waiting for the clerks to carefully examine their identification, money, or checks, fill out numerous forms, and blow smoke in their faces before the transaction was completed. I only knew that the transaction would be successful when the clerk started stamping, *bang, bang, bang*, and then scribbling initials over all the paperwork.

UN pensioners and those on the (often fake) invalid lists passed out by various political parties did their banking toward the end of the month, the same time as the staff were paid, yielding ever more impressive delays. One day, a tiny elderly gentleman in front of me in the interminable line got so upset at the slow pace that, after screaming and waving his arms demanding his money, he dropped to the floor with a stroke. This dramatic turn of events resulted in much further arm action and yelling by the surrounding patrons until first aid arrived and he was carted off. The tellers were unimpressed by this blatant attempt to get them to hurry.

My own interactions were less traumatic. It took upwards of three weeks for an electronic transfer to or from our bank in Oregon, and the credit union two doors away had to go through an American bank to move money. Once, just as I handed over a check for cashing, the clerk went on strike. With check in hand, he slammed the wicket shut and walked away. The manager told me to come back in two hours as this was a normal occurrence. I waited anxiously. Two hours later the check was cashed as if nothing had ever happened. "Normal" developed a whole new definition in my lexicon and we learned to keep plenty of cash on hand.

• • •

Banking was my particular dare. Glenn's was learning how to negotiate a crowd waiting for service. The revelation that Italians did not like to line up in a queue, preferring a more friendly method I called a gaggle, came as Glenn endlessly waited for our tax identification number, *codice fiscale*, shortly after we arrived. He got tired of being elbowed out of the way by people who arrived long after he had. Looking around, he saw a little old crone moving steadily forward. He sidled up and hung in her wake, looking like some furtive pervert until he got to the front of the line. This newly acquired skill stood us in good stead and he never again wasted any further time being overly polite when it came to waiting in a crowd.

We both marveled at the frequent strikes by aggrieved workers and nonworkers alike. Bank, gas station, and transport strikes were aggravating, but strikes by garbage workers, mail workers, teachers, tourist bus drivers, doctors and hospital staff, judges, journalists, TV presenters, and news agents were only background noise. Students and pensioners were always ready to march against the government. Judging by the papers and television, strikes and demonstrations were one of the national pastimes along with tax avoidance, soccer, and cycling. Coming from Portland, where workers generally submitted to whatever came their way with only grumblings of discontent, we were impressed by how many groups could march along the avenues to the main piazzas with their red flags, placards, and banners denouncing their opponents.

When in Rome . . .

Routine daily life beyond hunting and gathering also required a lot of changes in attitude. It also supplied us with amusement. Our evenings at home sometimes included the wonderfully awful Italian TV shows. After the news a woman in a suggestive dress read the next day's horoscope. Then came the many variety shows. *Spettacoli* were indeed spectacles with herds of scantily clad starlets flouncing around either a goatish male presenter who wore a cheap toupee or a female celebrity with tons of hair who was barely contained in her clothes. In either case, when the hosts weren't introducing talentless performers they spent their time either chatting with the studio audience or telephoning people in the hinterland: *"Ciao, Maria, come stai? Bene!"* A stupid question for a prize followed. The presenters must have had jaws of spring steel, for they never quit talking. Some productions were so amateurish that stagehands walked in front of the bouncing bimbos, hosts, or guests, and people tripped over cables strewn about the stage.

One channel showed movies from the 1930s and '40s. War films hailed magnificent (and, in the light of history, largely imaginary) Italian military successes. *The White Ship*, probably made in Mussolini's Cinecittà studio (built for propaganda purposes but later home to productions like *Cleopatra* and *Roman Holiday*) showed gorgeous nurses patching up handsome, slightly wounded pilots who had returned from heroically bombing defenseless Greece or Malta. Glenn preferred soccer along with occasional spaghetti westerns featuring cowboys sitting around campfires sipping tiny cups of espresso with their little fingers daintily crooked.

Far more interesting than the programs were the advertisements. Italy may be a Catholic country, but sex sells everywhere. Naked or barely dressed women were prominent on all European channels hawking eyeglasses, cars, tomato sauce, and, especially in the summer, ice cream frozen into suggestive shapes and slowly licked by a nubile young woman who had forgotten the top half of her bikini. One of the best ads was for butter, showing a split screen with one couple in bed reading and the other furiously making love because they used butter instead of the dull margarine used by the couple with their noses in books. After viewing the instructional scene we ensured that no margarine was on our table.

Another example of the genre was a gorgeous hunk coming down the stairs in his barely-there briefs. He opens the refrigerator to retrieve his brand-name jeans where they had to be stored to keep him cool. Still another showed a family sitting around the dinner table with a young couple giving each other smoldering looks while eating their pasta. She leaves the table for another room and a few seconds later he follows. Rather than the expected bedroom scene they meet in the kitchen where he helps her make more pasta sauce. An even more delightful ad showed gods and goddesses on a dusty ceiling fresco dropping their clothes into a washing machine where they were restored to Renaissance colors before magically flying back to the naked cavorting deities. It seemed that much of the legendary Italian creativity came out in their advertising.

Billboards lining all the major streets were also creative, but I couldn't imagine them in the U.S., with bare breasts and butts draped over cars or anything else that could accommodate female anatomy. Girls sitting on scooters, viewed from the rear, advertised underpants. These ads were often sponsored by my usual brand, the unromantically named Sloggis. At Christmas one year I laughed at an unfortunately matched pair of giant billboards. The first showed a naked woman lounging on her stomach with the bra she was advertising perched on her ample backside as she stretched out, showing off her shapely posterior and legs. The adjacent billboard had a gigantic picture of the stuffed hind leg of a pig, *zampone*, a common Italian holiday food.

Following Christmas came billboards for slimming prior to bikini season. The ads showed young women who were *snello e sodo*. Unsure what these words meant, I consulted our tattered dictionary. *Snello* meant slender, pretty obvious when looking at the picture, but *sodo*, firm, frequently referred to hard-boiled eggs. Indeed, it was easy to picture the firm bottoms as being halves of a hard-boiled egg.

The few ads that ever raised an uproar were those of a huge-breasted pitch-black woman nursing a newborn white baby (produced for a company peddling sweaters), and a crucified man whose high-fashion jeans were suggestively falling off. Even in open-minded Italy they got the desired attention and then some.

• • •

We constantly needed bus tickets. The little tobacco shops scattered in every neighborhood were our destination when we needed them or Glenn's favorite mints, the Salia brand. Some *tabaccherie* still had an old black-and-white sign saying *sale e tabacchi*, salt and tobacco, dating from the days when salt was a state monopoly. The shops no longer sold *sale*, but they did sell cigarettes along with lottery tickets and the special string and lead seals required to mail a package—a real disincentive to bother mailing anything. The most popular and cheapest brand of cigarettes was called MS, a not excessively clever abbreviation for *Monopoli Stato*. The state still retained a monopoly on local manufacture and all distribution except for those smuggled from Albania on aptly named cigarette boats and the ones available in our commissary. The shops also did a huge business selling official forms, paperwork being a national mania with requirements surpassing those of our very own Internal Revenue Service. The correct type of blank paper or document had to be purchased along with a tax stamp, a *marco bollo*, in order to file a report with the authorities for an incident like burglary. The rules were strict and applied even if you were trying to prove that you were alive after some bureaucrat inadvertently declared you dead.

• • •

The newspaper always plopped on our doorstep at dawn seven days a week in suburban Portland. No such convenience was available in Rome, nor was there a fat Sunday paper. During the week, I bought the *International Herald Tribune* in the office, but on Saturday we went to the local newspaper stand, *edicola*, for the weekend paper before heading out of town or continuing to the bar for our cappuccino and *cornetto* if we were going to hang around Rome. The Italian papers each represented a faction or party whose political views were trumpeted for the first five or so pages. One of anti-Catholic persuasion frequently printed a cartoon on the front page showing the pope naked. Papers cost about three times their price in Portland. This resulted in passengers on public transport straining to look over the shoulder of the person in front of them.

All around the stands were broadsheets fluttering in the breeze with big letters advertising *concorsi*, ads for training to take tests for various kinds of employment: 485 jobs in the Carabinieri, 85 jobs in ministries, or an unnumbered amount in the notoriously inefficient and slow post office—the signs varied from month to month. Jobs were scarce, unemployment high, and competition stiff. On a hopeful note that life would continue as usual, the following year's calendars were already on display by midyear. Outside the tourist area, where the focus was on dreamy Tuscan scenes, we were confronted with three varieties: Ferraris, naked women, and Mussolini. Glenn found the first two photogenic, but Mussolini was no sex symbol to either of us with his oversized jaw jutting out in the aggressive pose of a short-statured bully. His frequent appearance was a reminder of an idealized past where Italy was powerful and respected, and that he still had an ardent following.

The crowded display racks also held dozens of beautifully photographed fashion and home décor magazines with dream kitchens, as well as those for travel, cars, and sport. Alongside were stacks of titillating magazines, comics, and videos devoted to sex of every flavor, including Doberman Pinschers to appeal to the demented. All were in full view. No one else was concerned that they were often right next to the children's comic books and toys. Being prudish in Italy was a waste of time. I gave up.

XIII

Without a car the first few months, we did a lot of walking. Crossing major streets was exciting. In contrast to Portland where there was always a walk-wait sign to help the pedestrians and drivers stopped before the crosswalk, we sometimes felt that Roman drivers considered us to be targets. When we needed to cross the wide avenue near my office we tried to wait for a covey of nuns for safety. Less cowardly Romans raised their arms with palms facing outward while they blithely stepped off the curb into the void. But it was best to be nimble in any case wherever we were.

We also rode the bus, tram, and subway carrying all sorts of bulky and heavy things like chandeliers and two irresistible Persian carpets back to our apartment. Public transport was unpleasant due to crowding and grime, but it was generally efficient unless there was a breakdown or strike. Given the layout of the streets, some in existence since Rome's legendary birthday on April 21, 753 BC, the extensive bus routes were convoluted as they snaked around the monuments and newer districts. It was easy to get lost, which I did the first time I came home from work after dark, ending up on the military reservation before finding my way back home in a sweat.

Commuting to work involved first the bus and then the subway, called the Metro. The system had two lines, A and B, both dirty and jammed in rush hour, not bad in the winter because body heat compensated for the lack of heating, but miserable in summer with no air conditioning. The cars were dirty and covered in graffiti inside and out. The gravel between the tracks was a carpet of cigarette butts. Gypsies played their accordions while begging from commuters who avoided eye contact but dropped coins into the extended paper cups, hoping to get them to go on to the next car. Pickpockets and *frotteurs*, men who rubbed against me in a manner they enjoyed but I didn't, squeezed through the packed cars. Bottom pinching was out of fashion though, or perhaps mine wasn't tempting.

Our biggest travel nightmare, an *incubo* as the Italians often called it, was the interchange between the two routes at the main train station, *Stazione Termini*, where passengers burst out of the cars like champagne out of a shaken bottle. Thousands tried to get to the street, the train station, or the other line at the same time. Escalators were often out of service, adding to the jams. We heard Italians saying as they left the cars, "Now we are entering the Inferno." It was an apt comment and would have given Dante a challenge to decide which circle of hell he would have consigned the architects who planned the interchange.

Graffiti covered the Metro station walls, along with every other wall or flat surface in most parts of Rome. The most common motifs were an "A" in a circle, the anarchists' logo, and the star and circle of the Red Brigade terrorists, neither being comforting sights. It was easy to figure out the sexual symbols, which remained as popular as they were in ancient times. "Down with the USA" or similar thoughts were also frequent along with other, often left-wing, political slogans. At least I was spared the old fascist slogans of "To Dare, To Endure, To Win," or "Mussolini is always right." (My personal favorite, which did not appear daubed on walls, was "A nation of spaghetti eaters cannot restore Roman civilization.")

For all the inconvenience there was a consolation: sights and smells of food accompanied me on the early morning commute. When the Metro was above ground for a stop by the central wholesale vegetable market I could sample the atmosphere without shopping. In winter, wholesalers stood around small smoky fires made of broken crates while shop owners overloaded their *Apes* with shiny purple eggplants, bright red peppers, tomatoes, white onions, bunches of bright green broccoli, and small purple or dull green artichokes. In summer, the odor from piles of fresh basil permeated the warm, humid air coming in the open car windows, making me think of pesto sauce. My mouth watered at 6:30 in the morning.

• • •

I was eligible to buy a new car tax-free after the probationary year. After a month or so of dragging lighting fixtures, carpets, and small pieces of furniture onto the bus like itinerant peddlers, it became obvious that we needed to get some sort of interim transportation. The common practice among FAO employees was to buy a used car from another staff member. After looking at many postings on the office bulletin board we thought that we had found something that would do for that first year. It was described as in *ottimo* condition, which we thought meant "optimum," but turned out to mean "usually runs." At least *ottimo* was a step above *discreto*, "fairly good" in the dictionary, but when applied to a car meant "lemon."

Used car sales are the same the world over, and the old Renault we bought soon dropped its pretenses and revealed itself to be such a piece of junk that driving it in public was a humiliation. It was so awful that it fell below the standard "town car" many expats drove around Rome if they had a good one for the highway. A town car in Rome is not a Lincoln Continental but a beater with lots of battle scars and without radio or hubcaps or other desirable amenities. But it runs. By contrast, our chariot regularly stopped in the middle of a road and parts fell off without any intervention by thieves. We prayed that it would be stolen in its entirety, but local and Albanian theft rings wouldn't cooperate, though we left it unlocked on the street over entire weeks in the faint hope someone would take it. Meanwhile, the Italians all sped by in their new Alfa Romeos, Lancias, and Ferraris, none of which ever showed a dent or scratch, or in a tiny old *Cinquecento*, affectionately called a *Topolino*, Mickey Mouse, ideally suited for parking on sidewalks.

• • •

Traffic in Rome was as everyone described it: chaotic since time immemorial. In an effort to assert some order, Julius Caesar decreed that no chariots or wagons could enter the city from sunrise to sunset. We could imagine what it was like during the night with squeaking wooden cart wheels, bellowing oxen, and swearing carters trying to get through the narrow lanes. The single modern day without traffic was *Ferragosto*, August 15, the Feast of the Assumption of the Blessed Virgin Mary. On that day contemporary Romans were at the beach and the streets were nearly empty. Only a few sweating tourists remained, all desperately trying to cool off in the fountains.

In the year 1175, Alain de Lille said, "A thousand roads lead men forever to Rome." At one time there were twenty leading through the wall's gates: San Paolo, San Lorenzo, and San Pancrazio are among the memorable names. Along with the imaginary road that led me to Rome, the problem is that now about twenty-five actual roads currently lead to the ancient center. When the frustrated driver eventually arrives in the old city, there is no place to go beyond the labyrinth of narrow streets and a few central piazzas. The most frantic location was Piazza Venezia, where about ten streets come together. When we were on foot and not trying to cross the piazza we enjoyed the sight of the immaculately dressed traffic cop futilely gesticulating at the speeding cars. Standing on a pedestal, he looked like he was trying to conduct an unruly orchestra. Not that anyone paid any attention.

With the tortuous layout, city driving was a competitive sport where rules of the road were merely a suggestion timorously offered by the authorities. Whenever a red light did stop a procession of drivers, the number of lanes doubled or tripled—if the street was two-lane, at least five rows automatically congregated at the intersection, all waiting to race off when the green light flashed. (There was no worry about obeying traffic lights at night because most of them were turned off.) Like the Italians who didn't line up at the post office or bank, drivers maneuvered into intersections as far as they could go until they were bumper to bumper with the other cars. No one could move over to let an ambulance, police car, or fire truck pass. Shouting and honking in a slow game of chicken, the more aggressive got through a few seconds before the more fearful. But the road rage was short lived, and accidents other than those with two-wheelers were seldom to be seen in the city, the driving skill a higher level than first appeared.

Major intersections were crowded with men who washed your windshield whether you wanted it or not. Young Gypsy women showed what looked like horribly deformed feet and legs in an effort to extract money from sympathetic drivers. When their shift was up we watched them running like gazelles across the street to their next duty station.

Along with all the other distractions, we had to beware of drivers swerving across all traffic lanes from the farthest right hand lane to make a U turn in front of the cars going in both directions. There were other hazards too, like one dark, rainy winter evening when we came upon a woman pushing a man in a wheelchair in the middle of four lanes of rush-hour traffic, oblivious to the vehicles. Help Mercury!

Braver than we, no one else wore seatbelts, and when legislation was enacted requiring their use, many drivers donned a white T-shirt with a diagonal black stripe starting on their upper left shoulder, clearly showing their customary contempt for the law.

• • •

Despite the orderly layout of Roman military camps, geography, time, and decay dictated an absence of straight lines in modern Rome. The preference for sinuosity continues, with even the newest subdivision a maze of circles and angles and dead ends. The few straight streets built by Mussolini were bulldozed through ancient quarters. One leads to the Vatican and another is the Via dei Fori Imperiali, alongside the Forum. It was used for parades in his vain effort to recreate the atmosphere of the ancient Roman Empire. A series of bronze plaques affixed to an ancient basilica shows the expansion of the Empire, or if we walked backward, how it shrank again, a warning not heeded by *Il Duce*.

We used our *Tutto Città*, a detailed book of maps that came every year with the telephone book, to find our way. The *Tutto* was so coveted that if an apartment occupant did not get one from the building entrance immediately after delivery, it vanished, only to show up in the front seat of someone else's second or third car. Even with their detail, the maps didn't always help plan a successful route. The confusion in street layout led everyone to develop their own special way to get from Point A to Point B. When we asked for directions, each advisor insisted that his or her way was the fastest, but they were all equally contorted. Part of the problem was the *Senso Unico*, one-way system, which had little rationality. Trying to get to a hotel to pick up a friend, we drove on a one-way street until suddenly the street turned into a one-way going the opposite direction. Glenn had to back up in heavy rush-hour traffic in the rainy dark. His vocabulary had continued to broaden, and included ever more flamboyant Italian expressions and gestures.

Like most Italian cities and towns, Rome is roughly circular. Major roads become crooked chariot-wide streets with their name changed every block or two. Rather than Main Street or Park Avenue, the major streets in all cities are named for national heroes. Since there isn't an endless supply, every city and town invariably has a main road named after Vittorio Emanuele, Umberto I, Garibaldi, or Manzoni, in addition to prominent communists or socialists. Names are so similar that stories abounded about intrepid tourist drivers finding their way into a city center while the navigator was using a map of a different location.

One-way streets have the *Senso Unico* placard on a pole at eye level, easier to see than the obscure street signs affixed to the second story of some Renaissance palazzo where few notice them. Inevitably, this arrangement leads to confused tourists trying to find their way back to Senso Unico Street where they parked their car. One day while we were in our embassy, a perplexed American walked in. He neglected to note where he had parked and, after a day walking around sightseeing, he had no idea where he left his rental car other than a street named Senso Unico. No one could offer much help other than commiseration and, after he left, headshaking and eye-rolling. Another time an American couldn't remember the name of his hotel or where it was. Working at the consulate wasn't a job I aspired to after overhearing these cries for help.

In contrast to the repetitive names of the main roads, there was an enormous variety of names for the smaller streets, which demonstrated ever more Italian creativity. Whatever was actually located on streets named Tancredi Parmeggiani, Misericordia, or Padre Marino Colagrossi, the names were a lot more exciting than our former addresses, like 86th Avenue South. Some streets even had two names separated with the word *già*, meaning "formerly" because the street was renamed at some point, a not-uncommon event. Often, the street sign would indicate the significance of the name such as poet, singer, or philosopher. Some names were inexplicable, like the Street of Motorists. It was one block long.

Living not far from a military base, many streets in our area were named after lancers, frogmen, cuirassiers, and grenadiers. The martial names contradicted the neighborhood character with its quiet residential streets. Our apartment was on Divisione Torino, the Turin Division, at the intersection with Ragazzi del '99. A plaque was affixed to the outer wall of our building with a wreath hung below. The military wreath, common throughout Italy at many war memorials, was reminiscent of ancient Roman triumphal crowns. Made of tightly woven laurel leaves and small golden-colored balls, a ribbon in the Italian colors of green, white, and red served as embellishment. Our wreath was renewed once a year in honor of the "boys" of '99, the young men who became eighteen in 1917 and who were the last conscripts to fight the Austrians in World War I. They fought in the disastrous Battle of Caporetto in the Alps (one of the settings for Hemingway's novel *A Farewell to Arms*) and in the great Italian victories at Piave and Vittorio Veneto, the latter now the name of the street where the American Embassy is located. The plaque said: "Glory to the boys of '99, who in the most troubled hours brought to the Piave the smile of Italian youth and the desperate will to win."

XIV

The roads leading into Rome became our roads out to the rest of Italy and Europe. We wanted to take every advantage of weekends and the generous leave provisions the FAO offered, including a month's vacation time and numerous holidays. Until we got a reliable car our friends stepped in to offer many short day trips to nearby towns for a little sightseeing and long, companionable lunches.

Our first weekend outside Rome provided us with an indelible experience that finally put to rest any lingering doubts we had about moving to Italy. New friends, Peter and Maria, gathered us up for a trip to the Tuscan town of San Gimignano. It was February—cool, damp, but sunny. Our route took us through small hill towns and quiet fields until we rounded a bend and saw a city in the far distance, its skyline punctuated with what looked like skyscrapers, black against the blue sky. In reality it was close by and our destination, a twelfth-century walled town filled with ancient towers. Winter afternoon was already setting in. The low sun lit the cold medieval stones, beckoning us to bundle up and start exploring. The empty cobbled streets echoed with the raucous cry of jackdaws circling the churches, civic buildings, and towers. Built when the Guelphs, supporting the pope, and Ghibellines, the Holy Roman Emperor's faction, battled each other for power, each side tried to build taller than the other for military advantage. Now peace reigned and many of the towers had fallen or were crumbling with age, home for roosting birds and dangling vegetation.

Our hotel incorporated part of the ancient town walls. When I looked out our window I could see below me the tiled roofs of stone houses, laundry hanging limp in the damp, and small cars tucked into courtyards. The restaurant, decorated with medieval and Renaissance pottery and sculptures, featured a dinner menu suitable for the season with venison, wild boar, and red wine from nearby woods and vineyards.

The morning brought a slow sun rising over misty fields already emerald green with winter wheat. Cypress, olive, and umbrella pine trees completed the dreamy picture. We departed after breakfast for Montalcino. The rows of now-bare vines covering the hills had long since given up their fruit and golden fall leaves. Men were already in the vineyards beginning to prune the sleeping plants before spring arrived. We paused at a *fattoria* to buy thick red Brunello di Montalcino. The owner showed us his winery and helped load bottles in the car trunk while an elderly woman did laundry by hand in a tub placed underneath an old olive tree. Her hands were as gnarled as the tree's trunk from wringing out the cold, dripping garments over the years.

The Taverna dei Barbi was the venue for a lunch of freshly made ravioli filled with *zucca*, pumpkin, followed by grilled *bistecca*. Then, as if we were modern-day mendicants, we followed the Via Francigena, a medieval pilgrim route, to the Abby of St. Antimo. The rolling countryside was dotted with chestnut forests, vineyards, and olive groves. A few dead sunflower stalks, their heads declined as if in prayer, stood in fields waiting to be ploughed under in the spring.

Founded by Charlemagne in the eighth century, the *abbazia* had a "new" church and bell tower dating from the twelfth century while incorporating elements of the original. We crossed the greensward toward the massive door. The sound of a Gregorian chant at the hour of Vespers greeted us as we entered the nave. The church was empty except for a young monk whose voice filled the space. We listened to the sound in peace while gazing upon a magnificent carving of a crucified Christ. With eyes open and head to one side, he appeared to be listening too as he ascended to heaven.

We knew that we had found our Italy.

• • •

A year filled with events causing us to laugh, learn, enjoy, and sometimes wonder what we were doing soon came around. We now had the opportunity to buy a decent car tax-free. We took a train to Antwerp, the best place to pick up brands from all over Europe and Japan. We selected a zippy little red Alfa Romeo. It was a novel way to shop: look at auto magazines, check to see that the one we wanted was in the broker's catalogue, and pay the asking price. No test drive and no negotiation on the price or extras. Payment by certified check or money transfer only. It sounded simple. But it turned out to be a week of frustration when the broker would not accept our check drawn on the FAO Credit Union despite repeated reassurances from the manager that the check was the same as certified.

Phone calls back and forth to the credit union were to no avail. In a humiliating reversal of life's natural order we called Kathryn to ask her to wire money. After she finished chortling at our unexpected predicament, she accepted the challenge of trying to explain to our bank in Portland what we needed. Between the weekend, a bank holiday in Belgium, and the crash of the international money transfer system, we saw a lot more of Antwerp than we wanted, but the beer, French fries, and mussels dished up consolation. The city looked dark because I lost my glasses on the train and was stuck with sunglasses the whole time. A full week later we had our car. A month later I received my replacement reading glasses—it was August in Italy after all, the sacred month of vacation.

I managed to unload our old junker on an unsuspecting Egyptian translator. Every time I saw him in the hallways he looked at me reproachfully. I gave him a cheery wave as I passed by.

With our new wheels, we were now ready to start on number one in the game plan for our Italian sojourn: travel beyond where the train could take us. Countless local and regional maps along with hotel guides were consulted during the week. They were replaced one after the other when they wore out from overuse. We lived to travel, heading out early Saturday mornings before the Romans got going in order to avoid the traffic on the ring road leading to the *autostrada*.

The basic driving method on the *autostrada* for Italians was to pretend they were driving in a Formula One race. When one passed another, the would-be Mario Andretti narrowly avoided a "kiss," first to the rear fender and then to the front of the target car as he slipped out and back into the right-hand lane. The basic method for us was to stay in the "slow" lane until we wanted to pass. Then we'd look really, really carefully in the mirror, step on it as hard as possible, and swing out. If we lingered for one microsecond in the left hand lane an immense Mercedes or an elegant Maserati or Ferrari would suddenly fill our mirror, the driver furiously flashing his lights for us to get out of the way. I kept my mouth shut (most of the time) but my knuckles were white. Inevitably we saw an accident, an *incidente*, due to speed or carelessness. Glenn firmly believed that Fellini produced documentaries, and that a scene in his film *Roma* depicting the horrendous traffic mess on the ring road around Rome was an accurate portrayal.

Except on Sundays, when all but food transport trucks were banned, truckers from all over Europe, including Russia and Turkey, ramped up the thrills as they also drove as fast as possible weaving in and out between us, a *Cinquecento* or even a three-wheeled *Ape* loaded with tomatoes and eggplants. Trucks carrying enormous blocks of Carrara marble careened past. Herds of motorcycles sped by. Once the group was a wedding party with the bride's white dress and veil streaming out behind her as they passed us in a blur. Another day we overtook a *Cinquecento* slowly proceeding along the highway. It had a 50-liter wicker-encased glass bottle of wine or olive oil strapped to the roof. The bottle was approximately the same size as the car. The occupants didn't appear to be bothered by their lack of speed or the overload—Mercury or a guardian angel would do his best while they continued their energetic conversation, waving their arms, oblivious to danger.

At the first tollbooth on the *autostrada* a ticket is automatically issued to be given to the toll taker at the next intersection with another freeway or when taking an off ramp. We were heading for the Piedmont in the far north when I tucked one edge of our latest ticket into the air vent on the dashboard to keep it in sight. When we reached the off-ramp tollbooth the ticket had vanished.

We stopped and searched—no luck. When we explained to the ticket taker in fractured Italian that it was lost, the man went berserk, hurling *imprecazioni* ranging from "assholes" and "idiot foreigners" to outright obscenities. This went on for what felt like an eternity with cars piling up behind us while we shrank ever further into the seats until a supervisor showed up to take over and deal with the problem (us). He was rational but we still had to pay a huge amount, calculated from Rome instead of the nearby freeway interchange. We were shaken from the unlikely encounter, afraid that the first man was going to come out of the booth and physically assault us.

We reached the hotel and started to unload the car. I was on my knees looking for some maps on the floor of the front seat and looked up. There was our ticket deep in the air vent where somehow it had been sucked in. We were greeted with true Italian hospitality from the hotel owner, who spoke perfect English. Though I kept a rule never to complain to Italians about other Italians, we were so upset that I told her about the incident, repeating the wild man's tirade. She blanched when she heard the sad tale, complete with the more colorful and rude expressions, then picked up the telephone. In a few minutes our hostess announced that we would receive a refund of the excess amount with an apology. She topped up the good news with two bottles of red wine from her vineyard surrounding the hotel. From then on toll tickets were kept clutched in hand.

Another trip unexpectedly brought us back to America. A friend's daughter and her husband were stationed at a large American military base near Verona. We were invited to visit before touring Venice and the Veneto. We made arrangements to arrive on base late on a Friday night. The next morning we found ourselves in an impersonation of our former home surrounded by fast food outlets, smoking barbeques, obese people, and gigantic pickups driven with soldiers wearing camouflage and buzz cuts. It was a disconcerting geographic warp instead of the time warp among antiquities that we usually experienced. After dining on greasy hamburgers we began to worry about adjusting when my contract ended and we returned to the States after four years.

XV

Glenn is a country boy at heart and our more local excursions were his special pleasure. Often we drove north up the coast to visit Etruscan sites, a favorite with guests. They also enjoyed Subiaco in the hills southeast of Rome, where a medieval monastery clings to a rock face overhanging a gorge. Our visitors were fascinated with the church's grisly frescoes depicting all sorts of tortures—probably not the best sight just before we headed for one of the many restaurants in the tourist-filled town. The main church is built over the cave where St. Benedict retired in the fifth century after overseeing the construction of the great abbey at Monte Cassino. His lunch arrived on a rope lowered by fellow monks. His twin sister, St. Scolastica, set up her own establishment a few miles away. How she got her daily bread is not recorded.

If the timing was right, we went to pink-stone Spello for the *infiorata*, a festival with a carpet of flowers portraying religious themes carefully arranged on the narrow and steep main street. In a manifestation of the swift passage of life, we watched as priests trod the dewy petals into mush during the procession celebrating Corpus Domini Sunday. Sometimes our goal was Deruta for pottery or Montepulciano for their Vino Nobile. And sometimes we just circled a town on our map, hoping to find a good restaurant for lunch. We always found one.

On Sundays, crowds of bicycle riders in their bright club colors took over the entire width of the road so they could talk while pedaling, making it impossible for anyone to pass. Occasionally we had a glimpse of men relieving themselves near the roadside. I sympathized with them because rest stops and bars with their available toilets could be hard to find. At many wide spots along the roadside, prostitutes in skimpy clothes awaited customers no matter what the weather. The beautiful but sullen-faced women, trafficked by the Mafia, were frequently from West Africa, though a contingent from Eastern Europe and a few flashy Brazilian transvestites also competed for business. With only a crate or broken lawn chair to sit on and sometimes an umbrella for protection from sun and rain at their designated spot, the scene was more depressing than that in Rome.

Prostitution is legal in Italy but pimping is not. The occasional roundup often netted the local police, who were enjoying the prostitutes' favors in return for not prosecuting their pimps. While degrading in our opinion, prostitution frequently showed up in old Italian films by Fellini or Pasolini where the women were often pictured as laboring in just another occupation—purportedly the world's oldest. (I'd vote for bureaucrats preceding them.)

At the entrance to each of the little towns a post with a dozen or more signs pointing to the next villages confronted us. The signs were in no particular order although the one on the top usually said *tutti le direzioni*, "This is where you might be able to go from here." They were real head-scratchers and we often went round and round in circles until my slow reading of the unfamiliar names began to match what I could find on the detailed map of the local area. I turned the map this way and that trying to match the signpost to where I thought we were, often calling out, "Turn NOW," only to be followed by, "Damn—I think it should have been the next road."

Once we actually made it to our hilltop destination, the entertainment, at least for the locals, continued. The one-lane one-way streets, about the width of our small car, required us to fold in the side-view mirrors or drive over doorsteps, to the amusement of the inhabitants who were sitting outside preparing vegetables and chatting. When we hit a dead end or a sharp corner, Glenn's careful maneuvers provided even more comic relief to the onlookers who stood around or leaned out of windows to see what would happen.

Fortunately, we were only in one *incidente*. Unfortunately it involved the Carabinieri. On a sunny winter Sunday we were driving in the countryside north of Rome. Arriving at an intersection on a back road Glenn signaled, looked, and began to turn left. No one was coming—the road was empty. Suddenly a car came roaring at great speed over a small hill with the low sun behind it, blinding us until too late. Glenn swerved to evade the oncoming menace. The

Carabinieri's blue Alfa Romeo missed our red one by a hair's breadth. Their driver was not as skillful as Glenn and his car went out of control, careening into the roadside ditch. The car was scraped and the driver got a bloody gash on his knee but merciful Mercury intervened and no one was seriously hurt. We were terrified when the officers jumped out of the car with guns drawn and directed us to follow them to the nearest station. When we arrived we were confronted by the chief, the *maresciallo*, who sat at his desk, glaring at us. On the wall behind him was their organization chart. At the top was a crucifix, then a photo of the pope, then the president of Italy followed by photos of their current senior officers. We had heard that their patron saint was the Virgin Mary, so with all the high-powered signals emanating from them toward us we knew that we were up against a real problem.

We produced our documents, title, driver's licenses, and identification showing limited diplomatic immunity. After receiving a long lecture we couldn't understand, we were presented with a statement we couldn't read except for the bottom line showing the amount of the fine. Envisioning a scene where we were thrown in a dank cell with a bucket in the corner if we didn't cave in, we signed, dug out the cash, silently crept out to our car, and carefully drove away, anxious lest anything further happen. We suspected part of the anger was that they must have been driving at least 90 miles an hour, judging by the length of their skid marks. We often watched Italians argue their way out of a ticket but our skills were no match against the *maresciallo*, who probably had to explain the mess to his superiors. I'm sure that the story was embellished—stupid foreigners and all that.

When I took a copy of the document we signed to our insurance office the next day I received another lecture, this time in English. How was it possible that we could have been so stupid as to pay anything and sign a document agreeing that we were at fault? Humbled again, I tiptoed out of that office too.

XVI

We ate, we traveled, we befriended, and we learned to manage the demands of living in another country. Time passed much too fast. As the end of the four-year contract approached, I received an inquiry from the Forest Service asking whether I intended to return. With its suspension of our previous reality, and its interesting friends, travel, food, and wine, our Italian lifestyle supplied us with better opportunities than we ever hoped for. Like Dante's *Divine Comedy* we traveled through purgatory at times, but fortunately skipped the Inferno part. Many times we thought we reached our idea of Paradise, our *dolce vita*. Had we ever felt that way at home in the United States? No, we hadn't.

FAO expected me to stay on with a contract renewal. Despite the myriad attractions of our expatriate life, we never seriously considered settling in Rome, where challenges were always present. We saw that some of our friends and colleagues, longtime residents, slowly became virtual exiles as they turned their backs on their home country, and after they retired also lost touch with former colleagues. Many married Italians and then divorced, making them more isolated. They weren't Italians but they weren't Americans or British anymore either.

An additional problem was that I didn't have quite enough time in my US government pension plan to earn a full annuity; Glenn's early retirement had resulted in a reduction of his. And we missed Kathryn despite her frequent visits. It was as hard for us to wave good-bye when she boarded the flight back to Seattle as it was for her to leave the land of endless pasta and sunny sightseeing.

But we weren't ready to leave. It was a dilemma, the reverse of the one we faced when deciding whether to move to Rome, and far more painful. Sleepless nights thinking about the best course of action took up a month. Yes, no, yes, no—what to do? In the end, we decided that it wasn't wise to cash out my retirement plan and I gave notice to FAO. They were surprised. I was depressed.

The prospect of leaving drove me into a shopping frenzy, not that Glenn noticed much difference from normal. Having an entire shipping container available meant that we didn't have to worry about bulk. One departing friend dreamed of bringing containers of Rome's tap water home to ensure that her pasta tasted right. Maybe I could bring a small chapel, block by numbered block, like the nineteenth-century industrial barons? We packed up all the shoes I'd accumulated from the small artisans scattered throughout the countryside and local flea markets. Into the jumble went sweaters, and odds and ends of furniture and piles of pottery. We gave away the untouched liqueurs. We arranged to sell our Alfa to friends. When we went to the street where we parked the previous evening, ready to hand it over to the buyers, it was gone—stolen. The insurance money was more than we asked for when we negotiated the sale. I felt sad that our sweet car had probably gone to a chop shop or to the East to meet an uncertain fate.

A week before we left, we had an opportunity to pay a last visit to Marcus Aurelius to bid him farewell. His statue, like that of Mercury, played an inadvertent part of my life and the opportunity to see him in the flesh again was welcome. The statue's lengthy restoration was nearing completion and I didn't expect another chance to see him unless we came back to Rome as tourists. We were invited to a private visit in the Ministry of Culture's restoration laboratory to learn about the technical details of the statue, the painstaking restoration methods, and the construction of the exact replica now occupying its pedestal in the center of the Campidoglio. We climbed ladders that placed us within touching distance (no, we didn't) and admired the skill of the ancients. The statue with his outstretched hand now wished us Godspeed. His pensive expression seemed sad. We, too, were downcast.

In contrast to my first visit to Rome in an earlier life, this time I went to the Trevi Fountain. I was in a melancholy mood knowing that our imminent departure marked the end of an important period in my life. I had achieved the goal of travel but still wanted more. I worried about the future and what it would bring after losing the community of FAO.

Following tradition, I threw *lire* over my shoulder into the gushing fountain. Oceanus and his Tritons, busy managing the Earth's waters, didn't visibly acknowledge me. Colleagues brought a case of champagne to the office to see me off. Too soon the bottles were empty. The furniture was shipped. The plane was on the tarmac ready to take us first to Bangkok then Hong Kong, followed by a stop in Portland to visit friends and family and to pick up items we had stored. Then it would be on to Washington, DC, where a new job awaited me. The wheels went up and we soared over Ostia Antica and the blue Mediterranean in the reverse of our arrival. We were outbound to another life. I cried a little, knowing that Italy would soon be a distant memory.

• • •

I was assigned to a thankless job I expressly told the Forest Service managers I didn't want. Glenn went back to paid work as a courier for a medical lab company. (Picking up pee wasn't interesting, but the company had the best Christmas parties we've ever been to.) It was easy to manage our daily lives, and we didn't need to be stoics. We bought a home in Virginia in far less time than it took to rent the apartment in Rome. Bills were paid by check dropped in the mail instead of by cash at the post office. Grocery shopping was done in an hour on any day at any time. I stood in my new kitchen hugging the efficient and large appliances and watching the sink with the disposal really at my disposal. We learned to talk without moving our arms, stand in line patiently, not say *mamma mia*, keep to the speed limits (after a few speeding tickets), and park in designated spots. We tried Italian-themed restaurants, not always with a happy result. The ambience of Italy couldn't be duplicated.

No more long weekends in small hotels set in olive groves or villages that had grown organically from their hillsides. No more song of the bells that marked church services in our Roman neighborhood or those of the placid sheep. No more quick trips to France for a long weekend. Worst of all, no more Friday evenings of pizza and red wine shared with the many friends who so generously eased our transition into FAO and Rome. Exchanging Christmas cards and e-mails wasn't a satisfactory substitution for their daily companionship.

Luigi Barzini, in his book *The Italians*, asked, "What then is the fatal spell of Italy?" as he described Italy's great creative qualities and never-resolved political and economic problems. At times I felt like tattooing L-O-V-E and H-A-T-E on my knuckles to help decide how I felt on any particular day in Rome. But the positive invariably outweighed the negative. Like everyone else we complained at times, but like everyone else, we didn't want to leave. We tried to adjust back to the American routine, but the pull of Italy never diminished. It was no surprise when almost no one in the insular Forest Service was interested in talking about living abroad. Eyeballs glazed over and yawns were barely stifled. We were outsiders, adrift between two lifestyles with no easy way to accommodate our mixed feelings.

I developed a bad case of Italian fever. The symptoms of this incurable disease are a longing for fields of red poppies, olive groves, ancient ruins, pasta homemade by *nonna*, luscious fruit and vegetables, fresh mozzarella, and long lunches in the countryside gazing at the passing scene and talking with friends who are sharing the meal. I entertained the idea of embroidering "Home Sweet Rome" to hang on the wall. Tears sprang into my eyes whenever we drove near Dulles Airport and Alitalia flew overhead on its outbound flight. There is no known cure for this ailment, but temporary remission can be achieved by two-week applications of return visits—medication we took annually.

The roots of this longing for a life somewhere else probably came from family history. Various grandparents came from England and Germany, with stops in Ohio, Colorado, Japan, and Chile on the way to settling in Canada. I never knew any of them, nor did I have any idea why they left Europe. Even though they must have had stories to tell, no one was interested enough to record their history for me or any other of their few descendants. Were they wandering minstrels, Gypsies, or just part of the millions who departed in the late nineteenth and early twentieth centuries for a better life—those with a family motto of "serfs up"? Whatever the reason, the genes kept moving when my father left his prairie home in his teens to see the States. While an aunt was sent to a convent school in Belgium, and an uncle to a naval training academy in Chile, my mother only got as far as New York. She lived there for a time with her mother in tow while she studied ballet with a male teacher who barked like a dog. The only reminder my parents kept from their limited youthful travels was a walrus-hide Gladstone bag and a steamer trunk—always in my line of sight whenever I went to our basement storage area. Maybe they too had wanted to travel farther but circumstances were against them. They never said anything, but it was clear that I didn't fall far from the tree when it came to wanting to travel.

PART TWO

LA DOLCE VITA

XVII

Three long years after what I thought was the end of our Italian *dolce vita*, the siren call of Italy beckoned me to return. Another branch of the United Nations, the World Food Programme, FAO's sister food agency also headquartered in Rome, had an opening. In contrast to FAO with its emphasis on statistics and improved practices, WFP is much more adventuresome in its mission. Their staff specialize in delivery of emergency food aid to countries such as Ethiopia, North Korea, Haiti, Afghanistan, Somalia, and Sudan when they are stricken by tragically common famine, war, or natural disaster. WFP also supports food-for-work projects to improve infrastructure, and school feeding programs to encourage families to send their children to school, especially girls who are so often left without education and married off too young. The proposed job was chief of staff relations, similar to my previous work, plus management of a group who administered the many benefits offered to entice people to work in dangerous locations, often requiring them to leave their families behind. The position also offered opportunities for travel to some of WFP's work locations in Africa and Asia.

Glenn wasn't any more enchanted with DC than I. When I was asked to come for an interview in Rome, he whisked me out to Dulles airport and kissed me good-bye at the Kiss and Ride to wish me *buona fortuna*. When my prospective supervisor welcomed me to Rome with a kiss on both cheeks and treated me to lunch, I began to be hopeful that I would soon be standing in front of the Trevi Fountain again. The fates nudged the process along when history repeated itself with an opportunity for an early retirement from the Forest Service, this time for me. The offer to leave the government in return for a small payment arrived the same week as I received the offer from WFP. Oceanus and the Tritons had heard my departing wish at the fountain after all. I called Kathryn, who was now fully occupied with her own life. She said, "Go!" The first words out of my mother's mouth after we returned were: "Why did you come back?" She said she had no objection to our new departure, although I wondered even though she often said that, if she wished that she had an adventurous life when she was younger. Fortunately, she was living in Vancouver with nephews and their families close by and was still in good health.

Our unhappy DC interlude came to a close. As Terence opined in the second century BC: "How often things occur by mere chance which we dared not even hope for." We watched as our battered furniture was loaded into a shipping container yet again. Rome welcomed us back. Marcus Aurelius was also back on his pedestal, now protected in the Capitoline Museum with an exact copy in the piazza's center.

Our new home, again in EUR, was located on a street named for a suicidal midcentury poet. We found an apartment on the top floor, the *attico*, with a large and sunny wraparound terrace from which we could see the Castelli Romani. Roses were already blooming. We added a lemon tree, bougainvillea, and an olive tree to shade us and pots of orchids. Our kitchen was (marginally) better. We had a heating system that we could control rather than the inadequate system of the first apartment. But it was déjà vu all over again when we found ourselves sleeping on the floor while awaiting our furniture delivery. Happily, the air mattress didn't deflate and our furniture arrived undamaged, a big improvement over the misadventures of our first arrival.

The landlord on our first sojourn had kept his distance. This time around we found we had an unexpected problem. When we first viewed the apartment the owner was quiet, polite, and impeccably dressed in a suit and polished shoes. He was elderly and tall with thinning grey hair above piercing blue eyes. His wife, a picture of dumpy humility in her plain cotton dress and gray hair done up in a bun, silently smiled as she followed us around the empty rooms.

But a few days after we moved in, *il padrone*, a term that sounded a lot like *The Godfather* to us (*Il Padrino*) came to make his presence formally and firmly known. He presented his business card with a flourish. The engraving announced that he was a *Commandatore* although the word was carefully crossed out with two diagonal lines to graciously indicate that we did not have to use his title. (Old Italian hands told us that *Commandatore* was a basically meaningless honorific for someone who worked for the Italian state for a long time—or just another word for *pezzo grosso*, big shot, depending on your point of view.)

His innocuous demeanor changed as soon as we were in his clutches. Our new and fraught relationship was colored by sudden bursts of shouting and arm movements. His whole body expressed aggression and sometimes he stiffened up like a baby about to throw a tantrum. Although he didn't resemble Marlon Brando, our *padrone* continually made "offers" we couldn't refuse, as in "you owe me more money." Unwilling to let a lira slip through his fingers, he never hesitated to stand a few inches away and scream false accusations such as cheating on a bill for repairs to the heating system. When our telephone rang, the sound echoing off the terrazzo floors and on through the apartment, we hesitated to pick up the receiver, worried the call would be to announce another too-frequent visit to inspect his property. We mentioned his eccentricities to friends. They responded with the gesture for crazy: thumb to forehead, hand turning back and forth.

Il padrone continued to show up with regularity, apparently having nothing else to do. After he finished shouting at us he switched gears with gifts and repeated insistent invitations for meals at his home in Rome or stays at his villa in a small town in the toe of Italy. The gifts included figs from the garden of his southern home and foot-long animals made of almond paste—a fish at Christmas and a lamb at Easter, both filled with something like mincemeat. The office staff was always grateful for our regifting as it soon came to the point that the sight of marzipan made Glenn gag while I envisioned kilos of extra fat stubbornly clinging to my thighs. Not that the gifts were unattractive. The sweet lamb with creamy fleece and brown hooves was adorned with Christian symbols and a little white flag with a red cross sticking out its back. It rested on a mirror, all wrapped in cellophane. The fish came in Christmas wrap. The first time I unwrapped one I recoiled in surprise. The large staring glass eye and expertly crafted silvery scales and fins made the fish look all too real. Was a dead fish some sort of mafia message? Would a severed horse's head turn up on the doorstep next? No, the fish was a typical southern Christmas treat.

When we couldn't think of any more excuses, we accepted the invitation to Sunday lunch although we dreaded hours with strained communication and too much food. *Il Commandatore* insisted on driving us to his spacious and beautiful apartment in the Parioli quarter, where many diplomats lived. As we drove by a public hospital on the way, his wife turned to us in the backseat and gave the sign for warding off evil: the little and forefinger pointed downward. This gave us some concern about her cooking skills and the emergency ward we were passing. Their son and daughter, both in their thirties, unmarried and living at home, Italian style, were waiting for us when we arrived. They did speak rudimentary English, about equal to our Italian, so the conversation didn't lapse entirely although there was really nothing to talk about during the interminable *pranzo* with the lack of anything in common but the transfer of our money to the *Commandatore*. My jaws ached trying to keep smiling while throwing out a few conversational gambits that were quickly batted right back.

An Italian friend told me of her family's expression for bad cooking: *né sapore né amore*, cooked with neither flavor nor love. This was not the case with our landlord's wife. During the entire meal Mamma was in constant motion, presenting ever more heaping platters and bowls filled with food, urging us to have seconds and thirds while exclaiming "*mangia, mangia*," eat, eat!! The son and daughter tried to tell her that we could not eat everything, but she wasn't deterred. We started with three pastas: rigatoni, fettuccini, and orecchiette, all with meat or other rich sauces. Next came the meat: beef, pork, and chicken; followed by platters filled with mountains of vegetables; then salad. By the time we got to dessert, a large serving of tiramisu, we could hardly bear to look at it. Along the way we were offered martinis, white wine, red wine, and then *grappa* or *digestivi* after dessert. The *digestivi*, bitter liqueurs like *Amaro*, or Cynar made from artichokes, are an acquired taste, one we never mastered. We returned home after four hours and took our own brand of *disgestivo*, that is to say, antacids. We groaned for a while before going to sleep at five o'clock in the afternoon.

XVIII

Other than too many interactions with the landlord, our daily life this time around was more peaceful and organized. Mercury stood guard to prevent accidents or hospitalizations. But now work offered more *agita*. It was devastating attempting to locate surviving family members to make arrangements for life insurance payments after such catastrophes as the genocide in Rwanda or the depredations of the Lord's Resistance Army in Uganda, which resulted in the deaths of many local staff members. Plane and vehicle crashes took the lives of other staff. The worst times came when people I knew were murdered, including a young Dutch woman who was killed in a robbery in Burundi and an Italian man attacked in Rwanda. These events were not all that unusual for United Nations' staff but I had never been so directly involved before. The names on the memorial wall steadily increased.

My skilled assistant, whose watchwords were "*Ci penso io*," "I'll take care of it," spent endless hours arranging for repatriation of remains, an incredibly complicated process when bodies needed to be transported through several countries on their way home. These horrible events further opened my eyes to the dedication and bravery of the staff and the general nastiness of much of the world, some of which was now directly confronting me.

Travel took me to occasional meetings in easy places like Geneva, Brussels, or New York. Sometimes there was an opportunity to travel to countries more reflective of most of the real world when I took a few days after meetings to visit friends or tour in Jordan, Sri Lanka, or Tanzania. All had refugee camps or food aid operations that I visited. But what really brought the world closer to this sheltered American were two journeys that bracketed my time with WFP. Both supplied a startling and sad commentary to my life of contemplating what delights were awaiting in the local market or what kind of pasta sauce Glenn would invent on my return to Rome.

•••

I sat in the Frankfurt airport waiting to board the flight for Addis Ababa via Jeddah on my first travel to one of the most desperate countries WFP supported with food aid. Fellow passengers were Ethiopians, Arabs—some women veiled and others showing hennaed hands and feet—and Western aid and oil workers. When we landed in Jeddah a stewardess came on the intercom: "For those passengers not deplaning, please be sure to put away any alcohol and pornography." The departing unveiled women covered up. The rest of us felt hot night air enter the plane as we sat on the tarmac far away from the terminal. Not having any alcohol or porno magazines, I left my seat to look out the open door. The stewardess rushed up to tell me it was forbidden, lest my face pollute any stray man who might be servicing the plane.

It was late at night when the plane arrived in Addis. A man with a UN sign was waiting. We drove through an unlit city to the Hilton Hotel. I could hear loud music thumping when I briefly stepped onto the balcony before collapsing in bed. The next morning East Africa was before me in the guise of a huge and impoverished city. The hotel was surrounded by rusty tin-roofed shacks with a few modern office buildings in the smoggy distance. Below me was a large swimming pool in the shape of an Ethiopian cross. The nearby Kiedu African Dance Club was now silent in the early morning sun, replaced by the sound of chanting from the Ethiopian Orthodox church in the other direction. Flowering red flame trees, purple jacaranda, and pale green eucalyptus were scattered between the shacks spreading in all directions.

A woman sat in the hotel lobby roasting coffee beans over a charcoal brazier before grinding and serving the astringent brew in miniature cups—a perfect wake-up. I decided to walk up the lane to the gate while awaiting the driver who was to take me to the office. As I neared the road a horde of children and adults hanging around waiting for a guest to come near rushed toward me. Their hands clutched the iron bars while they shouted for money, money, money in every Western language and used the universal sign to ask for food:

fingers in mouth. I retreated, a protected prisoner, understanding why walking alone in the city would not be a good idea for a cowardly traveler on her first trip to the third world.

Emperor Haile Selassie's old palace still stood near the hotel. Worshipped by Rastafarians in Jamaica, he was long dead and the communist regime that followed was gone, too. I remembered the story about a discovery of a virtual sub-flooring of greenbacks hidden under the carpets when the palace was looted in the revolution that brought the communists to power. On a more accurate note, WFP friends told me about being caught in the crossfire during the fighting when the communists themselves were thrown out after a seventeen-year reign of terror. The city was headquarters for many aid organizations battling a never-ending hunger problem throughout the country caused by drought, flooding, exhausted land, and tribal, religious, and ethnic fighting. Meanwhile, arguments about how much aid, what type of aid, or any aid at all continued to rage, filling up journals, blogs, *Foreign Affairs*, *The Economist*, and offices of aid agencies and donors.

Many of the city streets were unpaved, and like so many impoverished places, the poor were rooting through the few garbage containers or the many open piles of refuse. Children in rags were begging or trying to peddle small items at every intersection. A few men stood by the roadside selling the tall woven grass tables used for communal dining. The tables showed up in restaurants as stands for trays lined with *injera* bread, which was used to scoop up lentils and spicy stews made with chicken, lamb, or goat.

Between bureaucratic duties I visited two projects where WFP food was distributed. First was a British charity offering health care to mothers of twins, not uncommon in this ancient and proud country, the only one in Africa never colonized. Babies were weighed, and food and nutrition advice was offered to destitute mothers. Next was a food-for-work project where men were digging pit toilets for their local community, which had no sewers. The men received payment in the form of food rations. Knee-deep in God knows what kind of muck, workers and crowds of onlookers were dressed in American and

European castoffs: sweatshirts with the logos of American basketball teams and universities, along with tattered blouses and pants with designer labels. This largesse, the shabbiest of donations, arrives by the container load to be resold for profit to the poorest of the poor crowding local markets. Was the young woman standing next to me wearing the old sweater I donated to a charity the previous year? It looked somewhat familiar, a discomforting thought about the relationship between the rich West and the rest of the world.

My itinerary took me to Kenya some days later. I arrived in daylight when it was safe for a UN vehicle to pick me up and take me to the compound where the many UN agencies were congregated. Outside the main business area Nairobi was full of shantytowns with hovels made of sticks, board, flattened tins, and corrugated roofing sitting amid raw sewage and refuse. The red earth supported a few cornfields, with vendors selling roasted ears nearby. In between the crowded slums and the small plots were schools and hospitals built by the Aga Khan charities. Their courtyards were filled with uniformed students and patients in their cast-off clothes. The UN complex of low buildings, surrounded by bird-filled trees, was an oasis in a sea of poverty.

Wilson Airport in Nairobi was busy even though it was barely dawn. Single-engine planes lined up for takeoff, one after the other. "Where are they going?" I asked. The answer: "To Somalia, to deliver khat." Bags and bundles of the narcotic herb were being loaded into other small planes while I waited along with several WFP staff to fly to Lokichokio. After an hour's flight near the Rift Valley, we landed on a runway where some of the parked planes had bullet holes to show for their efforts to provide aid in the protracted conflict in southern Sudan. The settlement, no more than twenty miles from the Sudanese border, was populated by the native Turkana tribe, Sudanese refugees, termite mounds, herds of donkeys and goats, and aid organization offices. Turkana people wearing only a few beads sat in front of their grass-covered huts, without interest in us. Dispirited refugees squatted in insufficient shade from the stick-roofed shelters. The isolated airstrip was used to air-drop food to starving Christian and animist Sudanese under attack from the Muslim Janjaweed militia. This militia, made up of nomadic tribesmen, was supported by the Sudanese government, who used them as a proxy to drive out the sedentary farming population and force them to surrender resource-rich land. Janjaweed means "devils on horseback," an apt name for the massacres and rapes they perpetrated. The militia sometimes pursued aid workers along with the rebels. Another bloody game in which the innocent starved.

The airport consisted of a fuel dump, small control tower, and several "rub halls," huge tents that aid agencies use to store emergency supplies. The tents held tins of cooking oil and grain and legumes ready to be triple bagged and loaded on an old twin-engine Canadian Buffalo airplane, a design known for its ability to take off and land on short airstrips. Sweating workers were slinging 120-pound sacks of food into the plane's cargo area. The sacks were to be air-dropped as the plane flew at an altitude of only 1,600 feet to help ensure the bags didn't break on landing. Food aid monitors had already marked drop points on the other side of the border awaiting the delivery. Village headmen were ready to gather the bags and oversee distribution to women who had registered their families, the amount doled out depending on the family size and ages. Did I want to go on a flight? Yes I did, but with no authorization from the Sudanese authorities, it was too much of a chance. Instead, I watched the plane lumber down the airstrip and take off over the brush-covered hills to return empty an hour or so later.

Lunch was served in a cafeteria used by the aid workers where Western food was supplemented by local food for the Kenyans. I was hungry after the early start and scooped up spicy goat stew, tough but tasty. The aid workers' simple accommodations had insect-ridden thatch-roof huts and communal showers. No TV. Only the most adventurous and self-sufficient took these jobs and even they didn't stay more than a year or two. Part of the reason for my trip to this remote airstrip was to talk to these workers to assess the need for expanding our counseling service, which attempted to assist them in coping with the rigorous and dangerous conditions. A need for the program was obvious when women food aid monitors told me about running for their lives and hiding in the scrub for days to escape the Janjaweed marauders before being rescued.

Mission accomplished and dusk falling, I was glad to get on the twenty-passenger plane for the flight back to Nairobi. On the homebound leg were a few WFP workers and several extremely tall, thin blue-black Sudanese, silent and dignified in their white robes and turbans.

My hotel was the Norfolk, with little plaques on some room doors where Teddy Roosevelt and Ernest Hemingway had slept, although Ernest was said to have spent most of his time in the bar. I sat on the veranda in the early evening watching businesspeople relaxing over bottles of Tusker beer and vans rolling up to the hotel entrance. The drivers slid open their doors and gathered up Americans wearing brand-new safari outfits. They were all trying to look like Robert Redford in *Out of Africa* as they ventured out to the bush for a few days' sightseeing in the game parks. Across the street, students were loudly protesting some issues at the nearby university. The power went out.

The breakfast buffet the next morning was extravagant in its variety and I assumed the fruit had all been carefully washed. Within two hours I was vomiting uncontrollably and having the DTs while lying in the UN infirmary. Although the doctor wasn't much impressed I had visions of a lonely death while being besieged by imaginary wild animals and ghosts. So much for my brave African adventure. After the more unpleasant symptoms abated, the office director's wife hauled me off to their home where I slept off the remainder of the problem, dozing with the faint smoke of the mosquito coil keeping me company.

My rescuers were hosting a party that evening. I managed to pull myself together and lurch out into the garden to make a late appearance. The house was a fortress: guards with their leashed German shepherds stood outside, broken glass topped the garden walls, bars covered the windows, and a safe room could be found inside. Talk at the party turned to the dangers in Nairobi: the chief of security for the UN had recently been murdered there in a carjacking. Out of the corner of my eye I could see two men leaping over a hedge. Good God, were we going to be attacked? No, it was the guards on patrol.

I wanted to do a little shopping before heading back to Rome. First, we went to a shopping mall. It was surrounded by high walls and had heavily armed security personnel in body armor strategically stationed throughout. Then we went to one more shop a half block from the hotel on a busy street. The driver pulled the car onto the sidewalk directly in front of the door so I could buy some beadwork.

The next evening, I waited for an old unmarked taxi to take me to the airport. It was too dangerous for a UN vehicle to drive the route after dark due to the many recent carjackings of their desirable, nearly new SUVs. The airport was in disrepair. Empty sockets stared at me in place of ripped-out video monitors. The flight back to the bounty and peace of Rome gave me time to think about the unhappy lives of those caught in the middle of never-ending violence. On a happier note, one of the brightly colored woven grass tables that I admired in Addis showed up in my office, courtesy of a friend who talked a pilot with the national airlines into throwing it into the cargo hold.

• • •

Toward the end of my time in Rome I participated in a review of WFP operations in Cambodia. The object of this trip was an assessment of various food-for-work projects, part of the effort to restore the ravaged country after the Khmer Rouge, headed by the brutal Pol Pot, collapsed. I wanted to see more of the world in which the United Nations operates—the world as it is, not as it should be—and a chance to learn more about the possibility of rebirth in devastated areas.

My colleague and I were delayed deplaning after our flight from Bangkok to Phnom Penh. Ground staff were still taking care of another plane whose tires were shot out by an important passenger in a display of petulance when he found his luggage was missing. When we eventually checked into our small hotel I quickly found out why the WFP's medical service gave me a tube of flea powder and a package of pills and potions before I left Rome. For $15 a night I had a thin mattress on a narrow bed, CNN, and a shower with an electric water heater affixed to the wall above the showerhead. Every time I stepped in to wash off the sweat I worried that I would be fried.

The city was coming back to life with scooters and bicycles maneuvering past buildings riddled with bullet holes and circling the Independence Monument, an ugly red sandstone replica of an ancient temple like those in Angkor Wat. Chinese gamblers filled new five-star hotels on the banks of the Mekong where shops sold French pastries and international newspapers. We ate along the river in one of the many crowded outdoor restaurants where snake was a major attraction on the menu. Another night, dinner was in an old French colonial home converted into a bistro. This time we were on a balcony watching thousands of geckos covering the walls and ceiling, so many I mistook them for wallpaper before speculating on what I was eating. The Russian Market, named for former shoppers who came to support the regime, was booming. The hot and airless covered area was filled with stalls piled with hand-woven silks, pottery, old carvings ripped from buildings, ornate "silver" gourds and teapots, and Korean robes. A shopper's paradise. I succumbed as usual.

We shared a small plane to Siem Reap with a crew of de-mining experts. I leafed through the colorful in-flight magazine of Royal Air Cambodge, all happy talk in defiance of reality. The route for the forty-five-minute flight took us over fields where millions died of starvation trying to produce rice for export under Pol Pot's regime. At one point I looked down on Tonle Sap, a lake whose waters flow into the Mekong River in the dry season. It was small but when the monsoon rains came later on, the river would back up to make it the largest lake in Southeast Asia. As we prepared to land at the tiny rural airport our plane circled over another lake, this one a perfect square built by the ancient Khmers as part of the enormous Hindu temple complex that includes Angkor Wat.

Before meeting with the local office staff in Siem Reap the country director warned that none of the local people wanted to discuss what they or their families did to survive during the dark times. Even without the admonition

I would never have asked if they had been collaborators or seen their families murdered. What I would have done in the same situation was a question I couldn't answer either.

The international staff had their own issues. One had recently married a Cambodian. He was applying for Cambodian citizenship but worried about being allowed to remain because internationally recruited UN employees were seldom allowed to serve in their home country. He would have to make a decision on his future. He showed me the wedding photos. The traditional Cambodian wedding ceremony, an oriental dream with everyone in brilliant blue, green, pink, and gold silks, was held at one of the temples, Bayon. With its crumbling towers carved as gigantic smiling bodhisattva heads serenely contemplating Nirvana, a more dramatic site was hard to imagine.

In a more realistic side of an aid worker's life, I talked with another young man about his inability to recover from the sudden death of his infant son. With no doctor readily available, the child succumbed from a fever in only a few hours. The tragedy encapsulated the hazards of living in difficult places and the need for counseling along with other support as a first line of help in such tragic situations.

First on our inspection itinerary was an orphanage, a recipient of WFP-donated rice. Children were supplied with food and schooling. The curriculum included traditional crafts and dance taught by the few who managed to escape the efforts of the communist regime. The regime's intent was to wipe out anyone who could be deemed an intellectual in their futile quest to remake Cambodia into a workers' paradise; i.e., hell. A young man proudly showed us his efforts at making a buffalo skin shadow puppet, one of the many arts nearly lost in the terror. What these children had seen in the killing fields was beyond my imagination.

We stopped at a warehouse used to store bags of rice to be distributed as food aid to ensure that the manager kept accurate records of the stores. The building was riddled with so many bullet holes in its outer walls it didn't need electric lighting for us to look around. Outside, a statue of a female rice harvester raising her sickle high in the ultimate communist posture presided over high-wheeled bullock carts carrying cattle feed to another depot.

We drove along roads built high above rice paddies where women bent over double as they planted rice seedlings in the mud. They'd look up from their backbreaking work to smile and wave as we passed by. Our destination was a food distribution site set up in a grove of trees near a large water wheel. The Cambodian Red Cross arrived in trucks loaded with bags of rice with the WFP logo, a stylized hand grasping corn, wheat, and rice surrounded by olive branches symbolizing peace, all in the United Nations color of sky blue. The workers also unloaded Coke bottles filled with cooking oil, along with paper twists of salt. Meager rations were handed out after each team leader signed that his group's portion of work restoring market roads had been completed for the week. Nearby, a mini market was springing up. People began picking over the small selection of tattered clothing. Balancing their food allotment and maybe a shirt or third-hand pair of tennis shoes from the market on their bicycles, they pedaled away to their homes built on stilts overlooking the paddies.

Our small hotel was similar to that in Phnom Penh. Flea powder was again advisable. Nearby, the Raffles Hotel had reopened, with evening performances of traditional dance and music accompanied by a lavish buffet with displays of tropical fruit and vegetables. Other hotels were under construction to accommodate tourists starting to fly in from Thailand. Their goal was Angkor Wat and other nearby sites built around the twelfth century by the Khmer peoples. WFP projects included several to help clean up and restore the area, which had fallen into ever more ruin during the Pol Pot regime. Workers were patching and sweeping while their children came out to beg as we talked with the supervisors. Other locations like Ta Prohm were slowly being strangled by nature, the press of grasping fig trees and other jungle vegetation unstoppable.

At the end of a day, we took time to visit Angkor Wat. Legless beggars lined the causeway built over a moat, land mines having accomplished their brutal work. A few young saffron-robed monks were in evidence; most of the others had been murdered in the holocaust. We slowly moved through the deserted complex looking at the carvings covering every wall. Voluptuous temple dancers, *apsaras*, had grapefruit-like breasts that seemed stuck on as an afterthought. Wars raged, monkeys danced, fish and turtles swam, and birds flew in the silent stones.

In the late afternoon we sat on a ledge and watched the sun set in the west and a full moon rise in the east, as they always have, no matter what lies beneath the light—whether more of the world's horrors, the possibilities of peace, or my comfortable, well-fed life.

XIX

My limited firsthand view of the privations of everyday life in the countries I visited where WFP provided food aid heightened the contrast with the banquet before me in Italy. I tried the dry high-calorie biscuits given to the starving and had seen the bags of rice, beans, and other basic foodstuffs distributed to those who were without any means to obtain food. When I returned home to Rome I was again in a land where, since the Italian economic miracle of the 1960s, food meant pleasure for all the population rather than a constant battle against starvation.

But like the millions WFP tried to help, Italy has undergone its own periods of privation and famine. The ancient Romans went to war to keep their grain supply flowing and passed out bread to keep the populace quiet. Malnourished peasants emigrated by the millions in the nineteenth and early part of the twentieth centuries, and people starved during and shortly after World War II. The contrast between tall, well-fed grandchildren and their elderly *nonni*, who hobbled along on legs bowed by rickets from their deprived childhoods, was a living history lesson.

It seemed ironic that food aid agencies were headquartered in a location where there was now such an abundance that we could never hope to sample it all. Despite the appearance of callousness it was a coincidence that they were located in food-obsessed Rome—postwar politics and the presence of the International Institute of Agriculture, which was founded by an American in 1908 to improve food supplies, combined to make Rome a good choice as the United Nations expanded in the 1950s.

Whatever its availability, the love of good food was bred in Italians' bones (or stomachs). In about 30 BC, Virgil rhapsodized about fat lambs and luscious wines in his *Georgics*. Apicius, a first-century AD Roman gourmet, compiled the first known Western cookbook, *De Re Coquinaria*. It was in wide circulation by the fourth century, an early version of *The Joy of Cooking*. Although we couldn't find many of its ingredients, such as flamingo tongues and rotten fish sauce, we did make dishes that the ancient Romans would have recognized such as fava beans and roast chicken with olive oil and garlic. From Petronius's *Satyricon*, written in the late first century AD, to Fellini's film of the same name 1,900 years later, through Etruscan and Roman wall paintings, to Caravaggio's sexy *Boy Holding a Basket of Fruit*, to the libraries of Italian cookbooks from Apicius until today, we could see that food has been central to Italians' imagination for as long as there have been Italians.

Part of our motivation to return to Italy and attempt to live the *dolce vita* again was to experience more of this gastronomic paradise. Our disappointing stops at the local supermarkets in Virginia pushed food back to the more utilitarian place it occupied in our earlier lives. Once we got back to Italy food returned to the disproportionate share of our mental pie charts it deserved.

We occasionally heard of people who didn't like Italian food. One story told of an American recruit who left a note on his boss's desk one evening saying he was leaving after a week because he couldn't stand the food. Another described how he hated gelato. A friend who lived in a hotel for nearly a year ate *spaghetti alla marinara* every night until a waiter told him that he wouldn't serve it anymore until he tried other foods. He tried another pasta sauce before reverting to the usual. Such a thought never crossed our minds.

Local food opportunities were similar to those near our first apartment, with the addition of a couple of restaurants. One produced superb pizza hot from the wood-fired open oven. Unlike the usual modest pizzeria, our new find had inlaid marble floors and original artwork on the walls, with prices to match. The dilemma there was whether to stick with the traditional *margherita* and *quattro stagione* or go with more inventive varieties like smoked salmon and capers on its own paper-thin crust blackened at the edges from the fire.

Rather than using an uninteresting but well-stocked nearby supermarket, we often walked to a small space set at street level of another apartment building a few blocks away. It was owned by two brothers who managed to cram in dozens of crates loaded with fresh fruit and vegetables on the floor and out the door, along with bottles of local olive oil and wine set on dusty shelves inside the shop. They welcomed us on Saturday mornings with a friendly greeting. We waited our turn while they gently fussed over a young girl with Down's syndrome who frequently arrived with her mother at the same time we did. Their care for the child and their efforts to pick out the best for us, while knowing we were only *stranieri* who would one day depart, were one of the many examples of the boundless Italian graciousness.

Again we had to make an effort to keep the shopping to an amount we could actually eat, given the limited capacity of our cupboards, our slightly larger refrigerator, and our (also slightly larger) stomachs. But the temptation to keep going was always there. When browsing the markets after the vegetable shopping was done, we looked for Sicilian capers packed in salt or semi-hard sheep's cheese, *pecorino*, from Siena. Melons were always perfect because the vendor asked if we were going to eat them that day or the next before he selected one by sniffing to determine its state of ripeness. If it was winter, Glenn bought lentils and *farro* for his soup pot. We found another vendor with olives the size of plums. A handful was enough to make a meal.

A few items never attracted us. I didn't like to eat (Peter) rabbit. He and his family were presented in butcher shops with little fur bits left around their paws as though they were wearing bedroom slippers, presumably to show they weren't cats. And neither of us would touch the illegally caught tiny songbirds eaten by aficionados in one crunchy bite. Traditional Roman dishes made of offal such as *pagliata*, calf intestines cooked in milk, never crossed our lips. Tripe or donkey sausage didn't look appetizing either. But everything else was just waiting for us to taste.

• • •

Bottoms up! That was our term for the myriad of middle-aged Italians we saw foraging for wild food in the countryside, bent over double with plastic sacks in hand. Pencil-thin wild asparagus and bitter greens grew in fields and open spaces. Fennel flourished in ditch lines. Mushrooms and chestnuts were gathered in the woods to be sold in local markets or taken home. Mushroom hunters in doubt of the safety of their catch could take them to a local pharmacy for identification and testing. We didn't go food hunting but our friends, Ray and Carolyn, picked up the heavy cones from umbrella pines lining the Roman streets to extract the nuts. Their hands got black from the sooty shell coverings.

Truffle hunting, though, was off limits to amateurs. Productive areas were kept secret to protect the pungent fungi that were auctioned off for thousands of dollars a pound. Jealousy among truffle hunters was so intense that competitors' truffle-sniffing dogs were sometimes poisoned. The small truffle grater I picked up in a local market still sits in a virginal state, the price of truffles being beyond our budget unless we had a few shavings on our restaurant risotto.

One frosty late fall morning on an outing north of Rome we watched as a farmer butchered a hog hung from a tree by its hind legs—maybe *prosciutto* was forthcoming. Boar, often from game farms, also showed up on the menu in the fall, most often as *cingiale alla papardelle*, a dish made with wide, flat pasta and lots of rich digestion-challenging meat. I felt like a stuffed boa constrictor after eating my serving. Venison, slightly less rich and gout producing, was frequently available at the same time along with all the other meat that Italians consumed. Despite hearing about the fabled Mediterranean diet with emphasis on fruit, vegetables, and fish for good health, every restaurant also listed many meat dishes on their menus, even for lunch. Following the lead of the lunchtime diners around us, we tried *bistecca alla fiorentina* in its namesake city, Florence, after a hard morning in the Uffizi Gallery. An inch thick, it was so large it hung over the plate. Our fellow eaters weren't daunted by the size, but neither of us could finish and unfortunately doggie bags were unknown.

It wasn't only meat that began its journey to our stomachs in the fall. As winter rolled around we snacked from paper cones of chestnuts roasted over charcoal braziers in cold piazzas. They typically came from forests in Tuscany where the trees and their prickly-husked nuts grew in abundance—so common that at one time they were the food of the poor.

When the olives ripened to a violet or dark brown color we stopped to observe the harvest, sometimes done by hand on ancient rickety wood ladders, sometimes from the ground using a stick to whack the silvery branches, or with mechanical poles that shook the olives into nets strung below the trees. The fruit was carted away to the *frantoio* for crushing and extraction in tall presses where green or golden extra virgin oil slowly dripped into vats or was poured into large glass carboys like those Glenn had rescued from the street-side garbage containers. We used oil by the liter. With a drizzle here, a gurgle there, or a single splash, it was imperative to keep plenty on hand along with that other staple, wine.

We received an invitation to try our hand at a *vendemmia*, grape harvest. A colleague who owned property in the Castelli Romani just south of Rome (often called the Alban Hills) recruited a group to pick his two acres of golden-colored grapes with the promise of a feast afterward. We were issued a short hooked knife and plastic bucket before being set to work. It was backbreaking reaching for bunches hanging from the vines strung overhead and we got sticky with the juice, our amateur efforts making a mess. I soon gave up, content with wandering into the kitchen, although Glenn soldiered on. A crowd of neighbor women hustled around stirring and simmering. Sweet smoke rose from the grill where sausages and steaks were on the grate. The long lunch was like those described in all Italian memoirs, the cliché of piles of food, vats of wine, and nonstop talk being entirely accurate. After lunch, the grapes were hauled off to the local agricultural co-op for processing. We were looking forward to an invigorating stomp, with dancing and singing while crushing the harvest, but being modern times, our feet never became purple with squished grapes and juice.

Even seemingly prosaic locations yielded unexpected culinary opportunities. *Autostrade* rest stops had enormous displays of local foods as well as full-service restaurants and bars with snacks. We had even more enjoyment from the fruits of foragers' or artisans' labors, either stopping by roadside stands or shopping at local markets in the countryside. Along the margins of many country roads were glass cases on stands to attract hungry drivers. Some displayed homemade cheese or sausage and others held *porchetta*, a whole roasted pig stuffed with garlic, fennel, and rosemary. The pork was cut to measure and placed between two slices of crusty fresh country bread, an irresistible treat. We did briefly worry about the safety of local production when a cartoon in the paper showed a man looking at the *porchetta* while the vendor asked if he wanted it with leaded, unleaded, or diesel flavoring.

A few chairs and tables were oftentimes placed near the stands where we could sit with other eaters watching them slice their salami, cheese, and bread with large pocketknives. Glenn thought that the knives were an excellent accessory so we went to Scarperia, a town in Tuscany, well known for artisans' knives since the Middle Ages, to select one. The next time we picnicked he looked like the rest of the *ragazzi* as he sliced our selections. However, he didn't use their technique of holding the food in one hand and using the other to wield the knife in the direction of their stomachs.

Squares of pizza baked in large trays were always available as takeaway from hole-in-the-wall shops in towns. For a lighter lunch we preferred *panini*, available in every bar, where we could sit with the locals taking in the scene. Besides ordinary *prosciutto*-and-cheese combinations in oval hamburger buns or between flatbread, more exciting sandwich varieties invited us. *Tramezzini*, made of crustless white bread filled with improbable combinations of artichokes, cooked carrots and peas, cooked spinach, and hard-boiled eggs, or plain grilled eggplant with a little peperoncino for seasoning, were often on our plates. I imagined what our stateside friends would think if we told them we liked to dine on eggplant sandwiches after the morning's shopping expedition. But they had long since decided that we were aliens anyway after dumping Portland and Washington for Rome.

Food festivals were everywhere in the fall. Cities had large organized events celebrating regional production of cheese or meat. If the celebration was for the *vendemmia*, fountains often were plumbed to turn water into wine, a reminder of biblical events. Political parties sponsored *festas* too. We stopped in a tiny walled town near Siena where the local communist party was holding a celebration with plenty of *salsiccia* and *bistecca* on the grill. But the most fun were *sagre* in small towns featuring some local specialty such as mushrooms, chestnuts, or truffles. If a specialty couldn't be found, anything else that came to mind would do, like the *Sagra di Toast* we came across deep in Tuscany. Festivities usually included processions of citizens displaying extravagant medieval or Renaissance costumes. They were accompanied by teams from each *contrade*, the town's administrative divisions, throwing short-handled flags high in the air. Often we watched a competition in some medieval sport like archery where the winners gained the right to display a religious statue or banner in the winner's *contrada*. The village band played. Fairgoers talked, drank wine, and ate while we thought about whether it would be realistic to buy property in one of the towns for a weekend retreat and become part of the local scene.

XX

What was Italy without pasta? Purportedly, Sophia Loren once said, "Everything you see I owe to spaghetti." I, too, ate a lot of pasta but unfortunately didn't get the same results.

Cookbooks told me that there are about 350 different varieties. Every location had its own specialty, each to be served with its appropriate accompaniment. Butter and sage, cheese (but not with seafood), various vegetables, shellfish, or meat complemented the pasta's shape and size. Names were creative. In addition to the light *farfalle*, butterflies, we tried the heavy *orecchiette* and *radiatore*, little ears and radiators, and the curiously named *strozzapretti*, priest stranglers. Tiny varieties were in the baby food sections of supermarkets. Deep in the countryside, we came across a factory with a large fresco of a German shepherd on one wall. It produced *pasta per cane*, pasta for dogs. Roman cats dine on leftover spaghetti. Mice like pasta too. In the middle of a pasta display in the window of an expensive restaurant in Milan we watched a mouse holding a broken-off piece in its paws, munching away, whiskers twitching in delight. It looked like an illustration from a children's picture book.

Our 1959 Michelin Guide was always fun to read because its commentary contrasted with subsequent straightforward editions. It had advice for the hesitant tourist facing a bowl of pasta: spaghetti must not be chopped up lest the tourist look foolish. Rather, he or she should take two strands on his fork and carefully twist it with the aid of a spoon while praying that it doesn't fall into the sauce.

We never saw Italians daintily winding their pasta with the fork held against a spoon. After a napkin was tucked in, the pasta was either deftly affixed without aid by the sophisticated, or quickly shoveled in and bitten off by the hungry. The remainder of the coarse bread always put on the table was used to mop up any leftover *sugo*. Italians' passion for pasta was amply demonstrated one afternoon when we observed an old gentleman eagerly awaiting his serving. As soon as the waiter set the bowl in front of him, he attacked it with two forks at once. On the opposite end of the spectrum of spaghetti-eating protocol, Glenn was singled out when he was dining with his Italian pals at his golf club. A couple of the men had brought their mistresses along for a treat. He heard one guest whisper to another: "Why can't he wind his pasta on the fork correctly?" His host, the old count, graciously intervened to explain (falsely) that he was new to Italian eating manners and would soon learn the correct procedure. Glenn asked at what age Italians began to be successful at gracefully eating spaghetti—the response was about age four. No wonder we were messy.

Glenn's favorite pasta is *spaghetti alla carbonara*, best eaten in the winter. Although the recipe came from a yacht owner friend, it is thought to be named after charcoal-burners who were busy in the mountains in all weather. Glenn's version of the rich winter dish is the number-one request from friends invited to dinner. While a pound of spaghettini or spaghetti is cooking, Glenn whisks three large eggs with five ounces of grated Parmesan cheese and a good grind of pepper. He then sautés six ounces of cubed *pancetta* in a little olive oil, and lets it cool slightly before adding it to the egg mixture. The cooked pasta is drained and poured into a preheated bowl. The egg, cheese, and *pancetta* mixture is quickly stirred into the pasta a minute or so before serving. The hot pasta finishes cooking the eggs.

Pasta was always our first choice but we didn't neglect rice, especially the Italian varieties for risotto such as arborio and carnaroli. Increasing Glenn's interest was a 1950 film, *Riso Amaro*, Bitter Rice, a dramatic look at postwar criminality and the backbreaking labor of female workers recruited to do the planting in the vast Po Valley rice paddies near Milan. The film was an exposé of the work that required the women to bend over barefoot in the cold water full of leeches and mosquitoes for twelve hours a day, rather like what I saw in Cambodia. The film also introduced Silvana Mangano. Her smoldering sexuality signaled the end of the era of my favorite black-and-white reflections of Italian life in favor of colorful and sexy movies starring Ms. Loren and Gina Lollobrigida. They both amply demonstrated the value of pasta over rice for those desiring a full Southern figure instead of the slender Milanese silhouette.

It wasn't all pasta and risotto. In hot weather lunch or dinner was an *insalata caprese*. Glenn sliced some tomatoes and interspersed them with slices of fresh mozzarella di bufala, the super-rich cheese made with water buffalo milk. He garnished his arrangement with fresh basil leaves from a pot on our terrace, and added a thread of olive oil along with some salt and pepper. That, some good coarse Roman bread, and a glass of wine made an ideal meal. Or, we had melon wrapped in slices of *prosciutto* followed by a bowl *of penne* with pesto sauce made with basil and pine nuts, pasta yet again.

As the weather turned to fall, Chef Glenn continued to experiment with grilling, soups, and more inventive pastas. He also continued to collect recipes by asking a friend, vendor, cook, or waiter how something was prepared and always got a delighted response. Chicken breasts browned in olive oil and then simmered in cream and sliced *porcini* mushrooms, courtesy of the owner of a small restaurant in an obscure town, thereby became another specialty.

We learned the gesture some Italians favored when something was especially tasty: forefinger to cheek, rotating it back and forth. I used it for Glenn's cooking efforts.

• • •

Of course we didn't just eat at home. Who would do that in Italy? Maybe only the most devoted mamma's boy, a *mammone*. With all the restaurants to try it was hard to choose, although we preferred local trattorias with their more simple menus. Décor was generally dull, the quality of the food being more important. The front door or window invariably displayed a standard sign announcing what day the restaurant was closed each week, the *turno*. With the exception of our newly found pizzeria and a trattoria whose inspired owner had placed a large copper bowl filled with dried pomegranates and chilies in the entryway, the usual interior view was a selection of football banners, pennants, and tarnished trophies, faded photos of friends or the odd celebrity, or maybe a moth-eaten stuffed fox or pheasant. Amateurish paintings hung on the walls. The sideboard often held a can of talcum powder to remove splashes of oil or sauce on men's ties in case they had an accident from not twirling their pasta correctly. No fancy plates, glasses, or silverware; all were made for utility rather than beauty. Knives, forks, and spoons were heavier and bigger than in the US. They really worked once we got the hang of it.

Of all the food we tried on our first tour, *fungi porcini* were the most memorable. On our return we never passed on the opportunity when they were in season. We had our maiden experience with the dinner plate–sized mushrooms available in the fall, on a trip to Cortona with Ray and Carolyn. While Glenn and I perused the dinner menu trying to make a decision, our travel partners took one look at the listing and ordered mushrooms for the main course. We were surprised that they were fasting, envisioning a few little button mushrooms sitting in the middle of each plate. When the dishes arrived, our friends raised their knives and forks ready to dig into giant grilled *fungi*, each one so large it filled the plate. They gave us a taste. It was as rich as beefsteak. After that first bite, whenever we saw them in their wooden crates displayed outside a restaurant their bosky smell was like the pull of gravity. We could still mentally taste them when we were in Virginia; another of our many reasons to return to Italy.

Food mistakes were few but once I had a language lesson in an expensive restaurant recommended by friends who got it confused with a more modest location with a similar name. The word for caviar is *caviale*; the word for cauliflower is *cavolfiore*. The caviar was delicious, the bill was horrendous. More suitable as a starter for someone on a budget, we looked for *olive ascolane*, large green olives stuffed with veal and/or pork then breaded and deep fried, a specialty of Ascoli Piceno on the Adriatic side of the peninsula. And one starry summer evening we began our meal with a half cantaloupe filled with crumbled feta and surrounded by red currants. I loved the small long-stemmed artichokes marinated in herbs and olive oil, so good I always ordered two when they were on the menu, and then could hardly eat anything else—unless *prosciutto* with melon or figs was available.

In summer, *pomodori al riso*, tomatoes stuffed with rice and herbs and sometimes served with wedges of baked potato, were often displayed on the restaurant sideboard along with other vegetables served at room temperature, *ambiente*. A Roman staple, I was inspired to make the dish after an English friend who had lived in Rome forever told me about her recipe. Newly married and living in modest circumstances, she learned to cook from her Italian mother-in-law. Her apartment didn't have an oven. Instead, she prepared trays filled with stuffed tomatoes to take to a communal oven for cooking. I pictured experiencing the romance of the old days, but such ovens are long gone. I stuck to my kitchen where the oven probably wasn't any better than the one used by neighborhood women. And at least they could talk, gossip most likely, while the bread baked or the stuffed tomatoes cooked.

While our oven was heating to 350 degrees (or thereabouts, given its limited abilities), I hollowed out six medium or four large ripe tomatoes, being careful not to pierce the skin, and reserved the slices off tops. After sieving the pulp to remove seeds, it was combined with ½ cup arborio rice, two minced garlic cloves, eight roughly torn basil leaves, a teaspoon of fresh oregano, and salt and pepper to taste. Using a little olive oil to grease a small baking dish, the tomatoes were placed in the dish before being filled with the rice mixture. The reserved tops were added and the tomatoes brushed with more oil. They baked for about an hour or until the rice was tender, then left to cool before serving, although it was difficult to wait.

We tried another Italian specialty, eels. They often came from Lake Bracciano, which has a town called Anguillara (*anguilla* means eel) overlooking the lake. Popular in Italy, there are some who have put forth the unlikely theory that, instead of the traditional lamb for the Last Supper, the menu was really eels garnished with oranges. Why Christ and his disciples would be dining on such an odd combination was unexplained. Eels were particularly associated with

Naples. I found an old Neapolitan recipe book containing a menu for Christmas Eve in 1839: fried broccoli, vermicelli pasta with salted anchovies, baked fish, more fish fried in batter, fried eel, roast eel, and a salad of cauliflower with olives, anchovies, and pickles. The eel-eating tradition continues. An English friend was married to a Neapolitan. She described the events of one Christmas when they loaded up their car trunk with a large tub of eels. By the time they arrived in Naples, the slimy eels had escaped en masse and were writhing all over their luggage.

Whether it was *fungi porcini*, *pomodoro al riso*, *bistecca*, or eels for a main course we usually had room for a light dessert. *Frutti di bosco*, a mixture of small berries like blueberries, raspberries, blackberries, currants, and gooseberries, or wild strawberries from Lake Nemi in the Castelli Romani, was a favorite. We also enjoyed frozen lemons hollowed out and filled with lemon gelato. We liked to eat them on hot days while lounging on the terrace of the Castel Sant'Angelo, originally Emperor Hadrian's tomb. While we spooned away we pictured Pope Clement VII pulling up his robes and scurrying along the narrow passageway connecting the Vatican with the castle as he escaped "holy" Roman Emperor Charles V's marauding troops during the sack of Rome in 1527. Perhaps cooks followed behind to ensure the expected luxuries were still available.

• • •

Part of our enjoyment in eating away from home was watching the Italians, for whom food means dining with friends or family unless making a quick stop at a bar. Despite living in the age of cell phones, conviviality was the rule and Sunday lunch was sacrosanct. First, everyone from babies to grandparents got settled; then lengthy discussions with the waiter about the day's offerings commenced: what was fresh, how was it cooked, what wine went with it. The menu was usually ignored because the cook was probably preparing some special not on the list. The words "pasta, *fungi*, *bistecca*" floated in our direction. Wine was poured and conversation began with everyone talking at once to each other—

food talk. If the speaker couldn't make himself heard over the din, he stood up to make his point. Antipasti arrived, then pasta or risotto with chewy bread to mop up the last of the sauce, then meat or fish and vegetables, followed by salad or cheese and dessert. Lastly, it was time for a *digestivo*. Meanwhile, the children—on a high from the caloric overdose—raced around the restaurant. Three hours later everyone staggered off. Why they were not hugely fat or comatose was yet another of Italy's many unanswered mysteries.

While dining out was always a culinary pleasure our Northern habits had to become adjusted to the slower-paced Mediterranean style. We typically ended up waiting endlessly for *il conto*, the bill. (More aptly, it is sometimes called *la dolorosa*, the painful one.) The restaurants opened at 7:30 or 8:00 p.m. for dinner. The Italians often came in later than we liked to dine with the result that when we wanted to leave, they were being served their main course. The waiters acknowledged our signal, the universal writing a bill in the air, with a nod. They put bottles of *digestivi* on the table to keep us quiet, with no charge if they liked us, then continued taking orders or serving without a further glance. It seemed as though taking our money wasn't all that interesting in contrast to the U.S. where waiters, who insisted on telling us their names, often brought the bill before we could set our knives and forks down. In Italy we were expected to enjoy an evening out, not be part of the night's turnover.

We found that Italians' enjoyment of being close to others while eating extended to *al fresco* dining when we took a picnic lunch to the Abruzzi, the mountainous area an hour east of Rome. We settled in on a high, empty plain near where Germans flying gliders during World War II rescued Mussolini from imprisonment. No one else for miles—at least we thought. Then a passing driver spotted us, jammed on his brakes, and pulled in. He and his friends jumped out and set up their picnic no more than ten feet away from us. They were soon followed by others, nearly enough for a small village, none of whom knew each other. Our private dining experience took on the ambience of a crowded restaurant.

A closer picnic spot was on the Appia Antica not far from the section where ancient cobbles with ruts worn by chariots are still to be seen. One Sunday after we set up shop we watched our Italian counterparts do the same. Nearby was a large family with grandpa in his sleeveless undershirt sitting at the head of a folding table piled with food, bottles of water, and wicker-encased jugs of wine. The women fussed around the table serving ever more food, the kids played soccer or ran in circles yelling and laughing, and the remainder of the men smoked and talked nearby, oblivious to other families right next to them doing the same thing. It was another quintessential Italian scene from a Fellini movie, his cinematic masterpieces being our infallible guide to Italians.

XXI

There is something atavistic about shopping in small shops or open-air markets. We often browsed in the stalls, so much more appealing than looking at goods neatly arranged in cavernous supermarkets with their deadening fluorescent lights and dearth of human interaction. Wandering past merchants calling me to look at their cheese, fruit, vegetables, shoes, sweaters, and piles of useless trinkets for our apartment took me mentally back into history, to the way everyone had always met their daily needs for food and other necessities. On Saturdays we sometimes went to the block-square Testaccio market with a stop at the divine food emporium, Volpetti, on the way. Both were located near a derelict former slaughterhouse, complete with a statue of a bull meeting his end looming over the main gate. The neighborhood is named for Monte Testaccio, a 100-foot-high hill made of broken amphorae that originally contained oil, wheat, and other commodities imported into ancient Rome. The newest additions to the pile were dated to AD 140. Longtime residents told us about the good old days when they could "rescue" some of the pots, but now it was fenced to prevent souvenir hunting.

Volpetti was one the best delis in Rome but the prices were astronomical. We tried not to drool on the displays of cheese, pasta, olive oil, balsamic vinegar, preserves, pâtés, whole *prosciutti*, and sausages. These temptations were displayed in the windows and in glass-fronted cases, hung from the ceiling, and piled on shelves and on stands in such profusion that it was hard to move among the cornucopia, the customers, and the staff passing out samples. We always found room for a few samples and an *etto* or two of some cheese or *prosciutto* to take home for lunch on the terrace.

More to our budget, the Testaccio market, a little farther out, had reasonable prices and a prodigious selection of beautiful fruits and vegetables, along with seafood and meat. In summer the fish smell permeated the atmosphere. It was wise to go early in the morning before the heat and odor got too intense. Best of all the goods, however, were the shoe stalls along one side. Fish smells or not, they were a gold mine because they sold the previous year's styles or overruns for bargain prices. I had difficulty worming my way to the front of the surrounding crowds despite using Glenn's technique of clinging to someone ahead.

I thought that shoes were a peculiar inclusion in a food market until I recognized that they were a staple as important as pasta and vegetables since the dawn of Italian history. One memorable fresco in the museum at Paestum (where three magnificent Greek temples still stand) depicts Venus wearing a pearl necklace, red shoes, and nothing else. It was probably painted around the fifth century BC, but it was easy to visualize a more modern Roman mistress in the same attire. Studying the variety of sandals on Roman statues could take a lifetime. Romans could buy shoes during the war when Italian troops were fighting in snow without boots in Albania and Greece, or at Monte Cassino. Even the pope was concerned with shoe styles, favoring red ones like ancient emperors.

Following a long-standing tradition of being shoe proud, I often left Testaccio market with a pair or two of shoes along with zucchini. But like looking over the vegetables before buying, I learned that it was best to curb one's enthusiasm after my one shoe *incidente*. I found a splendid pair of bright blue leather-and-black patent high heels and snapped them up after trying on the right one. I paid while the vendor placed the mate in the box and handed it over. When we returned home I tried them on only to find that one had a black sole and square toe and the other a light-colored sole and round toe. Maybe someone scrounged them from the garbage can after they landed there that afternoon. *Caveat emptor* as the ancient Romans said.

• • •

Sometimes late on a Saturday night if we were near the area encompassing the enormous Porta Portese flea market we heard the rumble of old iron-wheeled carts being dragged across cobblestones toward the enormous flea market in preparation for its opening at dawn. The flea markets always drew me in with the promise of bargains and unexpected finds. Unfortunately Porta Portese, the biggest one, was the single place in Italy Glenn actively hated. It was yet another manifestation of his true love that he went along as a lookout because of the numerous thieves. I carefully hid money in the deepest pockets of my jacket, but some shoppers were oblivious to the dangers. Early one morning we watched a parade running through the crowded stalls—first a little boy, then a midsize girl, and last an older girl followed by two Americans screaming, "Give me back my camera!" They all disappeared from view in the dense crowds. Like a native, I shrugged and went back to shopping.

To get to the market we had to decide whether to drive to a dusty, unpaved area where we paid off a man to "watch" the car, or to park in the FAO grounds and try to get aboard the crowded tram. When we parked at the lot, which was closer to the shoe stalls, we walked over a bridge lined with Rome's poorest sitting beside a few pathetic broken pieces of junk spread on the pavement in the hopes of making a little money: a worn-out pair of shoes, old radio parts, or a few books with broken spines. All was not always paradise in the land of the sweet life.

The tram was on a more scenic route but it put us at the beginning of the mile-long market, a long way from a side entrance near the stalls that I favored for browsing. Even in the early morning the tram was already jammed with bargain hunters as it trundled along the Via Marmorata, named after marble workers, past a fountain carved as a stack of amphorae in honor of Monte Testaccio's pile of potsherds, and then over the Tiber to the Portuense Gate. This Renaissance portal was built in 1644 as part of defensive walls put up to protect the Vatican during the Thirty Years' War. Instead of guarding against soldiers bent on rape and pillage it stood defenseless against the hordes of vendors and shoppers who congregated there, milling about and bargaining for treasures and junk.

Despite the modern goods and dress of the vendors, the market was straight out of a Pieter Bruegel painting. Hawkers stood on tables piled with heaps of goods shouting out their bargains. Fights between merchants erupted when one encroached on another's space. The inevitable Gypsies begged, pickpockets roamed, and portable tables were set up where slick men in shiny suits moved three walnuts or small cups in a blur while the surrounding crowd, complete with shills, bet on which cup contained the pea. Every once in a while the police ambled by. Thieves ran, gambling men picked up their tables and melted into the crowd, and payoffs were collected. As soon as the police passed by the gambles returned. A game of cat and mouse.

For a time during our first stay, large numbers of refugees from the collapsed Soviet Union and its former client states temporarily resided in Rome while they waited to be resettled. The Russians came to the market carrying all sorts of odds and ends, some of dubious quality or provenance. Fake amber, cans of purportedly fresh caviar warmed in the sun, Russian Army gear, painted wood boxes and Easter eggs, nesting dolls, and icons all rested on the ground. We gave a few coins to violin and accordion players playing melancholy folk songs from the countries they would probably never see again. After repeatedly buying a few trinkets for gifts, our recipients gently told us that they no longer appreciated our offerings of babushka scarves or pins with Lenin, Stalin, or hammers and sickles.

The variety of merchandise in the enormous market was seemingly without end. I usually aimed directly for the numerous shoe stalls and those that sold cashmere sweaters, some clearly used, but others suspiciously new. Good-quality shoes were sometimes to be had for $10, while four-ply cashmere sweaters went for about $25. In the fall, the stocking and sock vendors brought out patterned panty hose that were modeled on plastic legs strung from clotheslines. When the wind blew they looked like a disembodied chorus line of dancers kicking up their heels. We steered clear of the obvious fake antiques and piles of stolen fur coats, handbags, cameras, and watches. Bicycles were propped up in rows. They reminded me of those in Vittorio De Sica's heartbreaking 1948 film *The Bicycle Thief*, in which a desperate man searches for his only means of livelihood in another flea market. Baby chickens, puppies, and kittens were carried around in boxes. Ripped-off car parts and radios were heaped by the ton alongside plants for balcony gardens.

Several stalls sold used furniture and household goods. Old paintings, some with the paint flaking off, were propped up against chairs with their stuffing hanging out. I picked up a scene of a monk in his brown habit praying on his knees while birds flew in his cell window. When I looked closer I saw that they weren't birds—they were winged penises. I set it down after deciding not to buy it.

One vendor sold crystal drops from chandeliers that once graced ballrooms and elegant salons. We bought them for our Christmas tree. They always made me think of nineteenth-century petty nobility chattering or dancing away their lives as portrayed so unforgettably in the book and movie *The Leopard*. Could they ever have dreamed that their beautiful things would be lying in the dirt for the world to pick through and bargain over? A sad end to a lost way of life.

XXII

Our return to Rome not only gave us a chance to expand our food interests and our circle of friends, but also to continue watching the variety of people who come to Rome. Tacitus grumped, "All things atrocious and shameless flock from everywhere to Rome." Not much has changed in that regard from the turn of the second century AD.

We had ever more visitors, although none were either atrocious or shameless. Kathryn frequently hopped on a plane, first with friends in tow then with her fiancé, Steve, an architect who enjoyed looking at the glories built by his ancient peers and honing his culinary skills with Glenn over glasses of Nastro Azzurro beer. Glenn acted as chauffeur and tour guide, taking assorted relatives, friends, and friends of friends to the standard sights and the more out-of-the-way ones like Subiaco. After they saw the traffic none of them dreamed of renting a car and all expressed gratitude for what they saw as Glenn's bravery in the line of duty. When the subject of living in Rome came up, with the exception of Kathryn, not one had anything positive to say, especially after seeing our kitchen arrangements. They were shocked, *shocked*, by the lack of a dishwasher, air conditioning, clothes dryer, and other amenities like the wall-to-wall carpeting we had left behind without much thought. A life without all their North American comforts was not on their bucket list.

• • •

It hadn't taken long to determine the major differences between many of my first acquaintances at FAO and me. I grew up an only child, went to school without complaint, did my homework, anguished about fitting in, married my first boyfriend, and promptly settled down with a house and child. It was obvious to all that I was a real dullard compared with the lives of this piquant mix, many having repeatedly married and divorced nobility or coworkers. Others starved or were left behind in World War II as small children, were born in colonies and hated the natives, were unrepentant fascists, and/or had mistresses. Life in Portland was like the back of the beyond when regarding these colorful people.

Then I was introduced to new colleagues at WFP. Humanitarian aid workers are a breed apart, all having done something that was dangerous or brave in some far corner of the world. Our new friends, field workers temporarily assigned to Rome, experienced war, kidnapping, shootings, or contracted dangerous tropical diseases. After listening to their stories we felt ever more naïve and coddled, only daring to move to Rome, while most of them hated the city because it was too predictable.

To keep party conversation pleasant, talk of politics and religion was generally avoided unless someone wanted to ask us about American politics, always a subject of great interest. Which colleague was having an affair with another was an exciting subject, but far more gripping was talk about work. After liberal doses of food and wine the stories never stopped, with everyone trying to outdo the other. Typical conversation starters from those who had worked in the more gritty locations began:

"When I traveled up the river with the pygmies . . ."

"When Arnie and I brought in food aid by elephant in Cambodia . . ."

"Last winter in North Korea it was so cold . . ."

"When the harvesters served me deep-fried rats in China . . ."

A bit of bragging rights perhaps, but then again the stories were an accurate reflection of their lives, and true adventurers love to tell their tales. It wasn't all tall travelers' tales though—sometimes the conversation took a much darker turn:

"When my son was bitten by a rabid dog and we had to wait for the medevac plane . . ."

"When I was kidnapped and held hostage in Sudan, I thought that I'd never leave alive, but . . ."

The stories were fascinating, but combined with my modest visits to countries where WFP worked, I realized that while I loved being a traveler and expatriate I could never rise to the level of an aid worker. It was a disappointment to acknowledge my lack of daring. Some of our acquaintances had the mentality of war correspondents with their thirst for danger. It was a wonder that cynicism didn't overwhelm altruism, inured as they were to the horrendous sights they had encountered: starving children in North Korea, famine in Ethiopia, bloated dead bodies in Rwanda, raped women in the Congo, earthquake-struck villages in Afghanistan and Pakistan, refugees on the move everywhere.

• • •

It did indeed seem as though all the world's travelers congregated in Rome. Because the city was home to the Vatican, the Italian government, and three large United Nations organizations, including FAO and WFP (along with several smaller ones), there was a swarm of bureaucrats associated with the UN and with the many embassies accredited to both the Vatican and the government. A number of countries had institutes for resident artists and writers on fellowships, like the venerable American Academy. Or they offered language training and cultural activities to the general public. A NATO war college, as well as branches of various universities and schools with semesters abroad or degree programs, added to the transient foreign population as people cycled through their careers and studies.

Impoverished refugees of one sort or another—Sri Lankans, Filipinos, Russians, Poles, as well as many Africans—competed for menial work despite holding university degrees.

Colleges for church officials were scattered about the city, attracting those aspiring to the priesthood or already active in church-related professions. One evening we found ourselves in a restaurant seated next to a group of ten young American seminarians out for a lark. They postured like schoolgirls as they loudly giggled in high voices like something out of *La Cage aux Folles*, turning heads throughout the restaurant. It was some years before the scandals erupted, but it did cause us to be embarrassed about the unfavorable impression our co-nationals were making. But then again, over the millennia Italians have seen it all, so perhaps our sensitivities were unnecessary.

Besides the diplomats, refugees, bureaucrats, and church functionaries, millions of tourists crowded the monuments during every season. Some of the tourists were more noticeable than the rest of the herd. One day we were about to enter the medieval Santa Maria in Cosmedin when a horse-drawn carriage pulled up. Helped by a solicitous man, an overbuilt blonde picked her way on stiletto heels to the church porch where the Mouth of Truth is high on the visitor itinerary. She wore a transparent blouse and shorts that barely covered the top half of her bottom. We watched as she squealed with fake fright while bending over as far as possible to put her bright red fingernails into the mouth of the ancient sewer cover. Although she was an exhibitionist, she must not have been a perjurer because she escaped with all digits intact.

Tourists from Eastern Europe arrived in old, exhaust-spewing buses. The women were recognizable by their dumpy shapes, faded flowered housedresses, bandanas over their hair, and scuffed sandals worn with socks. The men wore short black leather jackets and cheap-looking pointy-toed shoes. From the other side of the world Japanese tour groups marched along, making sure to stick close to their minders. These short, elderly, often bow-legged people all wore sun hats and pale-colored pants and jackets. Unlike their taller and more daring children or grandchildren, they were often so timid that special stores with Japanese clerks were established so they could avoid interaction with Italian shop owners.

Rome was also host to a considerable population of permanent American and European exiles clustered mostly in the city center. Many of the oldest generation were artists and writers who settled in the 1950s or the following decades, drawn by Rome's benign climate and endless cultural treasures. We were acquainted with two elderly painters—one a British soldier who had fought his way up the peninsula and later married an Italian whose brother ran a high-end antique shop filled with treasures we could only dream of owning. He was one of Glenn's fellow golfers and produced excellent Van Gogh copies. The other was a German, whose father was in their consulate in Naples before and during the war. He painted Roman scenes. We commissioned a painting of the Appia Antica for what we considered to be an extravagant amount. His wife turned out to be a fancy antique dealer in London who, when she blew into town and saw the painting, demanded that we pay double. It, along with some excellent "Van Gogh" sunflowers, hangs on our wall to this day, but every time I look at the Appia I think of forking over the extra money. Especially annoying, he claimed that the view was from his villa's window, but some time later I chanced on a book with old photographs and there it was—exactly as he had painted it from a photo. And if he had a villa it must have been situated in the middle of the ancient road.

Even with all these disparate people there was one group in Rome that was conspicuous among the mixture of Italians and foreigners. They were the Gypsies, or Roma as they were sometimes called. These fixtures of city life had been the victims of discrimination since their arrival in Europe in the 1400s and blamed for things that they did not do, but we learned early on to be watchful when they were around.

I had always romanticized Gypsies, picturing the women with big gold hoop earrings and colorful velvet skirts dancing to fiddle music while the men, handsome and dark-eyed, sat around a campfire making copper pots in front of their painted wagons. Instead, we saw filthy, malnourished feral-child pickpockets dressed in rags holding cardboard to hide their hands or sounding wooden clappers to distract intended victims with the noise while they picked them clean. The young women tended to be thin with stringy reddish hair and dressed in mismatched dirty clothes, although they did have the long skirts of my imagination. They and their menfolk often were wallet and handbag snatchers who deftly reached through open car windows, snaked their way through crowds on public transport, and made lightning grabs on sidewalks.

The fireplug-shaped older women wore black dresses, shawls, and headscarves as they sat on the ground with drugged babies in their laps. They feebly reached out to passersby while muttering imprecations. The oldest lay in the middle of the sidewalk writhing and shaking in front of their begging bowls while we tried not to trip over them. The men stole cars, although they weren't alone in that occupation. Car alarms screamed all day and night long, and everyone we knew had either been robbed or had their car stolen, or most often, both. One coworker told me his home had been broken into seven times!

Driving by their many encampments on Rome's periphery, we could see new Mercedes surrounded by piles of garbage but only a single hydrant to furnish water on a communal basis. Newspapers and television frequently told stories about babies freezing to death in wintertime as they slept in unheated campers. The authorities broke up the camps and deported some of the inhabitants but the sad cycle started again immediately with human rights activists screaming that the Gypsies were being abused and victims of their activities screaming that they should be deported again.

Near the Forum, I stood by watching two men arguing with a young Gypsy, demanding the return of a wallet. She denied the theft, and in a last-ditch attempt to convince them of her innocence, pulled up her shirt to expose her bare breasts. Not at all impressed, the men didn't fall for the distraction. Seeing that she wasn't going to get away with her takings, she reached deep down under the waist of her long skirt and reluctantly returned the wallet. Not pleasant to contemplate.

Our visitors had incidents too. Glenn grabbed one Gypsy woman as she was about to relieve a cousin of his wallet while he was getting on the subway. Being forewarned, a visiting couple had nothing valuable with them, but another Gypsy made a lunge for the husband's inside jacket pocket. His wife was so enraged that she decked the woman, who was screaming bloody murder while still holding her prize—a candy bar.

• • •

Our new neighbors, actual Italians, were just as opaque as those the first time around. To our disappointment, a courteous *buongiorno* again accompanied by a nod or smile was the totality of our conversations. Shortly before our departure on the first stay we had invited all the neighbors in for prosecco and snacks. Everyone came and stayed companionably but no one invited us back. This time we gave up on any parties. We were destined to remain *stranieri*. The sole meaningful interaction occurred when our downstairs neighbor came up to tell us that our water heater was leaking into his apartment, a persistent problem in Roman buildings. He wore a frilly pink apron over his beautifully tailored business suit.

Many of the Italian women looked like Sophia, Gina, or other movie stars. And there were so many sexy men with clear-cut profiles who should have been on the cover of a romance novel—like Fabio with better grooming. But despite their handsome appearance, Italian men didn't seem to produce all that many babies, the birth rate being below the replacement rate. Whatever the reason for the demographic change, Italians loved the children who did come along. A big pink or pale blue bow was hung on the front door of the parents' apartment building when a baby arrived. A walk with a baby stroller was an occasion of great interest to passersby, who stopped and peered intently inside to get a look and coo about the little *tesoro* or *tesora*, treasure. We watched neighbors pulling their sunglasses back through their hair before pushing their heads right into the baby's face to get a really close look, as if some sort of alien had arrived.

The native Romans appeared to be as outnumbered as they had been in the waning days of the Empire. A "real" Roman, as we were told by a man who claimed to be one, was able to speak the *Romanesco* dialect. Not many people still had the ability because enterprising Romans went north to Milan and Turin to work in business and factories after the war, while the southerners, like our landlord, came to Rome to work in the huge government bureaucracies. Television also stamped out regional dialects over time. But whatever their original spoken language, Romans talked with their hands.

We understood useful gestures such as those signifying crazy, good food, or warding off the devil. But there were many other signs in this silent vocabulary for us to comprehend. Bringing a hand up with fingers and thumb tented towards the gesturer's chest while moving it to and fro and scowling meant "what did you expect (you idiot)?" Biting an index finger held sideways expressed anger, and bringing curved fingers of one hand from the chin outward conveyed "I don't give a damn." Drawing one's eyelid down with a forefinger silently conveyed "we understand each other" or "beware." One evening we sat facing the street in a hotel lobby while waiting for a friend. It was dark outside. Behind us and reflected in the window we watched a couple engaged in a nearly wordless argument. Ten minutes later the disagreement faded away after sufficient steam was released to wear out both sides' arms.

• • •

Glenn rejoined the golf club and I gradually became acquainted with two of the players, a retired general and the count, and their wives. They all spoke English better than our Italian and we often shared a meal where the conversation flowed in those two languages, plus a little Spanish and French and occasional smatterings of Swahili left over from our respective visits to Kenya and Tanzania. One never knows when the greeting "*Jambo, Mama*" will be useful.

The first couple was a retired Italian Army general and his voluptuous blonde wife. He occasionally played piano at a fancy American-style bar near the Piazza del Popolo. He was completely overshadowed by his wife. The blonde spent most of her conversational time describing her bedroom and how she liked to be "totally *nudo*," all the while running her hands suggestively up and down her curvaceous torso. In one burst of zeal she insisted on carrying the elderly count, who was taller than and as heavy as she was, upstairs to his apartment. This impressive performance made her look like a fireman with an old man slung over his shoulder. It was unclear what part of her was original issue. At least the parts we could see looked like she had had some "liftings," that descriptive word Europeans use for plastic surgery. Art and nature were running neck and neck.

Far more interesting was the second pair: the elderly Count Tommaso and his elegantly dressed and coifed Florentine wife. The countess, Francesca, petite with long brown hair, liked karaoke and energetically sold us sterling silver jewelry, picture frames, and boxes from a fancy shop in Florence as a sideline to her social activities. But the countess's obsession was to be ever thinner. On one visit to their home she insisted on demonstrating her new butt-reducing machine. We sat on their sofa trying not to laugh as we watched her skinny bottom go back and forth in a blur.

It was during a meal with this foursome that we learned how to serve polenta correctly. Glenn had either bought it ready-made at the *supermercato* or stirred up the instant kind, both methods scorned by purists. Originally a staple food of the poor in the north of Italy where it was eaten without any embellishments, the ground corn needed to be stirred over a fire in a large pot for about forty-five minutes. When *nonna* finished stirring it was poured on the wood kitchen table and cut with a copper wire. The golfers prepared it in the same manner, spooning the glop onto a breadboard and cutting the portions as tradition dictated, although we were served a rich meat sauce to heap over our helpings.

Glenn and Count Tommaso became good friends, yet he remained something of a mystery, with only faint allusions to his past life seeping out from time to time. His beautiful apartment was filled with fascinating objects, including autographed pictures of Victor Emmanuel III, the next to last king of Italy (who fled Rome in 1943), and his son, Umberto II. Umberto was king until a referendum in 1946 forced the whole family out of the country and turned Italy into a republic. Supposedly the count resided with the king for a time when his own home was bombed earlier in the war. A monarchist to the core, the count's preferred pizza was *margherita*, the colors of the country reflected in its ingredients: green basil, white mozzarella cheese, and red sauce. It was named in honor of Queen Margherita, who was of a fascist persuasion as well as being cowardly Victor Emmanuel III's mother.

The count had a full-length painting of his first wife, a daughter of Hungarian nobility, hanging prominently in his living room. What happened to her was never clear, nor was his current wife's opinion of the artwork. At some point his family must have been wealthy, as he spoke of a Renaissance villa and gardens near the Adriatic coast, recently restored by other owners. He had also been close to a branch of the Borghese family, teaching the boys how to ride. Once he showed Glenn a side road, remarking that up the road was a villa that would have been his had he not chosen the *bella* Hungarian instead of the Borghese daughter. He still maintained a lease on a small Borghese hunting lodge near Anzio. We occasionally went to the lodge for picnics but to my disappointment it wasn't much of a place. I had envisioned a palazzo with high frescoed ceilings and paintings of imperious ancestors staring at me, but instead it was dark with little furniture or decoration. Perhaps the Borghese appreciated an occasional taste of modesty from their usual digs.

Glenn drove the count to the NATO base near Naples, where we had shopping privileges, to buy some golf equipment. While they were passing by Monte Cassino on the way, he began to talk about his brother, who fought and died barefoot in winter conditions while trying to hold the line against the Allied invasion. He never explained his own military service, although he did allude to North Africa, where tens of thousands of Italian troops surrendered to British and American forces.

The count had a long career with the UN as a diplomat, lived everywhere, and knew everyone. He was also an energetic womanizer. Legions of secretaries in FAO had caught his eye. His beautiful current mistress sometimes came along with him to play golf and have lunch with the *ragazzi*. In old age he was still an imposing figure. When he was young he must have been the perfect fascist sports enthusiast, telling us as he did that he was the model for either the naked skier at the Stadio dei Marmi, another Mussolini project, or the naked horsemen surrounding the Square Colosseum near our apartment. We were never clear which it was (maybe both, maybe neither) but I preferred the horsemen version of the story so that anytime I wanted to, I could see him in all his former glory instead of trekking to the far side of Rome to the stadium where some of the 1960 Olympic events took place.

One day near the end of our second stay in Rome, he collapsed during lunch following the morning round of golf, felled by a stroke. When the other diners determined that he still had a heartbeat, they stood around gawking without bothering to call an ambulance. Glenn administered first aid, cleaned up the mess, and managed to get the onlookers to call for help. He later told Glenn that when the ambulance crew arrived at the hospital, they dropped him on his head. Fortunately the stroke was minor and his skull was hard. He was a tough old bird, playing golf and asking the cook for new recipes not long after.

XXIII

Just as easy as continuing to find great food and friends was the opportunity to continue with our "play dates"—arranged tours of the surrounding area. In addition to the staff association's events, other groups dedicated to wine, fishing, golf, and Italian art and culture also had offerings. Glenn became an adjunct member of the Canadian Women's Club (a gentlemen's auxiliary of one) courtesy of our Canadian friend Carolyn, enjoying being fussed over as the group toured Perugia or Assisi. We occasionally joined events with the American Women's Club through the embassy. But by far the most interesting experience was traveling with mixed groups, where it soon became obvious that Italians knew how to get the most out of the trips—eating, drinking, and enjoying whatever was before them. Our Anglo-Saxon ways were unimaginative, following the rules and paying attention to the leader, always in the bus on time, and listening dutifully to the guide no matter how uninteresting. That is, until we learned to do as the Romans did.

The Fishing Club meetings and actual fishing expeditions attracted mostly Italian men, but their short cultural and food outings were open to all. We signed up for them along with Ray and Carolyn, who also loved to travel no matter who was organizing the event. The Wine Club was international in membership. It held monthly get-togethers in the office after work, usually featuring a pedantic and soporific wine expert to whom no one paid much attention. We all impatiently waited for the droning to end and the tasting to commence, followed by an announcement of the next month's trip. These excursions always included a visit to a local winery, sometimes too early in the morning for us. Wine at ten didn't tend to mix well with the cappuccino and cornetto we had consumed only an hour or two earlier. Then, either before or after a three-hour lunch with more wine from a local *cooperativa* or vineyard, there was a cultural event, a visit to a museum, a tour of a *frantoio* where we watched the new green olive oil drip from the press, or some other agricultural operation, always with a well-informed guide.

On one occasion, the wine group was invited to a winery owned by two British staff members. The villa, vineyards, and winery were located in an isolated hilly area. A brooding, almost gothic-appearing ruined castle overlooked their red-tiled roof, which sheltered Turkish carpets and paintings of the local area. We toured the production facilities, tasted their excellent white wine named after the golden oriole, *rigogolo*, and enjoyed lunch on their spacious terrace. It looked like an ideal life. But having a piece of paradise was no cure for the intrusion of reality when the husband and wife later divorced and the property was sold.

Other excursions were to the nearby Castelli Romani. In the spring we went to small taverns to eat fresh fava beans with *pecorino*. The beans were heaped on wooden tables where we sat beside others on benches munching and sipping white Frascati wine. In the fall we helped test olive oil on grilled thick slices of Roman bread before buying a case of wine from the grower's estate along with bottles of his newly pressed oil.

The wine group included two elderly British retired secretaries, red of face and coarse of demeanor. Sadly, they were embarrassing drunks. On a day trip, before we had visited the first winery, one of the women, encouraged by the other over some imagined slight, verbally and physically assaulted an elegantly mustachioed Turkish NATO officer sitting in front of her. In the ensuing uproar everyone shouted at his assailant to stop, to no avail. The attack on his dignity, along with being shoved and hit on the head, was too much. He demanded that the bus stop in the next small town where he insisted on getting off with his frightened blonde American wife. The offenders were sent to the back of the bus in disgrace. This ostracism didn't bother the old girls a bit. Unrepentant, they tossed off their wine at lunch, acting as if nothing had happened. We didn't see the NATO pair again, nor did we learn how they got back to Rome or if diplomatic notes flew back and forth. The obstreperous twosome arrived for the next month's trip as usual but no one would sit near them.

We usually stayed in Spartan hotels on longer group tours where the rooms had one bedside lamp holding a 25-watt bulb and no shower curtain. We learned to remove the toilet paper roll to a safe place before turning on the shower after several occasions when the roll turned into useless mush. On our first overnighter with the fishing group we found an envelope by our silverware and napkin in the hotel restaurant. Not having any idea what it was for, we left our crumpled used napkins next to the dirty plate. We found them neatly folded in the envelope the following morning when we sat at our assigned place. We complied with this cost-saving measure from then on just like at home.

Once, on the way home after a trip to Rimini on the Adriatic coast, a Frenchwoman was discovered to have a small poodle in her capacious handbag. Italian staff members didn't like the dog and didn't like her, either. A screaming match ensued:

"You have a dog in there!!"

"*No.*"

"*Sì.*"

"You have no right to have a dog on the bus."

"He's not causing any problem."

And on and on, and round and round, with more and more people joining in to express their opinion. Meanwhile, the dog started to yap and struggle out of her bag, causing more commotion. The yelling match finished with the classic conversation stopper: "Why don't you go back to your own country?" For once, it was quiet on the way back to Rome with the dog, its owner, and the rest of the group keeping their snouts shut.

Another short visit took us to one of the most famous pre-Lent Carnival celebrations, held at Viareggio, a resort town patronized by the rich in the summer and people like us in the off-season. There weren't enough people from the UN so the tour operator recruited outsiders to fill up several buses. At least one fellow traveler turned out to be *male educato*, ill bred, when we stopped for coffee at a rest area. Glenn felt something and turned around to find an unknown woman draped in a luxurious mink coat with her hand in his back pocket, fingering his wallet—or maybe his bottom.

To work off all the food and wine our weekend group travels often involved evening entertainment, Italians always being exuberant party people who never want to quit for the day or night. Singing with the band and dancing, particularly to the inevitable infectious Latin American macarena and cha-cha, were the most popular. *Il treno*, conga line to us, was a fixture late every evening. We joined in the absurd line, holding on to each other's waists, snaking through the room. When we took our after-dinner stroll along the main street in one small town we passed the window of a restaurant. Faint strains of an accordion wafted out. We stopped to watch another tour group going round and round the room, all holding each other's waists chanting *"uno, due, tre—KICK!"* The procession bore a strong resemblance to paintings of medieval people going mad with dance during the era of the Black Death.

A shopping extravaganza was part of every group trip. I soon found that I was only an amateur when it came to this sport. Watching Italians shop was an entertainment in itself as they lumbered back to the tour buses loaded with bags and bundles. In Istanbul they had so much loot piled up in the aisles that we had to crawl over it to get to our seats. It was amazing anything was left in the bazaar.

When we went to Tunisia with the grandly and mistakenly named Diplomatic Golf Club (no relation to Glenn's club, which had an actual course with grass), everyone bought carpets. They were piled in the aisles, and when there was no more room inside, more were tied to the bus roof. Sometimes the fervor for bargains got out of hand. The leather luggage for sale on another trip looked tempting to one couple. The shopkeeper stopped them as they headed for the door. He grabbed their just-purchased suitcase and opened it to find they had nested additional luggage inside. After shouting and gesticulating, the shopkeeper won the contest and retrieved his goods. The rest of our group observed the dustup at a safe distance, but close enough so we could see the outcome.

The all-important dinner seating became an issue on a Mediterranean cruise where all the Italians wanted the late seating. With a scrum so thick and unmanageable, the purser threw his hands up and stalked off saying, "I can't take it anymore." As we neared each port, we glided into Italian soccer songs rolling over the water, thereby alerting the awaiting souvenir vendors that easy pickings were coming as soon as the gangplank was lowered. During a sightseeing tour on Rhodes, the group spotted a fig orchard next to a coffee bar where we stopped for a break. They proceeded to climb over the surrounding fence and help themselves to figs. We expected to see the farmer with a shotgun, but nothing happened (although we envisioned being thrown in a Greek jail as accessories to theft).

One venture is remembered for our own humiliation. Shortly before Easter, the staff association announced a trip to Seville. When we and Ray and Carolyn arrived at the airport, we found the flight delayed for hours. We four were the only non-Italians, and a merry lot they were as they milled around, talking and jostling impatiently. With no seat reservations, we managed to elbow ourselves into adjoining seats after a mad dash over the tarmac when the boarding call finally came. The plane was old and all safety instructions were in Japanese. Trusting Mercury, we sat back to watch the passing scene—not the clouds and Sardinia far below, but the hyperactive passengers who must have had too much espresso that morning. So rambunctious that they couldn't sit still, they stood or ran up and down the aisle to talk to their friends, like children on their first school outing. When we unexpectedly landed in Madrid to refuel (this on what should have been a direct two-hour flight) one fanatic smoker refused to stop smoking despite orders and pleas from the others. We were not allowed to disembark and were terrified the plane would explode.

Seville was lovely, with preparations underway for Holy Week and the fair that follows Easter. We watched men belonging to various religious confraternities dusting statues of weeping Virgins and polishing silver ornaments on the heavy floats they would soon carry in slow, rhythmical steps in the mournful Good Friday processions. Candy store windows were full of marzipan figurines of other marchers dressed in pointed hoods with eyeholes. Gypsies danced on platforms set up in the street. So different were they than the bedraggled Gypsies in Rome. The haughty women showed off their ruffled, polka-dotted dresses while the men, with smoldering eyes, tight pants, and high-heeled boots, exhibited their slim figures. At last, these were the Gypsies I had romanticized.

It was hot and sunny and we had too many sangrias and too much paella before walking around the center to see the fabulous cathedral. We gawked at its Moorish minaret, the Archive of the Indies, the intricately tiled Alcázar, and the former tobacco factory where Carmen rolled cigars against her tender thigh. It was all a pleasant blur from the strong drink and rich food. We were in a mellow mood—at least until it came time to depart.

In contrast to the modest places where we customarily stayed with our travel groups, we luxuriated in a five-star hotel featuring students dressed in eighteenth-century costumes serenading us with traditional songs in a tiled and fountained courtyard. All these happy memories instantly evaporated when we were accosted by the hotel manager when our group was checking out. He demanded to search our luggage for our towels, which were exceptionally thick in comparison to the threadbare scraps usually offered on our group weekends. All the other guests stood around watching us being humiliated. We didn't have them, had never considered taking them. After he yelled and shook his fist at us, we told him to go ahead and open our luggage. He backed off. Then we heard that a maid had picked them up when we were at breakfast but neglected to mark them off her list. Nevertheless, we were quiet on the return flight.

Despite these various embarrassments and misadventures we never hesitated to book the next opportunity.

XXIV

In the first century AD, Quintilian worried about the proper cut and draping of togas to ensure they would not be considered unshapely. Nothing much has changed in twenty centuries except for the invention of the sewing machine. While food is first in Italians' daily priorities, fashion is also of critical importance to the many who are concerned about presenting a *bella figura*.

I loved to venture to the beautiful and crowded Via Condotti and the surrounding area where the priests of high fashion showed their wares. Everything was luxurious in quality and design. Everything was also enormously expensive and the snooty clerks, seeing that we were not the high-spending young Japanese girls seen everywhere, shot looks of disapproval our way when we opened their shop doors to look around. The tittering girls hauled their treasures in bags with prominent logos, although sometimes the bags were about three inches square, containing only a key ring or some other trinket to announce to the world that they had shopped at one of the big-name houses.

The Roman middle-aged upper classes were well dressed and elegant, assured paragons of style. They were of average size or taller with slender builds. Women often had bleached or real blonde hair swept back with a tortoiseshell headband, or were redheads courtesy of henna. Almost no one wore bangs, or fringe as it is called. We were amused one day to hear a woman rush up to her bleached-blonde friend on the Via Condotti saying, "*Dimi tutto, bionda.*" "Tell me everything, blondie."

Elegant suits were in fashion, worn with heavy gold jewelry, a designer handbag with an expensive silk scarf tied around the handle, the latest style of sunglasses, high-concept shoes or boots, and, in the winter, a voluminous mink coat—the more fur the better. Fur coats were so large and heavy with their foot-wide collars, cuffs, and ruffles around the hem it was hard to imagine how the owners bore up under the weight. But somehow they intrepidly carried on. It was also impressive to watch the fashionistas adroitly negotiating the *San Pietrini* ("little holy rocks," or paving stones) in their stiletto heels. Mine always sank in the spaces in between and were ruined. In summer, the women's red toenails stuck out from handmade sandals. In winter they wore patterned stockings, reminding me of Renaissance paintings, although in the paintings it was the men wearing the fancy hose. Nearly everyone smoked while they ate, drank, and talked face to face or on their *telefonini*, cell phones. When they met on the street it was a kiss (air or full contact) on each cheek, and when they parted they waved backward, as if beckoning their friend to return.

On the opposite end of the fashion spectrum, many of the poorer Roman housewives were short and dumpy. They wore little gold drop earrings, a dark-colored housedress, an apron or a housecoat, and felt slippers or sandals definitely not designed by Ferragamo. They carried a plastic shopping bag or a plate of spaghetti to feed scrawny stray cats. Their hair was also often hennaed but for some reason it was frequently thin with lots of scalp showing. Maybe cheap henna isn't good for hair. I didn't try it but colleagues occasionally showed up with startling shades of orange, purple, and red. Elderly women carried on the tradition of black clothing for perpetual widowhood. They looked sad with their wrinkled faces, bent backs, gray hair pulled back in a bun, thick brown or black sagging stockings, and felt slippers. They'd hobble around the markets with their plastic sack or dragging little two-wheeled shopping carts to carry the few vegetables they could afford.

Men offered the same contrast. The wealthy were elegantly turned out and always looked as though they had come out of an expensive barbershop an hour previously. Their handmade shoes were freshly shined. Even for casual wear, they looked like they had just modeled for a fashion shoot to be published in Vogue *Uomo*, with cashmere sweaters artfully draped and a paisley ascot at their necks. Their designer label suits were beautifully cut, and in cold weather they often had a camel's hair coat slung over their shoulders. As with their female counterparts, their high-style sunglasses were on top of their heads when not in use.

The less wealthy men were as plain as their wives. And, like their wives, elderly men were also noticeably short. In winter, they wore heavy sweaters, scarves, and jackets with dark slacks. In summer, they often sat outside their shops on dingy white plastic chairs near the doorways that were hung with swaying strings of beads to ward off flies. The proprietor and his friends wore sleeveless undershirts while playing endless games of *scopa* around a small table, their attire hardly a fashion statement that would make Armani happy.

Glenn was unfavorably impressed by the men's handbags displayed in leather goods shops. He couldn't imagine himself carrying a "man purse," though his golfing buddies insisted that it was still a desirable fashion accessory long after the onset of cell phones, which replaced handbags for the younger set. I tried to interest him in ascots tucked into the neck of a sweater, but that didn't work either. With his khakis and blue oxford shirts he looked like an American—until these clothes wore out and we bought local, the cuts and styles looking nothing like Dockers or Nautica. Then tourists started asking us for directions.

Most of the professional office-bound staff dressed conservatively. Men often wore custom-made suits and dress shirts with their initials not-so-discretely embroidered on the cuff or pocket along with designer ties and handmade shoes. They always wore their jackets to meetings, no matter how hot the weather. Field-workers, in Rome for a meeting, frequently wore safari suits, making them look dashing. In summer, some of the younger female clerical staff wore as little as possible with brief T-shirts, sandals, and short, short skirts. So short that a friend said they were up to their *mariage*, French for private parts.

I tried to look like the rest of the professional women. They wore business attire except for one who wore so much jewelry that she was dubbed "the Christmas tree" in honor of all the brightly colored stones dangling from ears, neck, and fingers. Designer scarves were the most common accessory, tied or draped to show off the house label, Gucci, Valentino, or some other expensive brand. Fall brought sweater mania with angora, fur, sequins, beads, and other fripperies on brightly colored cashmere and wool. Winter was time for me to wrap a large wool scarf around my coat to keep out the damp chill. Inevitably, a frumpy American colleague wore old sneakers, making her look like a bag lady. Wanting to be different, I concentrated on improving my wardrobe, a pleasure in Rome although I knew that I would never have the style flaunted on the Via Condotti.

Members of Catholic religious orders were recognizable by their style. Franciscans wore brown robes with a knotted cord at the waists. Benedictines were in black; Dominicans were in black and white; nuns in black, gray, white, and gray-blue. Those of Mother Teresa's order were in white cotton saris with a blue border. The men were almost invariably white skinned. Elderly nuns were pale white, but the younger ones all appeared to be from India, Sri Lanka, the Philippines, or West Africa. Many of the orders' names were familiar, but one term was new to us—"discalced," meaning "without shoes" or barefoot, a real penance in shoe-mad Italy. We didn't see any bare feet, but there were lots of utilitarian sandals treading the pavements.

We peered in the shop windows in the "vestment district" near Piazza Navona, where clothing for the innumerable Catholic functionaries was displayed. Fellini's movie, *Roma,* features a satirical ecclesiastical fashion show, including priests on roller skates. Looking at the sumptuous ceremonial clothing for bishops and cardinals, it was easy to imagine him dreaming up such a scandalous scene. Basic black was available but many items had lace galore, and for the higher ranks, clothing in Roman and Byzantine reds and purples. In complete contrast were the windows with nuns' clothing, from the plain cotton bras and underpants shamelessly shown to the public, to simple sandals and dull-colored habits. Wrens versus peacocks.

The plain clothing of the religious orders seen on the street contrasted with the brilliantly printed cotton gowns worn by the tall black African ambulatory vendors. They called out *"vu cumprà?"* ("Do you want to buy?") to passersby. In turn the Italians derisively called them *vucumpras*. The men sold Mafia-supplied counterfeit DVDs and fake Gucci and Vuitton handbags, along with carvings of animals and masks. All this happened right under the authorities' noses. Wealthy acquaintances bragged about their bargains without concern for the illegality of their actions.

Manual laborers and mechanics commonly wore a blue jumpsuit, sometimes adding a folded newspaper hat or a handkerchief tied in little knots at each corner to keep their hair clean. Gloves, work boots, and hard hats were seldom seen though every work site had big placards mandating their use. Like seatbelts, no one bothered with safety equipment despite the heavy toll of industrial accidents.

The students looked similar to students everywhere in Europe: tall, attractive, and scruffy. Young women had tremendous amounts of long, curly dark hair, which they continually flopped around, especially when crammed in the subway during rush hour. It was imperative to keep my lips pursed, lest I get a mouthful. I had always thought that Renaissance paintings like Botticelli's *Birth of Venus*, with the beautiful creatures having impossibly abundant tresses, were an artistic fiction, but the artists must have been using real-life models. One of the most memorable sights in Rome was two young women on a Vespa weaving through traffic with their hair flying in the wind, not a care in the world.

Ah, but the military and other law-and-order costumes. For women who couldn't resist a man in uniform, they were heaven personified. Designed by the best Italian fashion houses, every group had its uniform. Traffic police wore snappy white in the summer; firemen had stylish scarves looped around their necks to match their rubber boots. Garbage workers wore their matching jumpsuits as they wielded witches' brooms made of twigs.

The best place for costume watching was the annual parade celebrating the Festa della Repubblica, June 2, 1946, when Italy sent the monarchy into exile and became a republic. We tried never to miss the celebration of the best in military and bureaucratic fashion. First came the Carabinieri honor guard, then dignitaries and troops in historic and ceremonial uniforms. Following along the wide Via dei Fori Imperali were nurses in their World War II nun-like uniforms, frogmen with flippers over their shoulders, and the crowd favorite, the Bersaglieri—Piedmontese sharpshooters. They wore round brimmed hats trimmed with bunches of iridescent capercaillie feathers that bounced as they ran to the sound of their trumpeters. Then came ranks of Yellow Flame tax police (imagine platoons of IRS agents), forest guards, and firemen, followed by Alpini carrying their climbing equipment and dressed in white ski outfits topped with a Tyrolean-style hat with a jaunty black feather.

But nothing could compare to the Carabinieri, who were magnificent when they dressed to impress for formal occasions. In addition to marching, they patrolled the piazza near the Spanish Steps on tall horses. The uniforms generally consisted of navy blue jacket and pants with a red stripe on the leg, a white leather strap across the chest, a small white box-like container (for what, I never knew), and a Napoleon-style bicorne hat topped with red and blue feathers. Sometimes they wore mirror-polished cavalry boots with tight white riding pants topped with a blue jacket with white lapels, rows of shiny brass buttons, and red cuffs. That outfit was complemented with a saber, blue cape, and tall blue hat with a red-and-white cockade. When they were on duty for state occasions they looked fit for Caesar's Centurion guards, with their silver-and-gold breastplates and helmets with long horsehair ponytails with a red feather pom-pom to one side. The costume was enough to give romance novelists fodder for years of heavy-breathing plots.

Besides being resplendently dressed, they were all tall, fantastically good looking, and perfectly groomed. It was obvious why so many of the UN clerks fell for theses gorgeous hunks. However, many jokes regularly circulated about them because their recruitment standards had been dismal in the past. They always worked in twos. One joke held that they had to be together so one could read and the other write. Whatever their intelligence, I found them a joy to behold.

XXV

La bella figura was particularly important when it came to weddings, not only in dress but in the style of the ceremony and feast afterward. Nuptials were sometimes performed twice; first in a civil ceremony followed by a formal church wedding. Thus, they were always big business and a fine opportunity to show off. One of the most popular events at the dingy and dilapidated exposition center was an annual wedding display called *Sposaroma*.

Without much to do on a weekend when the expo was in progress and wanting to be prepared when Kathryn and Steve set their wedding date, we went to the show for some ideas. We browsed among stands laden with marzipan cakes in the shape of the Colosseum, Trevi Fountain, and St. Peter's. Fireworks technicians advertised that they could shoot off colorful bursts for receptions continuing until dawn. Dozens of restaurants catering to the wedding trade had space to display tables dressed with lavish silver, china, and sets of wine glasses for every type of wine. The proposed menus went on for pages, pasta and more pasta along with meat and fish. Florists recommended filling the entire church with bouquets, sprays, and festoons attached to everything, including guests. We looked at samples of wedding favors, *bomboniere*, in sterling silver or Murano glass, and *confetti*, the traditional sugar-coated almonds in dozens of flavors and colors, including some coated in gold and silver. They were made into flower arrangements or placed in little bags, always in an uneven number like the gladioli we sometimes bought at flower stands. I made a note to myself that the *confetti* came from Sulmona in the Abruzzi Mountains east of Rome, where the same company had produced them since 1783.

Wedding gowns and grooms' outfits, modeled on runways or on mannequins, ranged from the most sober formal wear to the ridiculous. Most gowns were lovely, but some were my idea of a mother-of-the-bride's nightmare. These included a crochet model with empty spaces that left little to the imagination, and a black-and-white Little Bo-Peep outfit with a lace-up corset-like bodice, a shepherd's crook instead of flowers, and a large Marie Antoinette hat. Perhaps the groom was meant to be seen as a sheep or goat. Masculine outfits included tuxedo-like suits in sky blue or spring pea green as well as ultra-formal morning costumes with top hats. Somehow, none of the men's models looked right for the casual Pacific Northwest.

Often when we poked around a church we could see that it was set up for a wedding ceremony. If one was ongoing we stood at the back where no one would notice us, looking at flowers, well-dressed guests, the resplendent wedding party, priests in their vestments, and the sanctified surroundings. But one church, Santo Stefano Rotondo, rated as the last place in the world I would have wanted to be married. The mother of all churches if you like torture frescoes, it is one of the oldest circular churches still in existence, dating from about AD 468. Like so many of these ancient buildings, it is built over a pagan *mithraeum*, where sacrificial bulls had their throats cut in second- or third-century rituals.

During the Counter-Reformation the interior was frescoed in a cycle of vivid and grotesque scenes of martyrdom, a veritable catalogue of ways to dispose of people in excruciating, and in some cases, disturbingly culinary ways like deep-frying and roasting. While these martyrs died for their faith centuries ago, the faded frescoes reminded us of the modern world's abominations still centering on religious troubles. The last time we visited the church, it was set up for a wedding to be held on All Saints' Day, the day celebrating the Church's martyrs, the day before All Souls' Day, which honors the dead. It seemed a particularly inauspicious site and day. But then we often saw brides photographed in front of the Colosseum, which ran with the blood of slaughtered animals and gladiators in ancient times. There's no accounting for taste.

• • •

There is an Italian proverb, "Rain on a bride's wedding day is good luck." We were invited to three Roman weddings, each bearing no resemblance to the standard American occasion, or to each other in style. All were celebrated on sunny days. One was a civil ceremony conducted in a small deconsecrated church, the Complesso di Vignola Mattei. This building was first constructed in the sixth century, then became a home in the 1300s and part of a villa's gardens sometime later. It was furnished with ancient statues dug up from the grounds, adding to its romantic atmosphere.

Mark and Sophia were coworkers and partners. They decided to make their arrangement official because the groom was nearing retirement and it was mandatory to have a wedding before he retired if either of them were to have a survivor's pension should the other die. (Marriages after retirement were not recognized by the UN pension system, an incredibly backward view since remedied, but at the time it was cause for numerous hasty weddings.) Adding to the urgency, Sophia was preparing to go to Ghana for an assignment the following week. Both were British but they soon determined that it would take weeks to get the deed accomplished in England, because of the length of time to publish the wedding banns. It was too expensive to fly to the States, a possibility though neither was a citizen. The fallback position was a marriage in Italy, where it would usually take a month to get the paperwork in order and the wedding scheduled. They obtained a *nulla osta* certificate from the British Embassy affirming that there was no impediment to marriage and went to the Italian records office to get the remaining paperwork, a *promessa di matrimonio*. When they told a handsomely dressed bureaucrat (whose fly was unzipped) that they wanted to get married within eight days, he dropped his cappuccino in shock. After mopping up and zipping up, he agreed. In an astounding act of alacrity he issued the papers the next day, assigned a venue, and scheduled the wedding for the following Friday.

The presiding official, the local *assessore* or district councilor, wore her green, white, and red ribbon of office diagonally over her business suit. Mark and Sophia, in dress suits, sat in two tall, elaborately carved gold leaf chairs upholstered in scarlet velvet. Smaller chairs for the witnesses sat at each side. The short ceremony was performed to the recorded music of Vivaldi. Afterward, we all adjourned to a nearby restaurant for a long seafood luncheon. I didn't return to work that afternoon, being satiated after oysters, risotto with scampi, spaghetti with clams and mussels, followed by servings of grilled or baked fish including *orata, branzino,* or *spigola.* All this bounty was accompanied by champagne and white wine.

The next event was held on the Campidoglio, the site of Rome's founding in the Iron Age. The venue was the Palazzo dei Conservatori, which also houses part of the Capitoline museum complex. The wedding took place in the magnificent *sala rosa,* red room. With its crimson damask wall coverings, tapestries, and period furniture, it was justifiably the most favored and beautiful location in the city. The site was so popular that ceremonies only took a hurried fifteen minutes, with no time for music or arranging flowers.

The Palazzo, like many Italian public buildings, had a long history. It was erected in the Middle Ages atop the ruins of a Roman temple to Jupiter and later remodeled by Michelangelo in the 1530s. The inscription carved over the door to the sumptuous room said *Vniversitatis Tabernarior,* which meant it had been used like a guildhall where shopkeepers had settled their disputes in former days. The *pubblicazione di matrimonio,* banns, were posted on the wall outside the wedding venue showing names and dates of birth of those to be married, fun for snooping.

Our bride wore a traditional white gown, not that the guests noticed. Instead of witnessing the wedding, most of the invitees milled around in the piazza talking on their cell phones and waiting for the reception to begin. Ceremony over, we jumped into our cars and headed to a rustic restaurant about forty miles north of Rome in the ancient hill town of Capalbio, founded in the eighth century BC. First a prehistoric settlement, then an Etruscan one followed by the inevitable Romans, it was abandoned at the fall of the Empire. Capalbio gradually revived after the barbarian invasions, taken over by popes and powerful families until they too gave up, relinquishing the town to independence, country houses, art installations, and restaurants.

The food was as elaborate as the local history. Helpings of three standard shapes of pasta with their sauces were followed by piles of grilled chicken, pork, and beef. As usual, everyone was shouting and talking after a few glasses of wine. But then the party got a little rough when the groom, who tended to be combative, got in an argument with the local Carabinieri *maresciallo*. Evidently the groom had parked his car in a no-parking zone, which happened to be in front of the jail. The annoyed *maresciallo* threatened to throw him in the conveniently located lockup. His groomsmen rushed to the rescue and, after a discussion that was heated even by Italian standards, an accommodation was reached whereby his car was moved and he was released. The celebrations took up where they left off as if nothing had happened.

However, neither of these two events could compare with our inaugural Italian wedding experience on my first tour. My legal assistant lived on the Appia Antica in an old villa that he shared with a flamboyant French lawyer. The villa was a home that real or would-be expatriates dreamed about occupying. Marble fragments that had been dug up during construction were set into the walls. A swimming pool from ancient times was sunk in the extensive grounds, which were dotted with umbrella pines and cypresses. The rooms were filled with antique furnishings and paintings. I knew the French lawyer but slightly. However, because I was his housemate's supervisor we received an invitation to his wedding to an heiress. My assistant had told me about the arrangements for an elaborate reception to be held at their Appia Antica home, to which we had not been invited. In a complete social gaffe, I innocently mentioned this oversight, which then resulted in an invitation out of politeness.

The wedding was to be formal, and I was advised in no uncertain terms to wear a hat. After a wild-goose chase all over Rome to find one that was suitably elegant but not enormously expensive, I bought a little number to go with the red-patterned silk dress purchased especially for the wedding. I couldn't understand why the shop clerk kept tut-tutting when I told her that I didn't want a black dress. She valiantly persisted, bringing some delicious little black outfits for me to try. When we arrived at Trinità dei Monte, the French church at the top of the Spanish Steps, I realized the source of the shop clerk's dismay. All the other female guests wore black, appropriate European wear for all formal occasions and not limited to funerals. Feeling the all-too-familiar sensation of being an ignorant American, I shrank into a corner of the pew hoping that no one would notice me.

But all eyes turned to the bride when she entered the church in a low-cut strapless number, so tight it must have been sprayed on. Looking not at all virginal, she could hardly mince up the aisle. The groom wore a morning coat, as did his attendants. The wedding party tripped over videographers and photographers who continually got in the way. The service was conducted by a cardinal and two priests in splendid outfits. Greetings from the pope were read. By the time it was over we were ready for champagne and followed the crowd to the villa. To the sounds of a string quartet playing Neapolitan love songs on the candlelit terrace and the smacks of guests kissing the cardinal's huge jeweled ring, the groom opened the champagne bottles by swiping the corks off with a saber. He occasionally missed, breaking the bottle's neck and releasing foam everywhere. After the toasts we left. No one noticed. There's nothing like attending a party to which you weren't invited! I bought a black dress shortly after.

Watching these rituals I remembered Glenn's and my five-minute wedding at the home of two friends who lived on the rainy Oregon coast. In spite of, or perhaps because of, its drizzly beginnings, our union has endured, as has that of Kathryn and Steve. Their wedding day began with sunshine. It was drizzling by the time of the ceremony. The reception took place during a veritable monsoon. The Seattle setting couldn't compete with Rome, but we did have *confetti* from Sulmona, small silver bags containing seven silver-colored almonds closed with silver ribbons and almond paste wedding rings with their names. Instead of black I wore an Italian suit in a color called *tortora*, turtledove, to my mind a more fitting color.

Unfortunately for the Roman weddings, the proverb about weather turned into reality and all three of the marriages we attended ran into storms.

XXVI

In *Innocents Abroad*, Mark Twain wrote extensively about his visit to Rome although he added: "I wished to write a real 'guide-book' chapter on this fascinating city, but I could not do it, because I have felt all the time like a boy in a candy-shop—there was everything to choose from, and yet no choice." Twain had it right – where to start and where to stop. One reason it is called the Eternal City may be that it would take an eternity to see everything. We never managed.

• • •

One Saturday on our first tour I happened to notice some simple posters tacked up on nearby telephone poles between ads for French lessons and communist rallies. The flyer said that the Bishop of Rome was coming to our small local church the following Sunday. After we realized that this bishop was also the pope, we walked a block to the church the following morning. To our surprise, only about thirty people were waiting, some in matching sweatpants and shirts (a *tutto* or "all"), instead of a huge crowd dressed in their Sunday best. Two dogs engaged in amatory behavior to no one's concern. We surveyed this strange scene, completely the opposite of the pomp and cheering we had expected.

A convoy of five black limos eventually pulled up in front of the church. Photographers jumped out of the first one. The next several limos contained officials and the security detail. The pope came last. He looked just like his pictures, recognizable anywhere. The photographers busily rearranged the sparse crowd to make it look bigger. We were encouraged to join the small group meeting His Holiness, but since we are not of that faith it didn't seem appropriate in this intimate setting. The pope blessed everyone before the parishioners entered their church. Later that afternoon, we hosted a lunch party, and when our guests arrived we all rushed back to the church where he was still communing with his flock, now blessing a few children with beaming parents looking on. But the same aura of "no big deal" remained.

The casual affair in our neighborhood was in complete contrast to a papal encounter with visiting friends. Our car wouldn't comfortably hold six people on a hot day for the drive to the pope's summer residence in Castel Gandolfo, so we took a standard bus tour starting with a visit to one of the many tacky souvenir shops near the Vatican. There, we were encouraged to buy expensive rosaries to be blessed and sent directly to tourists' hotels. When we arrived at the papal residence, we stood packed in with hundreds of foreign tourists, some dropping to their knees or nearly fainting with joy at their coming proximity to the pope. All the while, we were guarded by soldiers armed with submachine guns standing on the periphery of the piazza or crouching on adjacent rooftops. When he finally appeared on his balcony we were formally blessed in many languages, although I felt no more holy than when we were at our corner church. Our friends, who were also non-Catholic, had tears in their eyes from being overcome with religious feeling. Whatever our own religious persuasions, we were impressed with the power the pope held over his audience, as have so many of his predecessors over two millennia.

• • •

Christmas in Rome was religious in sentiment. Santa was nowhere and the sound of endless loops of *White Christmas* and *Rudolph the Red-Nosed Reindeer* were missing. Since the Italians don't celebrate Thanksgiving there were also no Black Friday sales. (Alas, there were no Christmas sales at all because they were controlled by the government and only held twice a year, late summer and in January, with different dates for different cities.) Instead of decorations going up at the end of October, nothing was in evidence until December 8, the Feast of the Immaculate Conception. On that afternoon the pope traveled to Piazza Mignanelli near the Piazza di Spagna to lay a wreath at the foot of a column topped by a statue of the Virgin Mary. The Vatican was jammed with tourists attending services.

Our favorite sight was the delightful Christmas market filling the spacious Piazza Navona with toys, candy, and figures of a wizened old granny, *la befana*, who flies through the air astride a broomstick to bring treats to children if they are good, and coal if they're not. She arrives on the night of January 5 to ensure that the gifts are ready on Epiphany morning in remembrance of the Gifts of the Magi. But the "coal" on display is really black candy, so *bambini* are never very worried. When we strolled in the piazza, the sounds of happy children echoed off the magnificent buildings surrounding the area. They mixed with the one-sided conversations from their parents' cell phones and the sound of falling water from the three sparkling fountains.

Different sounds came from smaller piazzas where shepherds from the Abruzzi Mountains just east of Rome came to play their bagpipes, *zampogna*. The *Zampognari* are traditionally dressed in knickers, cross-wrapped leggings, and wool capes. We suspected that the outfits were only brought out during the holidays, and that, rather than returning to lonely flocks in the hills, the musicians tooled off in their Fiats to cozy homes and televisions. There they'd recuperate from their day collecting coins that we willingly donated after listening to their haunting music.

• • •

The life-sized Nativity scene by the obelisk in front of St. Peters was always beautiful as it rested within the welcoming arms of Bernini's magnificent statue-topped colonnade. But the exhibition of *presepi* in Santa Maria del Popolo, famed for its two Caravaggio paintings, was more intimate with little figurines dressed in native costumes from the world over. Nativity displays have been a tradition in Italy since at least the time of St. Francis in the 1200s. The most elaborate figures come from Via San Gregorio Armeno, a narrow street in the old section of Naples, Spaccanapoli, where artisans devote themselves to creating an amazing variety of theatrical characters—peasants in eighteenth-century dress with their carts and wheelbarrows, animals, cheeses, sausages, and baskets of fishes. They all surround the Holy Family, who are sheltered under an elaborate lean-to guarded by hovering angels wearing swirling Baroque robes.

The statuettes offering food in the Nativity scenes are emblematic of Christmas in Italy with its food traditions. Along the streets in the historic city center came a mouthwatering aroma from chestnuts roasting on charcoal braziers. Sold in paper cones, we found their taste irresistible on cold December days. "The Christmas Song" beginning with the immortal line, "Chestnuts roasting on an open fire" always came to mind as we munched while window-shopping along streets filled with luxuries from Gucci, Valentino, and Bulgari.

Piles of boxed *panettone*, the fruit-studded Christmas bread, filled supermarket aisles and were stacked in shop windows. We joined others holding on to the ribbon handles of their boxed treats, toting them on the subway or bus—gifts to the hostess or *nonna*, or just for themselves. Other seasonal foods were also abundant: *pandoro*, a sweet bread enjoyed by both ancient and modern Romans; tooth-breaking *torrone*, the flat sticks of nougat and nuts; *panforte*, a dense, dark, and chewy fruitcake from Siena; and *zampone*, sausage-stuffed pig's trotters often served with lentils.

Some shop windows were decorated, although none equaled that of an antique store where a tree was hung with small Greek and Russian icons each hanging from a ribbon. Having an attraction to otherworldly Byzantine-style Madonnas, I lusted after that tree's decorations without getting any satisfaction, given the prices. Our small and scraggly tree, the only kind available, was decorated with crystal drops taken from old chandeliers we'd found piled in heaps in the Sunday flea market at Porta Portese. As I hung the drops, I wondered again who had danced under the glittering lights in the eighteenth and nineteenth centuries, and what change of circumstances had caused their owners to sell them for a pittance.

Our tabletops held figurines for our own *presepe*: the knife grinder, the fish monger, shepherds, the Wise Men, a camel and donkey, and of course the Holy Family. Some of the figures came from the Christmas market (unpainted terracotta) and some from Standa, the local equivalent of a tiny Walmart (cheap plastic, but hand-painted in Italy), and a few from our trips to Naples.

Italians typically eat a large meal, usually fish or seafood, on Christmas Eve before attending midnight service. We reserved our holiday meal for Christmas Day. Butterball turkey showed up in our commissary, along with canned cranberry sauce. The sauce wasn't available in Italian grocery stores, and turkey wasn't a common commodity.

If we didn't have family or other visitors, we contributed to a potluck with friends. And after the meal it was time for a walk. Our favorite route was along the Appian Way where towering umbrella pines and cypresses, dark against the deep blue sky, line the ancient road. The paving stones are grooved from chariots from the time of the Roman Empire. Romantic ruins are scattered along the route, like those of the mausoleum of Cecilia Metella. The remains always put me in awe of the power and skills of those who populated the Empire two thousand years before my footsteps and long before Christmas was a concept.

• • •

Besides the haunting bagpipes at Christmastime, we never lacked for other opportunities to enjoy performances; fortunately, Italians did appear to be as musical as the stereotype. At least, most of them were. Every large city had an opera and even small towns had their theaters and town bands. We always enjoyed rural efforts but our real goal was to attend an opera performance at La Scala in Milan, the premier house in Italy and maybe the world. We had that good fortune after paying a hefty bribe to a friend of the Count Tommaso to get tickets for *Rigoletto*. It was a superb experience, never to be equaled.

We also managed a performance in the outdoor amphitheater at Verona, where everyone waved candles when the chorus of Hebrew slaves sang of their longing for their homeland in *Nabucco*. This song, which commences, "Fly, thoughts, on wings of gold . . . ," is the traditional Italian national anthem because of its association with the unification of Italy, a long struggle ending only in 1870.

There was a reason why it was far easier to obtain tickets to the Rome opera and symphony performances: like many Italian government–supported entities, the opera was a hotbed of political appointees, along with the standard hot-tempered performers and stagehands. The rubric of "the show must go on" wasn't applicable. When artists did show up, it was always a gamble as to quality, although the upper levels of the opera house were packed with claques who applauded with fanaticism even the most wretched performance. Cherubino in *La Nozze di Figaro* was so bad we grimaced, but the applause was wild. The sets for *Madama Butterfly* looked like they were dredged up from an American used furniture shop, with costumes from the Goodwill racks. More applause. Some of the musicians in the symphony never found any notes that they liked despite persistent attempts. Ever more applause, anyway. Santa Cecilia, the patron saint of music, must have stuck her fingers in her ears to blot out the discordant sounds.

When we went to the summer outdoor performances in the Baths of Caracalla all was forgiven because the setting was so dazzling. Merely sitting in the warm, humid air watching fireflies as the moon rose over the ruins and the umbrella pines was worth any number of lapses. The two most popular performances at the Baths were *Aida* and *Tosca*. All our guests loved them even if they weren't operagoers at home, and we never got tired of the productions no matter how many times we attended. When the dancers in *Aida* chewed gum and didn't seem to have ever seen each other before as they zigzagged off in directions the choreographer never intended, or stumbled into each other, we cheered as wildly as everyone else.

Our former neighbors, the Czech soprano, Jana, and the composer, Ada, continued to invite us to their concerts held in beautiful venues such as the Hungarian Academy, a sixteenth-century palazzo on the Via Giulia remodeled by Borromini the following century. Although the settings were old, the music was avant-garde. It often consisted of *brani*, fragments or short little pieces. Everyone in the audience was terribly serious. Local music critics came to listen, their positive reviews published in the newspapers the following day. Jana specialized in the music of Karlheinz Stockhausen, a pioneer in electronic music or "experimental noise" as one writer aptly put it. Her husband, the French-horn player, focused on the modern Italian composer Goffredo Petrassi. Our former upstairs neighbor, the composer Ada, wrote music along Petrassi's lines, i.e., both atonal and athematic. Despite our lack of understanding and appreciation of the music, the promise of a provocative experience ensured our attendance.

Jana's uncle from Prague, also a musician, came to Rome with other members of his string quartet to perform a more traditional program in the torch-lit courtyard of Sant'Ivo della Sapienza, built by Borromini between 1643 and 1660. The church, one of the most architecturally interesting in Rome, has a spiral ramp over the dome evoking the Tower of Babel. Like the performances at the Baths of Caracalla, the lovely ambience of a summer evening added to the melodies and offered a much more rewarding event than formal winter concerts.

Other entertainment options included the Cinema Pasquino, one of the only movie theatres in Rome showing English-language movies without dubbing them into Italian. The cinema had a roof that could be opened on warm evenings, a useful amenity because it let out the smell of marijuana being furiously smoked by students who sat in front. A friend told us about the time it started to rain and management began to close the roof. Unfortunately a cat was sitting on the movable part enjoying the scene and maybe the marijuana. Its tail got caught when the roof closed. After hearing the yowling they managed to reverse the closure and release the animal, who rapidly headed for another venue for his evening excursion.

On a warm evening we were lined up in the narrow alleyway waiting for the ticket booth to open. Across the alley was a well-known fish restaurant where diners were enjoying an outdoor meal. A *barbone*, bum, began walking back and forth in a furtive manner with a waiter repeatedly shooing him away. Suddenly, the disheveled man ran up to the roped-off dining space and on the fly grabbed a large platter of expensive seafood from right under the noses of a couple. The astonished patrons were left with open mouths, and knives and forks waving in the air. Taking off at great speed and never dropping a single shrimp or oyster, the intrepid *barbone* headed around the nearest building with the waiter in hot pursuit. Round and round they ran until the frustrated waiter finally gave up. The ingenious bum sat on a ledge to enjoy his free meal at a safe distance from his tormentor.

• • •

Despite all the distractions of music and movies, Rome's real cultural attraction was the art. I enjoyed studying art history in college but nothing prepared me for the total visual assault. Our neighborhood offered fascist art from the 1930s but the *centro storico* piled twenty-eight centuries one on top of or beside the other. It was nearly impossible to travel anywhere in the center without finding something old that was new to us or new to the world, with excavations continually bringing treasures to the surface. Museums that had been closed for decades were opening up again or exhibiting items that had been in storage forever. The many art venues regularly had "blockbuster" exhibitions mounted from holdings throughout the world. Smaller galleries exhibited newer artists. For a time we dragged guidebooks along on every expedition, diligently reading the narrative and studying the layouts of churches, museums, and forums. We went on guided walks with experts and we watched television programs featuring more experts. We were drowning in art.

When the Greek and Roman statues in the Vatican Museum all began to look alike and the paintings of saints, Annunciations, and Crucifixions ran together, we gave up the guidebooks and surrendered to concentrating on the more comprehensible minor delights. We absorbed the sights by osmosis, looking closely at one aspect of a sculpture, fresco, or mosaic. We touched sun-warmed stones to imagine whose sandals had trod there or picked a leaf of laurel growing next to a monument while thinking that the tree's ancestors might have supplied a wreath to crown some victorious emperor home from war on the Empire's far frontiers. We trailed fingers over the moss in a fountain, or tasted dishes made from ancient recipes still served in restaurants. Instead of endless trudges through the major museums we went to the smaller ones like one on the Caelian Hill, which displayed slave collars along with other domestic items, giving us a more intimate glimpse of the reality of life in Roman times. Sitting on ancient chunks of marble looking at the vestiges of the past, we tried to picture what they had originally looked like and wished it could all spring back to life for a few moments. We picked one or two streets to see in depth. I became interested in early Christian mosaics with their glittering red, green, gold, and blue, all the figures so flat yet so alive with infinite promise when the light played over the tiny glass tesserae. It was restful to contemplate them in ancient churches on quiet afternoons.

What good fortune we had to be able to idle when our visitors joined the millions of other tourists rushing from the Palatine to the Colosseum to the Vatican in one or two days. But we wanted to experience the passing scene in other places as well.

XXVII

Like Mark Twain, we could become overwhelmed with Rome. His cure was to press on to Naples and the south. We often followed Twain's advice and found an Italy far different than the center and north. Coming from the mossy Pacific Northwest with its oyster-colored sky, and where the definition of better weather often meant a paler shade of gray, the warming concept of "the south" dictated our destination for many long weekends or more extended trips.

Determined to be on the road as frequently as possible, we didn't fool around with a junker or wait for a year to buy a car when we came to Rome a second time. Glenn bought us an Opel Calibra, large enough to stand up against Mercedes and Lancias on the road. Some days I thought that he loved that car more than me as he eagerly jumped in the driver's seat to head out of town on our excursions.

The dangerous two-lane coastal road started a few blocks from our apartment. It led past Glenn's golf course and towns established by Mussolini with 1930s modernist architecture. They were part of *Il Duce's* grandest reclamation project, the draining of the malaria-ridden Pontine Marshes to improve agricultural production. The marshes had been depopulated since antiquity due to endemic malaria. The mosquito-infested high water came from ancient deforestation on the surrounding steep hills and storm surges on the flat plain. As far back as 312 BC, there are records of unsuccessful attempts to reclaim the land. In his drive to re-create the glory of his imperial forebears, Mussolini turned his energetic eye to the problem. He employed thousands of laborers in the 1930s who worked under harsh conditions to drain the marshes and build new towns. The disease wasn't fully eradicated until the 1950s, and now the land is productive with farms and dairies.

On the way to wherever we were heading in the South, we made sure to stop at one of the small shops adjacent to the many dairies, *caseifici*, selling the fresh results of water buffalo standing in mud peacefully producing milk for mozzarella. Cholesterol be damned, tasting the cheese, so soft and drippy it could barely hold its round shape, gave us *forza* to carry on.

The black buffalo looked incongruous to us but they are longtime residents, brought to the peninsula in the seventh century by the Goths. The animals were originally used solely for plowing muddy fields, but by the twelfth century gourmets were making cheese from their milk. Basil is native to the Mediterranean, but the tomatoes, the other element necessary for our *insalata caprese*, had to wait for Columbus. Lucky for us, we arrived after the divine combination was invented.

The road south sometimes led us to the beautiful water gardens of Ninfa, built into the remains of a small town abandoned for six centuries due to wars, banditry, and malaria. In 1920, the heir to the ancient Caetani family married an Englishwoman who made it her life's work to turn the castle and churches into gardens full of purple wisteria, lavender, rosemary, irises, and roses, all growing among the ruins and cypress trees. Streams with clear, sparkling water ran throughout. Swans graced the ponds. We ambled in the gardens, delighting in the combination of English garden design precepts mixed with half-fallen medieval buildings. It fully lived up to its description as idyllic. But the nearby town of Norma, built high on an isolated cliff overlooking the garden and nearby farms, soon brought us back to the reality of the south, where incomes and educational levels are lower than the industrious north. The inhabitants all looked poverty stricken and some had hideous growths. After a wretched restaurant experience (eating *pasta alla norma*, no less) we brought a picnic on the next garden visit.

• • •

One wedding anniversary, Glenn took me to an elegant hotel at one of the beach resorts at San Felice Circeo, an hour or so south of our home. The name alone was attractive, although it may have simply meant Saint Felix of Circeo, a saint I could never find on any list. More to my taste was a translation to Happy Saint Circe, a nice pagan touch similar to saints named after Bacchus, Janus, Venus, or Apollo. Circe was the enchantress who imprisoned Ulysses nearby or, in other tales, had her tempting calls ignored when he and his crew stopped their ears with wax to avoid them. The beautiful coastline is called "Riviera d'Ulysses" in memory of these mythical events and the descriptions by Homer and Virgil. More prominent and factual are the watchtowers built in the Middle Ages to protect against real Saracen raiders.

It was mid-February, not a popular time to visit Italian beach resorts, though it was already spring in the south with flowers in bloom. We looked forward to a quiet dinner at the hotel's highly rated restaurant, with no enchantresses or Saracens to alarm us. But when we drove up to the beautiful white building draped with brilliant coral-red bougainvillea, we found dozens of gigantic black Mercedes and Lancias in the drive with swarthy people emerging. The men flaunted heavy gold necklaces and scarred pockmarked faces. The women all looked like they could hold their own in any alleyway brawl. Then the tough-looking bride stepped out of her limo and the party started. And it never stopped. The noise from the music, yelling, and breaking glasses continued until dawn, when the local version of the Mafia finally wore out from their revels. Meanwhile, we were shunted off to the coffee shop for our anticipated dinner. There we toyed with our food while watching a file of small ants march down a wall and across our plates to share the uninteresting meal. Romance didn't flourish that evening.

The next day we ran into what appeared to be yet another wedding, although at first glance the bride and groom were smaller than typical, maybe dwarfs like those collected by the aristocracy in the past. As we walked along the seafront, a procession of cars sounding their horns passed by. The first car had a cameraman filming the car behind, a Rolls-Royce convertible with a boy and girl in the backseat, each dressed in white satin, the girl in a wedding gown and veil and the boy in his shiny suit. They stood waving to the onlookers, the photographer and a string of honking cars behind them. Surely the Italians didn't do child weddings. No, it turned out to be a first communion, celebrated in flamboyant southern style.

• • •

When the southern coastal road crossed the Volturno River, we were in the real south. Once we stopped in the sad town of Santa Maria Capua Vetere where a colosseum rivaling that of Rome in size still stands. Spartacus trained there and in 73 BC began his unsuccessful slave revolt. Visions of Kirk Douglas and Jean Simmons came to mind. But despite the historical site, it was another town best avoided where, like Norma, the poor inhabitants looked nothing like movie stars. Many had goiters. Living conditions were squalid and some of the streets were unpaved and deep in mud. Vendors sold perfect-looking strawberries, but we passed on the opportunity after looking at the dispiriting ambience.

Nearby is Cumae, where the Cumaen Sibyl spun out her prophecies. We viewed her lack of charms on the ceiling of the Sistine Chapel where she is studying her books and scrolls. Of the five sibyls, she's the ugly one, rendered with aged and masculine features and a weightlifter's upper body and arms. The sibyl was reputed to have shunned sex—Michelangelo painted her legs and feet primly poised together. Her fame rests on offering nine books of prophecies to an Etruscan king of Rome in the sixth century BC. He declined to buy them because of the cost. She burned three and offered the remainder to the king at the same price. He refused again, whereupon she burned three more. He gave in and purchased the last three at the full original price. They were kept in the Temple of Jupiter on the Capitoline Hill in Rome to be consulted in emergencies—not that they did any good, as the Empire and the books are both long gone.

When she was "alive" she sat at the end of a 145-foot-long trapezoidal tunnel cut through solid rock. The tunnel and the surrounding remains of an ancient Greek city and temple complex are located not far from Lake Avernus, considered to be an entrance to Hades. Virgil described the sibyl's fearsome power: "Through the amplification of her hollow vaults, the sibyl cast her warnings, riddles confused with truth."

She had a peculiar end. She asked Apollo to let her live as long as the number of grains of sand she held in her hand. Apollo granted her wish but because she forgot to ask for enduring youth, she slowly withered away, ending up in a small jar. In the end only her voice was left, and that, too, is long gone, thus preventing me from asking her any questions.

The tunnel had a few openings for light cut into the cliff facing the sea. We stumbled along in the dimness. By the time we reached the end it was easy to think of the ancients quivering while awaiting some word on the future as she wrote their destiny in riddles confused with truth on leaves to be placed at the tunnel's entrance. The mood was unsettling and we didn't linger, anxious to return to the emotionally cleansing sunlight.

We were transported to the eighteenth century when we emerged into brilliance after one visit. A funeral cortege was passing by. In the lead was an ornately carved Baroque black wooden coach about the size of a tank, drawn by six black horses with black plumes on their bridles. The coach was glass-sided with a tall gold-and-silver lantern on each side, a gold railing across the glass, and a gold cockleshell adorning each of the lower sides. The wheel spokes were as elaborately carved as the coach body. On top were two screened domes to dispel the odor of decay. We could see a coffin heaped with flowers resting on a red velvet bier inside the coach. Incongruously, the driver and his helper sitting on the carved and painted high seat were wearing ordinary slacks and windbreakers. No bewigged footman in sight. A dozen cars followed the coach as it slowly made its way along the road. They were hung with funeral wreaths so big that they were nearly buried in flowers. Were they headed to the cemetery or to Lake Avernus and the underworld to see the deceased off on his journey to an unknown destiny?

XXVIII

When we followed Twain's advice and went to Naples, the usual traffic mess became a nightmare as soon as we reached the suburbs. Using the sidewalks as a road was sometimes the best method to get through traffic. Driving in the rest of Italy now appeared to be as orderly as in Switzerland.

Crowding and noise, squalor and ostentation, laundry strung across narrow streets, noisy Vespas and motorbikes, Baroque churches and ugly concrete apartment blocks make up the fabric of a city that cannot have changed much in spirit since the Greeks got there in the eighth century BC. Mark Twain summed up his view of the situation by sniffing: "'See Naples and die.' Well, I do not know that one would necessarily die after merely seeing it, but to attempt to live there might turn out a little differently than expected."

While one is not likely to die in Naples unless you're part of a Mafia gang, a more appropriate motto might be "see Naples and get robbed." We were paranoid when visiting, trying to be as inconspicuous as possible, wearing no watches or jewelry, much in contrast to the Neapolitans, who were often extremely flashy in dress and behavior. The stories about crime were legion, but the sights and setting of the ancient city brought us back many times.

Our first destination was always Spaccanapoli, the area that cuts through old Naples. There we elbowed our way through noisy crowds frequenting bars and shops or carrying on life in the middle of the streets. Our immediate goal was the Sansevero Chapel, to us the most unforgettable sight in the city. The small eighteenth-century church is filled with sculptures, most on the subject of death, loss, and mourning for the departed relatives of the builder. He was the excommunicated Prince Raimondo di Sangro, who dabbled in hydraulic engineering, pyrotechnics, and alchemy, among other esoteric pursuits like finding boys suitable to be *castrati*, forever sopranos, for church and opera performances, when he wasn't overseeing the construction of the chapel.

A few of the sculptures are rather ordinary remembrances of family members, but two of the larger-than-life funerary monuments are rendered in minute, scientific detail, with the hair and fabric looking as if they couldn't possibly have originated in a block of cold marble. The monument to the prince's mother, who died when she was only twenty, shows her as a beautiful young Vestal Virgin covered only by a gossamer veil. She is leaning against a broken monument symbolizing a life cut short. The inscription celebrates her social graces, manners, intellect, charity, devotion, and loyalty. I couldn't imagine a more moving tribute. Another sculpture, dedicated to his father, depicts a man, aided by a spirit, struggling to free himself from an immense net symbolizing sin or ignorance. Each knot and twisted cord is perfect. We wanted to put our fingers through the spaces between the dusty draped marble rope and his contorted body to help free him.

The centerpiece of the chapel is the unforgettable *Cristo Velato*, Veiled Christ, by Giuseppe Sanmartino, carved in 1753. The white deathly cold figure of Christ lies on a mattress set on a dark gray, heavily fringed bier. His head is resting on two pillows. The crown of thorns and the instruments of the passion lie by his feet. The entire body is covered by a transparent shroud that exposes the body while covering it at the same time. The shroud's folds emphasize Christ's death agony, from the veins on the forehead and the concave ribcage, to the marks of nails on hands and feet. We stood silent and alone in our thoughts looking at the suffering so vividly carved in stone. Michelangelo's *Pietà* cannot compare in emotional impact.

When we descended to the lower level of the chapel, a different aspect of death, so fascinating to Neapolitans, confronted us. Two life-size fleshless bodies—a male and a female—composed only of their skulls, bones, arteries, and veins stood in glass cases. The woman is pregnant and has one arm raised menacingly while her eyeballs stare at the onlooker from across the centuries. Supposedly the bodies were injected with a liquid that turned the bones and vascular system to stone. Less mysterious, recent research determined that the vascular systems are composed of wax, wire, and silk draped on the skeletons, although that doesn't relieve their gruesome appearance. In a true demonstration of the spirit of the eighteenth century, some say that the bodies are those of servants who gave up their lives in the name of science. Willingly or not, who knows?

Overwhelmed by these marvels after one visit, we emerged blinking into the bright light with friends Maria and Peter. The street was filled with locals in sweaters and old jeans or tracksuits. Despite warnings from his wife, Peter was dressed as the American he is with a new striped designer polo shirt, expensive running shoes, and khakis. He also had a camera around his neck and his wallet in his back pocket. Suddenly a blur passed by and just as quickly Peter had a scratch on his arm. Glenn saw a man turning a corner at high speed. We stopped and looked around. We couldn't see anything out of the ordinary— wallet and camera were still in place—so we continued on our excursion. The sun rose higher and noon came and passed. We were getting hungry.

"What time is it?"

"Oh my God, my Rolex is gone!!!"

• • •

On the Sybaritic island of Capri we found our dream home, 777 steps above the sea. Perched on a rocky promontory near the town of Anacapri, it overlooks the sparkling Bay of Naples with Vesuvius in the distance. The town is jammed with day-trippers escaping the anarchy of Naples, with the idle rich coming out at night from their luxury hotels, or if they are really lucky, their own villas. The front door to my dream, the Villa San Michele, is so modest it is easily missed by tourists walking along the narrow street. The villa was once owned by an eccentric doctor, Axel Munthe, a Swede from Lapland who was enchanted by the quality of the island light. He was well known both as a society doctor, treating the neurasthenic rich along with Swedish royalty, and for treating the poor who were stricken by cholera, which regularly plagued Naples.

Munthe fell in love with Capri on his first visit as a child and searched for the right place for his home. He found that place in 1887, where there was room for a house open to the sun and wind and the sounds of the sea like a Greek temple. It took him over a half century to complete his home, gardens, and a small bird sanctuary. Stones from one of Emperor Tiberius's villas, a peasant's hut, and a small chapel were incorporated into the complex, adding to the atmosphere. The chapel, painted brilliant white, sits on a steep hillside among umbrella pines and yellow-flowering broom falling away to the cobalt-blue water far below. Standing guard by the chapel entrance is a non-Christian Etruscan sphinx.

The magic began when we opened the villa's door. Although not a spacious house, its atmosphere told us of a man who knew how to fill his life with beauty and mystery. The décor reflects his interests by incorporating simple local crafts with statues and fragments from the Roman era. We shared his passion for this incomparable place when we wandered through the house, admiring the antiquity-filled loggia draped in purple wisteria and the subtropical gardens on the way to the belvedere. There we sat by a crouching Egyptian sphinx overlooking the bay and eternity.

In some horrible punishment from the gods, Munthe developed an eye disease that left him nearly blind and unable to tolerate the bright light he so loved. He returned to dark Sweden where he recounted his life in a quirky autobiography, *The Story of San Michele*. The house and grounds are now owned by the Swedish government, who use it as a cultural center where visiting scholars reside. It was hard to imagine that they could get much work done in such a scenic setting. I would spend the time contemplating the flow of history while the material world dissolved into the numinous infinite.

XXIX

Most rushed tourists heading south go to Pompeii and Herculaneum where they are forced to submit to being herded around like sheep by guides grasping their shepherds' crooks or umbrellas while yelling to their flocks in dozens of competing languages. We were fortunate to be able to avoid the crowds when we went to nearby Villa Oplontis in the modern and crime-ridden town of Torre Annunziata where tourists seldom visited. After we parked our car in a guarded lot next to the police station we could walk at will through the enormous villa with no one to bother us. Never specifically mentioned by ancient writers, it was probably constructed in the first century BC. The villa is on the oldest known map of the Mediterranean world, the *Tabula Peutingeriana* from the fourth century AD, copied by a monk in the thirteenth century. Indicated by a small drawing of a house, it is shown along with little drawings of Herculaneum and Pompeii, the memories of these buried places still lingering after two hundred years. Like its well-known neighbors, the villa was buried in the eruption of Vesuvius in AD 79. Pliny the Younger described the catastrophe: "In the other direction gaped a horrible black cloud torn by sudden bursts of fire in the snake-like flashes. . . . And then came the ashes." The wooden window frames and shutters turned to stone by the enveloping ash attest to this disaster.

A hundred rooms have been excavated. It was impossible for us to take them all in, so we wandered through the cavernous spaces until we were overwhelmed. The Romans turned out cold statues of gods and emperors by the gross. But the frescoes decorating every wealthy homeowner's walls gave us insight into real and warm daily life—their beliefs, hopes, and dreams. The main part of the villa, my idea of fresco-heaven, is covered in near-perfectly preserved brilliantly colored designs representing several different schools of art and the mindset of the times. The colors are as vivid as the day they were painted, with the deep Pompeian red made from cinnabar, red and yellow ocher, malachite green, and cerulean blue. So new-looking we should have been able to turn around to see the painters coming through the echoing halls just back from a "quick coffee" ready to pick up their brushes again.

Painted views of open windows have columns behind which other columns sprout that, in turn, lead to idealized landscapes set further back in the scene. Foliage, fountains, and festoons abound. Illusionistic metal and glass bowls and vases sit on shelves and tables, and birds perch on the edge of water basins. Beautiful gardens with fruit trees and more birds flourish. In contrast, the artists in the other rooms limited themselves to colored squares and rectangles, often in red, black, or white with small idyllic landscapes inserted as part of the scheme, a style popular during the reign of the sober Augustus. Those from the time of Caligula and Nero run riot with a fantasy of panoramic vistas, aerial perspective, architectural framing, and classical scenes of unhappy love. By then more of everything was the painters' goal. It was positively dizzying to speculate how it would be to live in such an overwrought environment, one that was brought to such an abrupt and unforeseen end.

Among the ornamental elements are swags of leaves, wheat stalks, and pomegranates supported by ox skulls. Known as *bucrania*, they are said to signify sacrifice. We often noted the design on churches where so frequently pagan names and themes mix with the Christian overlay. The masks of comedy and tragedy are another frequent motif in the villa, which in the context of this grand home seem to foreshadow its doom, especially since it is often associated with Poppea, Nero's wife until he murdered her by kicking her in the stomach late in pregnancy.

The frescoes featuring human figures were the most appealing; many looked like our neighbors or people on the street. We amused ourselves trying to guess whose ancestor they might have been. "Don't you think that one looks a bit like Signora Salvatore?" we questioned as we stared at the walls. It didn't seem that Romans have changed all that much. Put modern clothes on them and no one would notice that the frescoes were two thousand years old.

Roman-style angels hover in the air, sometimes with delicate transparent or dainty bird wings or sometimes without, all dressed in diaphanous gowns, feet dangling in the void as they effortlessly float. Others have wings as sturdy as those in the Renaissance. Shepherds gaze out over the landscape as they lean on their crooks like Glenn's golfing buddies, resting on one leg with the other bent in front, leaning on their putter waiting for the preceding player to make a move. With few exceptions, such as the figure of Silenus, pictured as old, fat, and bald, humans and gods are in perfect physical condition, the men well-muscled and the women shapely with no excess fat anywhere, all in well-groomed good health. It was pleasant to think that the ancients were all so attractive, but surely many must have looked like us, flab and all.

Taking us back to reality, the domestic quarters demonstrated Roman hygiene with toilets separated by sex and supplied with running water. Most touching was the scratching on a nearby wall done by a Greek slave, "Remember Beryllos." I promised not to forget him.

When we went to Pompeii without guests who only wanted to see the main sights, we entered via a back way leading to the Villa of Mysteries, separated from the main complex by a long path lined with tombs. This villa, ignored by rushed day-trippers, was part of an agricultural complex and still contains a large wine press. Numerous bodies of workmen trapped and turned to stone were found in the rooms where they died. We were attracted by a room filled with larger-than-life figures devoted to the cult of Dionysus. Among many scenes, all painted with a background of Pompeian red, are those of initiates sacrificing a goat, reveling in drunkenness, and unveiling a sacred phallus. Then there is the most enigmatic: a young woman with her head in the lap of an older one, possibly seeking protection from a winged woman who is about to lash her. Scholars have endless happy hours arguing over the meaning, which may have had something to do with marriage rites or the initiation into the cult. Whatever the meaning, we found the scenes distinctly disturbing but fascinating all the same. I always thought the Romans were highly rational with their roads and armies, but it turns out they weren't any more than we are.

• • •

South of Naples, we often followed the narrow road to the lovely towns of Ravello and Positano on the Amalfi Coast, where more of the beautiful and rich relaxed and shopped for handmade sandals and bikinis in the summer season. The towns cling to the hillsides amid wildly twisting roads, lemon groves, grand hotels, and Michelin-starred restaurants. After looking at all the pottery shops and tiny grocery stores we decided that the inhabitants worshipped lemons. They were hanging outside in bouquets, loops, and bunches, made into *limoncello* for an aperitif and painted on tables, pots, and butter dishes. Wagner came to stay in Ravello to compose parts of *Parsifal*; we came to stay to compose ourselves in the spring sunshine when tourists were few. We walked along paths that overlooked the bay. Framed by umbrella pines and lichen-covered statues, the view was still balm to the soul as it had been for the ancients.

The Duomo, the town's cathedral, founded in 1086, is graced with mosaics of fantastic animals and the sinuously curling designs typical of the period, often called *Cosmati* work, after two brothers who popularized the style in medieval Rome. The elaborate layouts consist of strips of small triangles, squares, and other shapes made of red porphyry, green serpentine, gold glass, and black marble in concentric, intertwined, or other geometric motifs set into white marble. The shapes often curve around large disks of colored stone as they move across the surfaces, snake-like. When set into floors, the connecting circles make the paving appear to be in motion, making me want to dance along the otherworldly design to reach a state of grace like Turkish whirling dervishes.

On an earthy note, the large freestanding pulpit is supported by six spiral pillars in turn supported by six anatomically correct lions, three females with three males standing behind them. The females have their tails off to one side, waiting. The priest must have had difficulties keeping the parishioners' attention with this visual competition. The religious iconography escaped us but the quality of the sculpture was superb.

XXX

Conditions in the far south, below the luxurious Amalfi Coast, are vividly described in two old but timeless books, Carlo Levi's *Christ Stopped at Eboli*, published in English in 1947, and Ann Cornelisen's *Torregreca*, published in 1969. Both books explore the culture of the south—its superstitions, poverty, corruption both petty and large, and the enduring efforts of the peasants to survive. *Christ Stopped at Eboli* was made into a film but the area has attracted few writers or filmmakers to help me interpret the vast and often lonely land.

South of Amalfi the *autostrada* narrows and the countryside becomes barren and broken with steep rocky hills. Human sensibilities changed too—when I browsed in shops attached to gas stations, I found weird ceramic liquor bottles shaped like Hitler's and Mussolini's heads. Near Eboli, the town memorialized in the title of Carlo Levi's book, the highway divides. The main road continues south to the toe, another turns toward the sea and Paestum, and a little farther on a third road leads inland to the little-visited interior. The saying "Christ stopped at Eboli" refers to the jumping-off point for the road and railway to the interior, where Christianity never fully overcame superstition and witchcraft.

The coastal road once brought us to a small fishing village where in a timeless scene, an old woman sat leaning against an upturned boat as she stared out to sea. She was little and wrinkled. Her hair was in a wispy bun and she wore widow's black except for a faded apron. We watched her sit, head in hand, motionless like some momentarily idle Penelope awaiting a Ulysses who would never return. Small boats were drawn up on the pebbled beach at the little port, nets drying in the sun. Fishermen whiled away the hours awaiting nightfall when they would be put to sea again with their brilliant acetylene lamps to attract the catch. The town straggled along the seafront. Houses had strings of bright red peppers hanging from eaves or walls to dry in the sun. Men guided mules dragging lumber to a building site. Glenn and I ate in a restaurant where the other customers were a man in a bowtie and his bulldog in his collar, both sitting in chairs enjoying their meal.

Sometimes we drove to Matera on the instep, settled since Neolithic times. Carlo Levi described the countryside, called Lucania in ancient times and Basilicata in more modern, as a limitless wasteland of clay ravines without shadow, where bandits hid in caves. He highlighted the locals' belief in spells and werewolves. An anti-fascist doctor, writer, and painter, Levi was exiled from Turin in the north to this remote and impoverished area in 1935. The provincial capital, Matera, was where he bought quinine and other simple medical supplies to treat the malaria-ridden peasants. It still had its old town made up of hovels carved into the soft yellow-gray volcanic tufa cliff interspersed with Byzantine, Romanesque, and Baroque churches. The surreal sight with its spontaneous architecture, where the roof of one cave house serves as a road, stairway, garden, or terrace of another, reminded us of an Escher drawing.

The living conditions during the time Levi described were horrific due to lack of water and sanitation. Malaria, cholera, and other diseases plagued the peasants living with their animals. By the 1950s the government forced the abandonment of the area due to unhygienic conditions and the collapse of some of the habitations. A more modern town grew up around the deserted historic center, completely atypical for Italy. Restoration began in the 1970s and travelers like us come to stay in the once-abandoned homes, now redone as tourist attractions. The similarity of the old town to sites in Judea has led to several movies filmed on location, most notably in recent times Mel Gibson's *The Passion of The Christ*.

One Easter in Matera (purportedly the sunny south) we nearly froze in a snowstorm while watching the local version of an Easter parade. Late-night torch-lit processions, with mournful music and statues carried from a church with doors featuring skulls and crossbones to the cathedral, imparted a Spanish impression. Like everywhere in Italy, the churches have frescoes and statues of tortured saints: Agatha with her breasts on a dish (she's the patron saint of bell founders), Lucy with her eyes on a dish (patron saint of the blind), and

Sebastian (patron of archers and soldiers) being shot with arrows. He was so lushly imagined in Guido Reni's painting in Rome that he always looked to us as though he was enjoying the experience. Also popular were Lawrence being roasted on a gridiron (patron saint of cooks) and Catherine being broken on a wheel before being beheaded. She is patron of a bewildering assortment of people: potters, spinners, lawyers, and unmarried girls. I found it hard to understand the fondness for these grisly depictions but did have a personal favorite, Peter the Martyr. He always has a meat cleaver neatly buried in his head from one ear to another while looking totally unperturbed. He's a patron of inquisitors and midwives.

• • •

The heel of Italy, where the Ionian and Adriatic Seas meet, was more like Greece and Albania with its sugar cube houses, white and baking in the sun. At the entrance to the small town of Castellaneta we came across a larger-than-life blue-glazed ceramic statue of a man dressed as a sheik welcoming us. We stopped and hopped out of the car to inspect the unexpected sight. It was none other than the original Sheik of Araby: Rudolf Valentino, or as he was known to his friends, Rodolfo Alfonzo Raffaello Piero Filiberto Guglielmi di Valentina d'Antonguolla, born there in 1895. Valentino's string of names reflects the history of the town, settled in the Bronze Age, and successively conquered by Greeks, Romans, Visigoths, Ostrogoths, Byzantines, Longobards, Normans, Swabians, Spanish, and then the French before Italy was united. The statue was erected by the city fathers, Valentino apparently being the single claim to fame for a poor town with such a long history. The town itself, like so many in the area, seemed almost abandoned at midday with shutters tightly closed and only a few dogs sleeping in the dusty streets baking in the sun.

When we turned northeast toward the Adriatic and its blindingly white towns with Norman cathedrals towering over their harbors, we found groves of gigantic olive trees, their size rivaling those in the Garden of Gethsemane, spread out over the rolling hills. Their trunks, some at least twenty feet in circumference, were in fantastic shapes—writhing, hollowed out, and tortured, reflecting the equally dramatic history unfolding alongside them. Olives were originally brought to Italy by the Greeks between the eighth and fifth centuries BC, and these trees could have been some of the original nearly immortal symbols of peace. We easily imagined an ancient philosopher engaged in dialogue with his students under the shade of the small silvery leaves, which could be mistaken for little fishes weaving through bright water as they rustled in the faint breeze.

Between the olive groves the road wound through the countryside where oranges, lemons, and figs flourished in orchards, prickly pears sprouted on top of dry stone walls, and capers and wild fig trees pushed out of cracks. Along the edges of the fields, or scattered about in their midst, small stone structures dotted the landscape. Called *trulli*, they were built by peasants for storage or as ovens. Made of limestone without mortar, they came in cones, igloos, and ziggurats. Around Alberobello the structures grew much larger and often several were connected together to make houses, small hotels, or junky tourist shops. These *trulli* are the fancy models, round with white-tipped conical roofs painted with pagan symbols and a pinnacle topped off with a ball. No one is sure when they were constructed but travel writers love them because they look like they were designed by Disney.

Castel del Monte to the north was always our last, and most enigmatic, stop on a southern circuit before returning to Rome. Completed in 1249, it was built by the Holy Roman Emperor and King of Sicily, Frederick II, the most learned European in that dark, bloody, and unlearned era. He spoke six languages and patronized the arts to a degree not seen since the Roman Empire collapsed. He also translated works from Arabic on falconry and founded the University of Naples when he wasn't fighting for control of the peninsula and parts of Germany. His many castles, found all over the south, followed the typical massive and menacing design of the era but Castel del Monte, modest and mysterious, is unique.

The building sits high on a lonely, windswept wildflower-covered hill. Frederick participated in the Crusades, crowning himself King of Jerusalem, and the Eastern architectural motifs for the Castle may be based on the Dome of the Rock in Jerusalem or the Islamic eight-pointed star in recognition of his ties to the Holy Land. Two stories high, eight-sided with octagons at each corner, it has eight rooms on each floor with an eight-sided courtyard in the center. Some see the design as an ancient symbol of eternity, a sundial or a calendar with light lining up through the windows on the summer and winter solstices. There is speculation that the design served as the basis for Umberto Eco's intricate novel, *The Name of the Rose*. Wandering around the empty rooms, it was easy for us to visualize the story. A mystery in design and function without a moat, a drawbridge, or space for soldiers, it seems unlikely that the castle was made for defensive purposes. Some believe it was built to house a harem, an idea the king picked up while crusading, or that it was a hunting lodge. Poor Frederick died the year after it was completed so in any case he did not get much enjoyment from either languid concubines or fleeing animals.

Whatever its use, we could sit among the wildflowers looking out to a distant sea or back to the empty hulk—the hulk that offered only a few hints of the lives of its long-gone inhabitants. *Sic transit Gloria mundi.*

XXXI

When not on land looking around, opportunities to travel south by sea were available in the summer. We had owned a sailboat in Portland but keeping one in Italy was out of the question because the expense would eat into our precious travel budget. Being a boat owner's friend was a much better arrangement. Glenn received an invitation to help a retired American who had remained in Italy with his British wife. Their French-built 11-meter (36-foot) boat was moored at a marina north of Rome. The friendship started in the manner of most boat owners with an invitation to scrape and paint the *Virginia*'s hull. After demonstrating competence and an ability to accumulate ship's stores from the commissary, Glenn progressed to full crew member on trips along the coast of Italy to Greece, as far as Turkey, and back to Rome. His sea bag, a cherished memento from his navy days, was always ready for sailing season. Since my idea of sailing is making sure that my drink stays level, I was happy to remain at home except for one trip from Turkey as far as the Greek island of Paros where I disembarked and cheerfully hopped a flight home to return to work.

The twice-annual trip to Greece or the reverse always brought pleasures and surprises. On the way they sometimes stopped in Capri or its sister islands to take a break. When they reached Reggio Calabria on the tip of Italy's boot, the sailors could visit the city's single claim to fame, the Riace bronzes. The two Greek life-size hyperrealistic nude warriors, cast in bronze around 450 BC, were lost in a storm on their way to Rome. Bone and glass eyes, silver teeth, and copper lips and nipples speak to the astounding technical proficiency of ancient craftsmen. Like so many finds, they turned up by chance. In 1972 a scuba diver near the hamlet of Riace was diving off the Calabria's Ionian coast. He saw a hand sticking out of the sand. Thinking it might be a corpse from a Mafia hit, he soon found it wasn't flesh after all. It was bronze.

Greeks and Romans alike feared the Straits, where lay the rocks and whirlpools of Scylla and Charybdis, the ancient sailors' terror recounted in the *Odyssey*. Ulysses watched Scylla's whirlpool too closely and lost six men to Charybdis' six voracious heads on the opposite side. Aeneas and his crew sailed the long way around Sicily rather than get caught in the terrifying waters. Passengers sailing with Mark Twain on the way to the Holy Land after leaving Italy weren't worried; some whose geography was shaky rushed on deck during the passage to see what they thought was Sodom and Gomorrah. Rather than the terrible currents that claimed so many mythical and real men of old as they rowed for their lives, the danger for modern sailors like those on the *Virginia* was from passing ships, especially the many ferries going back and forth from Reggio to Sicily.

The time passed quickly on the *Virginia* as it sailed toward Greece or the reverse passage. Mostly there were calm blue seas with occasional sightings of leaping swordfish being chased by fishing boats, or turtles and whale sharks lazing and dolphins frolicking. A fishing line trailed in hopes of a fresh dinner. Sometimes at night, cruise ships ghosted dreamily with all their lights on, like the one Fellini wistfully watched as a child in the autobiographical movie *Amarcord*.

When close to the southern Italian shore the sailors could see the rough terrain of the Aspromonte Massif where bandits and kidnappers hid from their pursuers. At the edge of the sea stood empty castles, monasteries, and churches formerly occupied by medieval overlords, monks, and priests. Also visible was the lonely Doric column at Cape Colonna, marking the last vestige of a temple dedicated to Hera by the Greeks in the sixth century BC when Magna Graecia flourished.

Occasional summer storms, especially when making the long night sail between the toe and the heel across the Ionian Sea, made it difficult to see oncoming freighters. On one stormy trip the haven of a tiny port on the heel beckoned, but the rough seas made it particularly hazardous. The boat's depth meter read zero in the trough of the waves as they shot through a narrow breakwater opening, barely avoiding crashing against rocks.

Rather than the prospect of physical dangers, sometimes the crew was the excitement. On another passage a Latin American feminist along for the ride didn't like the cut of a port captain's jib when he asked her a question about her passport. A raging argument then escalated so far that the *Virginia's* captain feared the boat would be impounded before he could calm the situation.

Once, the sailors nearly lost their anticipated dinner. After they dropped anchor in a small port for the evening, the first mate, Anna, went shopping while Glenn and Captain Bob attached a new grill to the stern railing. They didn't do a good enough job and the large and expensive fish Anna had just purchased from a local fisherman slowly and inexorably slid into the water as the grill tilted. The nearby yachtsmen smirked as they observed the tragedy. But no way were the sailors going to lose their dinner. Using a treble hook, fisherman Glenn snagged the fish from the bottom of the harbor. After tightening up the grill they slapped the fish back on the coals. Oily harbor water added perfect seasoning to the meal. Thus, another day passed in the always-unpredictable adventure of sailing.

• • •

As every boat owner knows, nothing involving a boat ever goes according to plan. This truism was amply demonstrated on one voyage. A following sea (waves headed in the same direction as the boat) lapped against the *Virginia's* stern the first night out on one voyage to Corfu where the boat would be moored during the summer. It was windless. The lights of Anzio glittered in the near distance. Captain Bob, taking the first watch, was motoring through the fishing boats and their nets off Anzio. Bored, he decided to pump out the bilge while Anna and Glenn slept before taking their turns on watch. Sometime after finishing his chore, Bob put the boat on autopilot for a minute to descend into the cabin for a quick look at the chart. But as he put a foot on the stairway, he saw a pending disaster instead.

Glenn awoke when he heard the captain shouting for Anna and then for him when she, sound asleep, did not answer. After he jumped into his sea boots, always ready beside his bunk in the bow, Glenn saw that he was ankle deep in rapidly rising water. Rushing to the stern through the main salon, he noted that the rubber lifeboat, *gommone*, used as a tender or in case of emergency, was still neatly stowed under the table, not yet inflated.

"Shall I get out the *gommone*?" Glenn shouted up the ladder to the deck.

"No. Check the sea cocks!!" was the response from the captain.

Water was gushing, although there was no evidence that the boat had hit anything. Quickly, Glenn checked the sea cocks, valves for draining wastewater from the galley and toilet out through the hull. All were closed. Next he lifted the engine cover. Water was spurting everywhere. Bob turned off the engine. Glenn tried to start the electric bilge pump. Nothing happened. Bob began to work the manual pump on deck. That action somehow made it possible for Glenn, still below deck, to start the electric pump. But he had to hold the starter button in the "on" position to keep it working.

When the first mate awoke and stepped into the water sloshing around her bunk, she went into a panic, crying to Glenn:

"We're going to drown, we're going to drown!!"

"Don't worry, we're close to Anzio."

"We're going on the rocks!!"

"We're close, but not too close."

"I can't swim that far!!"

"Don't worry, we won't sink!"

First responder Glenn distracted her from her terror by assigning her to the electric pump. "Keep your finger on the pump" was the mantra. Keeping her finger on the electric pump switch finally started to produce results, and the water level began to drop. The immediate emergency was over but Anna remained terrified. She climbed up to the deck for a few minutes of fresh air before going below again to keep pumping. She began to vomit, overcome with the fear of drowning. Between the gagging, she gasped, "I can't breathe!" Glenn held her head over the rail, telling her that she must be breathing because he could hear her.

Glenn went back below to work on the engine, checking for broken hoses or a cracked block, while the captain steered the drifting *Virginia* away from nearby rocks, boats, and fishing nets. The problem was revealed as the water level slowly dropped: when the captain had finished pumping the bilge, a strong following sea created a siphoning effect. This effect sucked water backward through the pump, filled the bilge, and then began to fill the cabin as well.

Dawn came and along with it calm on deck and below. The sodden sailors limped into a small port for several days' rest, to make basic engine repairs and to attempt to dry out the cabin and the food stowed under the floorboards. But for the rest of the voyage every time they opened a can there was a surprise— the labels had all floated off.

The next port was Capri, where the sailors moored amid gigantic yachts. When it came time to leave, the anchor couldn't be weighed. The struggle to get the boat free furnished hours of entertainment for rich yachtsmen and their crews and guests, who idly watched while holding their drinks, cell phones, and cigarettes. With no success in sight, Captain Bob gave up and hired a diver. The diver found that the anchor had become hooked to a heavy naval anchor chain lying on the bottom of the long and narrow harbor. After the boat floated free, they slunk out of port. But problems with the half-drowned electrical system continued, causing repeated stops to undertake ever more repairs. Despite the near miss, Captain Bob, ever the optimist, preferred to trust Mercury and life jackets rather than inflating the *gommone* until they reached Corfu, where it was used to go ashore from their anchorage.

The passage was days behind schedule and I was getting lonely at home. Finally I got a call from Brindisi that Glenn was going to be getting on the overnight train on his way home. The next day the sailor appeared with his sea bag full of laundry slung over his shoulder, his watch cap perched on his head, and a lot of stubble on his face. A month later Glenn related his fraught adventure, knowing by that time it was too late for me to fret about his safety.

The story cured me of wanting to venture into a small boat on the open sea, but it didn't deter Glenn at all.

XXXII

Although it had been part of the Bourbon Kingdom of the Two Sicilies before the unification of Italy, there is really only one Sicily. Glenn had sailed near enough to see smoking Mount Etna, but neither of us had set foot on the island. The little I knew derived from three old movies. *Salvatore Giuliano*, directed by Francesco Rossi in 1961, recounts the life and death of a murderous bandit. He was backed by a resurgent and well-organized Mafia springing back to life when the US Army moved north after the invasion of Sicily during World War II. Giuliano's one claim to fame beyond murder was his desire to have Sicily annexed to the United States. The scene in the film of his ancient mother heavily draped in black keening over the dead body of her son is straight out of the *Iliad*. The film, in black and white, perfectly captures the harsh light of the south, so strong that even if it were photographed in color the white buildings and black shadows would not look any different.

A second film, Antonioni's 1960 effort, *L'Avventura*, is a tale of ennui among the bored rich. It was so long and obscure I never quite finished watching it despite the evocative settings of rocky volcanic islets, faded *palazzi*, and towns with large Baroque churches and small populations.

More enlightening was *The Leopard*, taken from the book by Giuseppe de Lampedusa. Burt Lancaster is perfect as the exhausted landowning prince staring at the inevitable end of the Bourbon Kingdom and his own way of life as Italian unification comes to pass. The film vividly illustrates the sense of fatalism pervading the *mezzogiorno*. The word, meaning the middle of the day, signifies the hot, dry, and impoverished south where the burning sun always shines as if it was noontime and nothing fundamental ever really seems to change.

One Easter we decided it was time to see the island that makes up the football kicked by the boot of the mainland geographically—and if some politicians in the north had their way—politically, too. Our friends Peter and Maria, who were soon to leave Italy to return to Virginia, had found a tour that looked interesting. Rather than drive ourselves some other time, we joined them as a last chance to celebrate our friendship before their departure.

Like everyone else, my first thought about Sicily was the Mafia, in this case the Cosa Nostra rather than other branches like the Camorra in Naples, or the Sacred Crown and 'Ndrangheta in the far south of the mainland. Begun as armed groups hired by landowners for protection in the nineteenth century, when Sicily was moving from feudalism to become a reluctant part of Italy, the thugs gradually evolved into powerful clans. Eventually these clans would hold a vise-like grip on the economy through protection rackets, extortion, sabotage, drugs, prostitution, and murder. The political establishment regularly wavered between denunciation and complicity. Allegations that politicians and even the Church accepted funding or agreed to look the other way appeared in the media from time to time.

When we checked into our hotel in Palermo, the manager warned us about the dangers of walking in the adjacent botanic gardens at any time or the city in the evening. We immediately began to worry that our visit was a mistake. But all was peaceful and, instead of being mugged or shot, I received an unexpected souvenir courtesy of some careless mafioso. One morning as I strolled along the nearby waterfront watching the ferry from Naples disgorge its passengers, I glimpsed a gold chain-link bracelet lying on the sidewalk. It winked at me in the sun. I looked both ways to see if some guy with a gun was heading my way. The walkway remained empty. I winked back and shamelessly picked it up.

The Renaissance skipped the city, where massive medieval Norman churches and civic buildings competed for our attention with those of curly eighteenth-century Baroque design. The city's atmosphere expressed poverty and decay. Vacant lots with neighboring buildings propped up by timbers looked like they were remnants of unrepaired damage from bombings in the War. *Palazzi* were crumbling and the opera house was shuttered tight. The shops didn't look prosperous either. If there was the equivalent of Rome's Via

Condotti or Milan's Via Montenapoleone, we didn't see it. But we did find a derivation of the pastel men's suits on display in the wedding expo in Rome. Every men's clothing shop had a display window filled with Easter colors—powder blue, maroon, rose, and yellow models. Maria and I tried to get Peter and Glenn to try them on but they balked.

My main interest in this dubious city was the glory of the Palatine Chapel, the intimate space used for worship by the Norman kings. The chapel, built between 1130 and 1140, is a dazzling riot of gold and other colored glass tiles, inlaid semiprecious stones, and marble. Although the stories told in mosaic are standard Christian, much of the work was done by Muslim craftsmen, experts in such work, and ironic in today's world. I couldn't imagine what it must have been like when priests chanted, candles flickered, and incense clouded the air, with Christ looming over the altar and the worshippers. Truly otherworldly.

The most famous site is the cathedral in Monreale, a few miles above the city. Another product of the ruling Normans' desire to glorify themselves and God, the twelfth-century mosaics in the enormous cathedral are so overwhelming that I couldn't take it all in, let alone attempt to have an understanding. The gleaming gold walls are made of millions of *tesserae*, tiny glass tiles, depicting the Christian message. The magical small squares brought the flat depictions of ceremonies, blessings, and stories to life as I watched the light slowly moving across their surfaces.

In the apse a gigantic Jesus calmly gives a blessing to his flock while portraits of saints and tales of sinners and miracles cover every other surface high above the floor. The scenes provide a mystical feeling in the soft light to all who gaze at them, even in our skeptical age. With their dreamy scenes of idealized life, pornographic activity, and strange religious rites, Roman frescos and mosaics entertain me, but Christian mosaics always pull me into their otherworldly glow. I think of the clever minds that designed them, the humble hands that set the tiles, and the endless procession of souls who were instructed, inspired, or comforted through the ages.

Although the work, commissioned by the Norman kings, doesn't have the power of the more vivid and original Byzantine work in Ravenna done some six centuries earlier, many of the scenes in the cathedral were compelling. God creating the heavens and earth, Christ healing the leper (whose disease is represented by black squares), Noah's sons rushing to cover up their drunken, naked father, and the Apostles standing around a table listening to Christ (although one is looking at the food—a decapitated chicken resting in a bowl). It was impossible to see them all. The unlettered worshippers must have been in awe (and suffering from stiff necks from looking upward).

But what would they have thought if they were around some centuries later to see what is called the Chapel of the Crucified Christ, the most egregious example of Baroque architecture I could imagine, with dizzying twisted columns and riotous designs? The ensemble is a clashing and exhausting mash-up of inlaid stones, bas-reliefs, and statues. While timeless Bible stories grace the nave and speak to all, the chapel, which alternately repelled and fascinated me, focused solely on giving new meaning to glorifying man's cleverness over the divine.

• • •

Our tour group assembled a few days after we arrived in Palermo. When we four climbed on the bus, we found that instead of our usual group of Italians or mixed United Nations employees, we were with a group of American tourists. Many of our group had Sicilian roots—the descendants of the millions of starving poor who had emigrated from the island to the Americas in the nineteenth and early twentieth centuries. Our fellow travelers talked among each other about what villages their families had left. As we were driving along the south coast, one of the elderly men asked the driver to take a short detour up a country road. The driver obliged. The man became agitated and moved to the front steps of the bus. We came to a junction near a small town. "Stop right here!" he shouted. When the door opened he jumped out next to a field filled with tomato plants heavy with ripening fruit. He dropped to his hands and knees, kissing the ground his father had trod upon before desperation drove him to a passage in steerage to the New World. We all applauded as our emotional traveling companion climbed back on the bus while wiping tears from his cheeks.

As I looked out the bus window and then at the itinerary, I could see that the weeklong tour wouldn't be long enough. It would take many more trips and much more intensive reading to begin to understand the cultural web woven by the island's many invaders. We saw an island whose inhabitants mixed Greek temples and theatres, Roman ruins, Arab-inspired food and place names, Norman mosaic work, and Baroque churches, all presided over by a smoking volcano. It wasn't a soft scene like Tuscany but it was one that would call us back in the future.

Not so far from the memorable tomato field, we arrived at the fourth-century Roman villa at Casale. The house with its baths covered about thirty-five thousand square feet. The floors were covered with stone mosaics, the colors mellow with age. The contrast between the shimmering biblical themes of the Norman churches and those decorating the floors in the villa was striking. Horses race around the Circus Maximus with the Aventine Hill in the background, cupids fish or drive carts pulled by ostriches, and musicians play. Gods and goddesses cavort, and exotic animals are hunted and carted off to the arenas to meet gladiators who triumph over them. Lovers embrace as always. But we knew there was truly nothing new under the Southern sun when we came to the gymnasium. There, mosaics show women wearing bikinis exercising with dumbbells, getting ready to throw a discus, racing, and playing with a ball. A referee awaits contest winners with a crown and olive branch in her hands. An early Olympic contest or another strange ritual? A guide said they were ladies of easy virtue and that they soon lost their bikinis after the ceremony. Whoever they were they were fitter than I was.

The floors were a lesson in the vast difference of concerns between the pagans and Christians—the earthy and earthly pagan life of the here and now that changed over time into a Christian wait for heavenly reward. As our tour continued, it appeared that the Sicilians had managed to combine the two concepts of good living.

Among their many delights was food. The Greeks were devoted to Dionysus, and the cult of the grape remains exemplified by vast acreages. The Romans brought rich recipes such as those with goose, and the Byzantines arrived with a fondness for sweet and sour. But it was the Arabs whose culture had an indelible culinary influence. They came with apricots, sugar, citrus fruit, melons, rice, saffron, raisins, nutmeg, cloves, pepper, and cinnamon. Much later, Spaniards arrived with cocoa, prickly pear, corn, turkey, and tomatoes. The resulting opulent cuisine reflects the mixture of the inhabitants and their food preferences, a mélange of flavors different from the rest of Italy.

Food, always food! A scene in *The Leopard* describes a banquet featuring a mountain of pasta, a *Timballo di Maccheroni*. In his novel *The Viceroys*, written in 1894, Federico de Roberto describes the monastic life: "The monks lived according to the motto 'Good food and drink, not forgetting a little gentle exercise.'" The maxim was an apt reflection of our own guiding principle for life in Italy.

But what is a week to sample such a variety? The answer was "not enough," but we did our best to try the food reserved only for the wealthy (and monks) in the past, but now on display in every restaurant, delicatessen, and market. We started the day with juice from the blood-red Sanguinello or Tarocco oranges with our coffee and *cornetto*, already anticipating lunch and dinner, where the menu always listed so many dishes of interest that we would never have time to try them all.

When it was time for a real meal, *spaghetti al nero di seppia*, pasta with calamari ink sauce, *involtini di pesce spada*, stuffed swordfish rolls, and dozens of other seafood dishes were on the menu. There was salty *bottarga*, pressed tuna roe, grated on linguine or served as a slice with oil, parsley, garlic, and peperoncino. We tried *pasta con le sarde*—sardines, fennel, saffron, anchovies, raisins, and pine nuts served over *bucatini* pasta, a bit exotic for our tastes but reflective of the island's history. I liked it but the mixture didn't make it into

Glenn's repertoire—a rare event. There was also *pasta alla norma*, with a sauce full of eggplant, from the Sicilian province of Catania—not the town of Norma south of Rome where we had eaten the doubtful meal after visiting the gardens at Ninfa.

Caponata, also on every menu, is a mixture of eggplant, onion, celery, green olives, tomatoes, sugar, vinegar, and capers. It was also another acquired taste, with the sweet-sour mixture lingering on our tongues. Better was the *insalata di finocchio e arance*, a salad composed of oranges, fennel, onions, walnuts, olive oil, and sea salt from vast salt pans on the coastline. Glenn made some notes to try it out when we got back to Rome, although he skipped the walnuts.

Dessert included fragrant jasmine gelato, the high-calorie *cannoli* full of ricotta, jewel-bright candied fruit, chocolate, and sugar, or *cassata*, a cake with similar ingredients and covered with a layer of almond paste. Sicilians seemed to have a real sweet tooth, with pastry shops filled with these and other marzipan treats for Easter, including the lambs similar to those regularly presented by our landlord and passed on to my staff.

Between meals we continued our tour with visits to Greek temple sites dotting the landscape, some surrounded by wildflowers so thick and tall we watched caretakers hack through them with machetes to make pathways. The deserted monuments were bathed in a hot glare while the nearby deep blue sea sparkled as if diamonds had been sprinkled over a field of sapphires. How the Greeks must have enjoyed life in times of peace as they worshipped Zeus, Demeter, and Persephone and watched the plays of Aeschylus and Euripides in the theatre in Taormina!

The city, set high on a hill, is a glory of Sicily. It was beloved by hedonistic nineteenth-century English travelers for its own beauty and that of the young men and women whom they photographed in provocative poses. We stood on the balcony of our hotel room looking at the sea; at smoking, snow-capped Mt. Etna; and at the Greek theatre where performances are still mounted. The main shopping street was lined with art galleries, confectioners, and designer shops doing trade with the Easter visitors eager to part with their money. Intoxicated by the sights, we considered buying a painting depicting a mother in Sicilian costume with her young daughter leaning against her. They were taking a short break next to an old fountain before filling their water jugs. The scene was kitsch but the artist had captured what we wanted to see as an ideal Italy, nothing like real peasant life. The canvas was large, expensive, and overly sentimental. We didn't buy it, settling instead for a small scene of fishermen and the sea, more a memory of Glenn's sailing experience and the real sights we had seen as we traveled along Italy's long coastline. Yet the rejected picture has remained in our minds' eye—a scene of warmth, family love, and contentment. What more could be asked of life?

XXXIII

Despite my generous leave and holiday time it wasn't always possible to travel to Sicily or northern Italy for a week. Etruria, now the regions of Tuscany, Umbria, and Lazio, was always a pleasant destination for easy day trips and weekends to view the remnants of other long-gone inhabitants of Italy; in this case, the Etruscans. We saw the countryside as yet another Italian dreamscape, with golden sunflowers and wheat, fields of brilliant red poppies, olive groves, vineyards laden with grapes in the fall, and hill towns scattered across the landscape. Sections of aqueducts, deserted castles, and isolated monasteries embellished the timeless scenery.

A lingering haze gave distant hills a blue tint and a mystical and immaterial feeling in summer and fall. Lanes leading to villas and farmhouses were lined with cypress and umbrella pines, sometimes in a repeating design of two exclamation-point cypresses separated by a round-topped pine. As we drove along back roads through volcanic hills full of caves, I always expected to round a bend and see an Etruscan standing beside the road silently watching us.

In *Etruscan Places*, D. H. Lawrence not only wrote about myriad tombs but also about the multitude of wildflowers in the fields. We, too, were enchanted by their variety and color. The bright red poppies were scattered everywhere. Some fields looked as though a can of scarlet paint had been carelessly spilled by the gods onto ripening wheat. Sleek horses and foals grazed knee deep in pastures filled with this brilliant beauty. In springtime, poppies, daisies, grape hyacinth, anemones, asphodel, and primrose made a Persian carpet of red, white, yellow, blue, and purple under olive trees with their tiny white blossoms.

During the summer, ubiquitous commercially grown sunflowers added more color to the landscape. Their yellow faces beamed happiness at us from fields along the roads between hill towns. In the fall, the round-domed Etruscan tombs near Cerveteri were covered with wild cyclamen that looked like pink shooting stars.

The most frequent word applied to Etruscans is "mysterious," although we looked at their artifacts in every area museum, along with the Villa Giulia in Rome. They flourished between the eighth and second century BC until the Romans finished them off, destroying their temples, writings, and the language itself. Several hundred words have been deciphered from inscriptions in stone or metal, but they're mostly on the order of: "Here lies . . ." Unfortunately, the interesting information like their recipes, stories, and poetry are lost to the ages.

Judging by what's left of their civilization, Etruscans had their slaves spend most of their energy on tomb building. The tombs were filled with painted Greek or locally made vases in Greek design, bronzes, elaborate gold jewelry, small boxes for ashes, and full-size sarcophagi with representations of their occupants sculpted on the lid and classical scenes on the base. Modern tomb robbers armed with long rods to poke into the earth still find and loot underground tombs on their nighttime excursions. Fake or real artifacts were always available in the Porta Portese flea market.

We saw hundreds of tombs carved out of tufa or dug into the ground. They came in many styles—columbaria, houses, temples with columns, and freestanding houses called *dado*, meaning "dice" or "cube." Cliffs are honeycombed with tombs. The soft rock has steps to the entrances, but many now lead nowhere but the infinite as the stone has crumbled away with time. We had a sense of unease when we climbed up for the view, thinking of the dead long since disappeared from their resting site.

Everywhere we went there were empty sarcophagi—in church courtyards or interiors, resting on top of city walls, sitting in museums, or decorating local city halls. Some had melted with time, the carved faces and bodies indistinct, while others were so well preserved that they looked like they were fresh from the stonemason's yard. The deceased are often resting semi-upright and look as if they expect to be served another glass of wine at any moment. Some lie flat on their backs with their feet propped up on pillows, presaging the carvings on Crusader tombs. A man often wears a flower garland around his neck and holds a libation bowl, a *patera*, with a raised center that some say represents Earth floating in the heavens. Sometimes the dead man holds a scroll with his destiny inscribed. The woman might be holding a flower garland or a mirror. They often have an expression reminiscent of early Greek statues and the Mona Lisa, an "archaic smile."

What were they thinking? Was the afterlife as pleasant as predicted when the augurs read the livers of sacrificed animals? Whatever their thoughts, they looked at peace to us. In contrast to the empty rock tombs, broken and open to the sky, the contented faces on the sarcophagi made me feel better about the future. If they were enjoying it, why wouldn't I be able to have the same experience—although not too soon, please Mercury.

• • •

Using Lawrence's book as a guide, we developed an easy route for explorations in Etruria, especially if we had guests who were bored or overwhelmed with Rome's never-ending sights. Cerveteri, up the Via Aurelia and full of traffic since 241 BC, was the first stop. Our usual goal was the nearby necropolis of Banditaccia with over a thousand family-sized tombs mimicking the cities of the living in design and layout. The structures with rock bases and rounded tops (*tumuli*) are now covered with grasses and flowers. We strolled along ruts from ancient funeral wagons worn into the soft rock roads dividing the tombs. We looked in the dark, empty structures, some partly filled with water, their contents long ago looted or carried off to museums, while wondering about long-forgotten lives and if local inhabitants had Etruscan genes.

One of the most beautiful relics, the so-called Sarcophagus of the Newlyweds, is now in the Villa Giulia Museum in Rome. Sculpted in terra-cotta in the sixth century BC, the couple recline on a couch, with an extra pillow for the husband's elbow. Their slight smiles, as though they were pleased with themselves, are directed at us. His right arm curls protectively around her shoulder as she rests against him. Both have their hair done in Rastafarian-like dreadlocks hanging neatly over their shoulders. I couldn't help wondering if they died young or the sarcophagus was prepared as a wedding present to be used in the far future. Not my kind of wedding gift but, in comparison with all the drooping angels and weeping families so common in cemeteries from the time of the Greeks and Romans to the present, this sarcophagus offered a much happier perspective on life—past, present, and future.

The stop after Cerveteri was usually Tarquinia, the home of two of the first Roman kings, Tarquinius Priscus and the wonderfully named Tarquinius Superbus, and some good restaurants. Near the town is a constellation of about two hundred underground painted tombs. The colorful frescoes covering the tomb walls and ceilings are fully deserving of the appellation "mysterious," with their absence of any perspective and little sense of proportion. The style is almost Egyptian, but less sophisticated with their lack of detail.

Presumably the paintings represent Etruscan life or what they believed awaited the dead. Men frequently have bronzed skin, recognizing lives spent outdoors, while women are pale. Some are blondes, said to signify that they were prostitutes hired for the evening party (and maybe that blondes have more fun). If life was really like this, the Etruscans spent their leisure time lying on couches drinking and listening to musicians playing the double flute or lyre while watching jugglers or dancers. Naked servants bring cups to sustain the merrymakers. Dancers whirl, holding their hands in such contorted positions they reminded us of temple dancers in Southeast Asia. Flower garlands hanging on the walls behind the merrymakers add to the festive air. Sometimes a figure is shown presenting an egg to another, a symbol of rebirth as in our Easter eggs. Sporting events are illustrated, complete with referees for wrestling matches. Fishermen with birds flying above and dolphins below decorate some walls. For funerary art, most of the scenes were a lot more fun than medieval depictions of poor sinners consigned to the flames of hell in the hereafter.

But there were are also a few disturbing elements, at least in the way the Etruscans sent the dead off on their journey to eternity: two men using a stick to whack a third who is on his hands and knees, and a man with a sack over his head surrounded by attacking dogs, blood dripping. One tomb features two men having sex as an angry bull approaches. On the other side of the wall a man has sex with a woman as she reclines on the back of another man, this time with a bull resting while gazing directly at us. What could it mean? No one knows, but we enjoyed speculating as we did with so many other sights.

• • •

We sometimes visited Pitigliano, which suddenly appeared on its clifftop when we approached from the deep valley far below. The cliff, golden colored, is honeycombed with Etruscan tombs. Those along the steep road with its hairpin turns leading us to the *centro storico* are still in use, but not for the dead. When their wooden doors were open, we could see wine or oil in wicker-encased jugs, or a three-wheeled *Ape* or a baby-sized *Cinquecento* automobile, instead of sarcophagi. Although the town is living and the buildings and Renaissance-era aqueduct are the same lovely color as the clifftop, we found it forbidding, with what appeared to be empty windows staring out over the valley below. At one time the town was called "Little Jerusalem" in recognition of its large Jewish population, but after the ravages of war only a few were left. Even though the inhabitants bustled on their daily rounds like all towns, it had a melancholy aspect, a reminder of many horrors. We seldom lingered.

Narrow tracks cut deeply into the rock connecting Sovana and Pitigliano. Some of these Etruscan tracks are forty feet deep and so narrow that in places they resemble tunnels. Just wide enough for hikers, they are always deep in mossy shadows, and overhung with creepers, leaning trees, and other vegetation, making them damp on even the hottest days of summer. Another place where an Etruscan could pop up, although the only people we saw were like us, dressed in jeans and T-shirts on day hikes.

Sovana, a picturesque hamlet of about a hundred residents, was a good place for lunch. The tiny town, once powerful, is now somnolent. Named as a bishop's seat in the fifth century, it was reputedly the hometown of Gregory VII, one of the most powerful medieval popes. Over the centuries it was owned by everyone from the Etruscans to the Medicis. They all left bits and pieces of walls, coats of arms, churches, and a castle before malaria killed off the populace. Not much is left except for an interesting church, a few restaurants with lovely terraces for dining, and a workshop specializing in high-quality copies of Etruscan pottery. What always made the town an anomaly to us was the extra wide and single street, which on a hot, dusty afternoon looked like the perfect place for a Wild West shootout, Etruscans versus Romans, or maybe the Aldobrandeschi clan versus the Orsini.

Our usual last stop was for a post-lunch stroll across an arched Roman bridge built on an Etruscan foundation high above a river. The narrow pathway brought us to a fortified early medieval abbey remodeled into a castle in the twelfth century. It changed hands numerous times before ending up in the possession of the Church. They used it as a customs house at the border of the Vatican States until their temporal power ended with Italian reunification and the area became the Province of Lazio. It now houses a small museum where we could look at a few dusty objects and contemplate how the procession of Etruscans, Romans, medieval clans, Renaissance condottieri, and princes of the Church faded into travelers on day trips like us.

XXXIV

There was always more to see in Etruria. Many weekends were spent slowly poking around the countryside with no particular goal in mind. Something interesting always turned up. We stopped in small inns for lunch where lamb chops were thrown directly on a grate over an open fire to sizzle while pasta was cooking. When we stayed in country hotels in isolated locations, we looked for a spot to lie on our backs in the evenings, so we could watch the millions of stars silently shining on Italy.

It seemed as though a small town was perched on every hilltop, and like the waves in the ocean, each one was different yet the same. Many towns are so small they are called *frazioni*, meaning hamlets or fractions of another larger town. Most are built with dark volcanic tufa but some glow golden or rose colored in the sun. All but the smallest have a church at the top and a castle in various states of decay or restoration. Occasionally we could see huge cranes towering over walls as the town fathers slowly repaired the damage from war and time. Within the walls life went on, although sometimes only because a family restored their ancestor's home for holiday use after moving to Rome. We could peek through open windows and doors to see remodeled kitchens, new televisions, and other indications of modern times. A delectable smell of pasta sauce came from kitchen windows and from unpretentious shops where fresh lasagna was made for those who didn't have time to cook. Other little shops had flowers, vegetables, and fruit carefully arranged in their miniscule storefronts sandwiched between offices of the various political parties or those of the *pompe funebri*, undertakers. Artisans busied themselves making picture frames, mending shoes, or painting ceramics. Butcher shops and dry cleaners bustled with business. Women bought knitting supplies for their winter projects in the *merceria*, which also sold thread, hosiery, and shoulder pads for the home seamstress.

But despite the liveliness in the towns, the unstoppable passage of time was evident. Large death notices were pasted on walls between fading and tattered posters for the small circuses that had come to town in past years. In winter, old men wearing heavy sweaters under their jackets along with scarves and caps followed the sun as it passed around the piazza. They were living sundials as they moved like dozing cats while they smoked and discussed the latest political crises or how the hometown soccer team was faring.

In the Maremma, the western part of Etruria, long-horned white cattle graze or are herded by cowboys like in the Wild West. One town, Scansano, attracted us for its red wine with a hint of blackberry adding to its aroma. Morellino di Scansano is produced mostly from Sangiovese grapes like Vino Nobile di Montepulciano and Brunello di Montalcino. Some wine writers describe the taste of Morellino as including chocolate, cherries, and plums. Not being sufficiently sophisticated to discern these finer points, we sniffed and tasted only the flavor of its namesake, *mora*, Italian for blackberry. A case or so often found its way into the cool storage room on the ground level of our apartment building.

Montemerano, filled with flowers at every doorstep, balcony, and window, was another stop on some outings. One of Italy's most beautiful towns, we loved it for the delightful Madonna della Gattaiola, the Madonna of the Cat Door. This beautiful Renaissance virgin was painted on a door sometime in the 1400s, and moved to the church at an unknown date. She wears a red top and dark blue skirt and stands with her hand on her heart, her head inclined modestly, with a richly designed orange screen behind her. But in a complete contrast to the heavenly scene, a round hole near the blue gown's hem has been chiseled out. This serves as an entry for the church cat to pursue any available mice lurking in the nave, another nice combination of the sacred and profane.

We have a friend who lives in another town an hour north of Rome. Her address is on Via Etrusca, a perfect name for visualizing the continuing Etruscan influence. The little town, set high on a cliff, has no tourist attractions but is kept alive by commuters. Our friend lives in an ancient row house thought to be between four to six centuries old, the year the building was actually erected long forgotten. Ancient oak beams still support the floors below and the roof above. The stone walls are over a foot thick, with room for niches to display her many artworks collected around the world. At night, when there are only glowing embers in the fireplace and the red wine bottle is emptied to the dregs, the silence is as complete as it must have been when her home was new. A few streetlights shine over empty narrow streets, through arches supporting the age-old structures, and the closed shutters in our bedroom. But early in the morning we hear the Vespa engines being turned on. As we walk the few blocks to the small shopping street early in the morning, the bar owner is firing up the espresso maker. The *giornalaio* puts up his racks with the day's papers featuring the latest political scandal, while fruit and flower vendors pull up their metal shutters and move their wares outside their shops. Life begins anew as commuters head for the train station and their jobs in Rome while we plan another day of sightseeing.

• • •

It was Ferragosto, the big summer holiday. We went to Bevagna, near Assisi for the festivities. We arrived about noon in the small town. By that time the morning traffic had cleared out and the local policeman, looking smart in his summer whites, had nothing to do. He stood near the town wall bored and without a care, swinging his whistle in one hand and idly scratching his crotch with the other.

We booked a hotel in a palazzo dating to 1710 constructed from an earlier building erected between the fourteenth and seventeenth centuries on Roman ruins. The hotel enclosed a garden with a disused well surrounded by bright red geraniums in pots. Heavy purple wisteria flowers hung from vines winding over the walls. The lintel over the side door caught our attention. The owners told us that it was a fragment of marble from Roman times carved with an arrangement of ox skulls and swags hanging between the horns, the *bucrania* we had seen in the Villa Oplontis frescoes. In the morning we lazily studied the eighteenth-century frescoed ceilings in our room while listening to the bells and chanting from the monastery across the narrow street. The words carved over its door were "*ora et labore*," pray and work, the Benedictines' motto.

The town was alive with other music too. A lovely little theatre, inserted into the Gothic Palazzo dei Consoli in 1886 for the good citizens' pleasure, was opened in the early afternoon for a piano concert including Mussorgsky's *Pictures at an Exhibition*. This theatre was typical of those in many small towns with its painted curtain showing romantically imagined ancient scenes and three tiers of boxes surrounding the main floor, everything done up in red velvet. We helped fill the seats along with other appreciative holidaymakers. Afterward, we all poured out into the streets to start the early evening *passeggiata*, strolling and chatting in preparation for the big event later in the evening.

The piazza was filled with white plastic chairs facing a temporary stage fronting the twelfth-century Church of St. Michael the Archangel, severely damaged in one of the many earthquakes that periodically shake Italy. Above the rounded arch over the carved main doorway was St. Michael himself, his raised sword attacking a winged devil. Below St. Michael were carved ox skulls hung with garlands, the *bucrania* motif again.

We occupied two of the chairs for a free concert of arias sung by winners of a recent regional contest. They were accompanied by a thirty-piece orchestra, which punctuated the vocal selections with overtures by that enthusiastic Italian composer, Rossini, always good for creating a happy mood. The crowd went wild as each young artist took the stage. Music soared into the warm and starry night sky. Maybe it was the setting and the youthful eagerness that created the spell, but their performances outranked anything we'd heard in Rome or Verona.

This event was followed by a community dinner with a local band playing music from the sixties and seventies and everyone talking, eating, and dancing no matter what their age. A *nonna* danced with her grand or great-grandchildren, young men drank too much wine, young women giggled and flirted, and the middle-aged talked and watched.

We lingered a long time before returning to Rome that evening.

XXXV

One of my favorite small churches is The Madonna del Bagno, nestled inconspicuously near the main road to Deruta. It is famous for painted ceramic tiles affixed to the walls by worshippers in thanks to the Virgin for rescue from near death. In the seventeenth century, an itinerant merchant, one Christopher the Mercer, found a ceramic fragment on the ground. Fourteen years earlier, a Franciscan monk placed the little piece, painted with a primitive image of the Madonna and Child, in an oak tree for safekeeping. The story continues: The merchant returned the fragment to its place and prayed to the image to save his dying wife, whom he did not expect to see alive again. When he returned home from his travels he found her not just alive but "out of bed in perfect health, sweeping the floors." This housekeeping miracle gave rise to the fragment's veneration.

The church, built to commemorate the event, became a magnet for ceramic artisans from nearby Deruta, a center for majolica-decorated terra-cotta tableware and decorative items since the Middle Ages. The local inhabitants expressed gratitude for their own personal miracles by making ceramic ex-votos, thanking the Madonna for her aid in times of danger. The original image of Madonna and Child, painted on a broken cup, still survives. Its depiction of a small Madonna holding a large, fat Child who in turn holds a globe is a delight to all mothers. The colors are simple blue and yellow on a white background, still the predominant colors on traditional Deruta ceramics.

Glazed terra-cotta plaques made by local artisans eventually covered the small church's walls. These tiles had a partial miracle of their own: about two hundred were stolen in 1980, but about half were recovered to grace the walls again. There are now about six hundred plaques covering every aspect of human misery averted by the Madonna's grace. Although varying in shape they all have a disaster scene, the Madonna and Child in a tree, the initials

"P.G.R.," sometimes written out as *Per Grazia Ricevuta*, for grace received, and sometimes the year. Folk art in style, they depict scenes of people being miraculously saved from falls off roofs or out of trees, attack by animals or bandits, or floods, fire, lightning, earthquakes, plague, and the dangers of childbirth. While most plaques are from the seventeenth and eighteenth centuries, reflecting the rigors of life in those times, more contemporaneous disasters are also pictured, especially auto accidents, and one memorializing a man who survived imprisonment in World War II. They all are colorful and hopeful, but also a reminder that whatever can go wrong will go wrong. I thought about commissioning one to celebrate my brush with death when I fell in the Rome subway or our avoidance of jail after the crash with the Carabinieri.

• • •

"*Cigni, cigni . . . cigni!*" "Swans, swans . . . swans!" the little boy cried out as he carried his pail holding yesterday's bread to feed them. They and their cygnets were gliding around the mill pond's still waters, leaving small wakes trailing behind. We were staying at a hotel converted from a fifteenth-century water mill built on a little island and over a small river, the Clitunno. The grounds were the scene of a wedding reception, with guests dining in the garden by candlelight until daybreak sent them home. We looked at the romantic scene from our window above the garden and river while hoping the newlyweds' life would continue to be as idyllic as it appeared that evening.

Floodlit and reflected in the mill pond, a small temple rests among cypress trees on a hill above a short stretch of ancient and worn stones of the Via Flaminia. This golden-hued stone building is the lovely Tempietto di Clitunno. It would look at home anywhere in the ancient Roman world with its porch fronted by four columns, two carved in a spiral design and two with fish scales. A pilaster on each end completes the entrance. They all have the beautiful acanthus leaf Corinthian capitals supporting the classic entablature and pediment. But instead of sculpted Roman gods, the pediment has a cross, grapevines, and flowers with a Latin inscription, "Holy God of the Angels Who Made the Resurrection" on the architrave. Faint shadows of frescoes depicting Christ and Saints Peter and Paul still decorate the interior. Like many ancient buildings, the argument as to the temple's origin goes on. One school decided that it is a true Roman temple turned into a church in the third or fourth century; another dated it to the eighth century, positing that it was made from remnants of the classical temples surrounding the nearby lake, the Fonte di Clitunno.

Whatever its origins, we were as enchanted with the temple as so many others have been. Andrea Palladio, the great Renaissance architect, as well as the French classical painters Poussin and Lorrain, were enamored. Lord Byron waxed lyrical when he visited in 1816. In *Childe Harold's Pilgrimage* he tells us: "And on thy happy shore a Temple still/Of small and delicate proportion, keeps . . ."

The setting, so redolent of the past, always made me mindful of the continuity that so characterizes Italy and how I was part of that endless procession, pagan and Christian, rich and poor, native and foreign, who all shared in its eternal beauty. The temple remains my most beloved Italian place—a site where I could become one with those who came before.

The mill pond is fed by the river Clitunno coming from the nearby Fonte, a lake famous in antiquity. In Roman times the sacred lake's clear waters were used to bathe white cattle before they were sacrificed to the gods. Caligula consulted a nearby oracle. I wondered if the mad emperor posed a question before he made his horse a senator—and what advice the seer might have offered. Pliny the Younger, in his letters written about AD 108, described hills covered with cypress and the lake itself surrounded by ash and poplar trees, its cold water so clear that one could count coins tossed in for luck. Earthquakes changed the landscape in AD 446 and the sacred site was abandoned to time.

While the Tempietto is not much visited, the lake is still in existence, although now surrounded by a dusty parking lot instead of temples. Tour buses by the dozens disgorge their passengers to sit under the surrounding poplar trees, enjoy their picnics, and buy souvenirs, the past out of mind.

• • •

On another adventure we were lost at midnight somewhere around Lago di Vico, one of several volcanic lakes north of Rome. The road home was the Via Cassia, a Roman consular road built before 187 BC, still heavily traveled in its modern guise. The festival at Ronciglione, a small city known for its modern Pre-Lent carnival, was finished.

The infamous Carnival of Rome is no more except for children wearing cute costumes, some paper confetti (not the almonds from Sulmona) tossed around, and fried pastries called *frappe* temptingly displayed in bakeries. The original event, celebrated since ancient times, was an orgy with Romans wearing costumes and masks to disguise themselves and their behavior. Renowned for food, fireworks, and riderless horse races where the animals had girths studded with nails to make them run faster, it also featured elderly Jews being forced to run through the streets and criminals being marched or dragged along while they were tortured to death. These entertainments presumably kept Romans from thinking about their own unhappy lives and the pending dreary Lenten season. Berlioz celebrated it in his *Roman Carnival Overture* and many painters idealized the festival, but Ronciglione, like the Carnival we had visited in Viareggio on the west coast south of Genoa, had civilized it into a happy celebration for all.

In our somewhat more enlightened time, floats pulled by local farmers' tractors carried towering *papier mâché* figures lampooning politicians, both Italian and American, sometimes obscenely. Little children dressed up as ladybugs, pirates, and princesses. Adults in elaborate Renaissance costumes bowed and waved as they proudly walked along the route. Riderless horses, minus the ancient abuse, clattered on cobblestones. Everyone waited for the show's climax, the Carabinieri. Dressed in their best Napoleonic-era costumes, they raced tall horses through narrow, steep streets over and over to the crowd's cheers and applause as they stood close to the buildings or sat on balconies throwing candy and confetti everywhere.

After a long, wine-infused dinner it was late, cold, and foggy. It was time to go, but the traffic leaving town was the typical nightmare. We couldn't find the Via Cassia. As usual, the few road markers didn't offer much more than "*tutti le direzione*," and we could hardly see them anyway. Our map was utterly useless in the fog. Lost, we stopped near the middle of a road, hoping that no one would run into us while we puzzled over what to do next. We were surrounded by empty cornfields, their rotting stalks barely visible beyond the ditch line. As we sat in the quiet of the night we thought we could hear faint singing. It gradually became louder and louder. A glowing light appeared. Out of the fog, a tractor pulling a float slowly emerged. A dozen people were hanging on, partying with wine and song, not willing to give up on their festivities. They stopped by our car to point the way before slowly disappearing back into the fog as if they had never existed at all. Yet another surreal scene Fellini would have adored.

PART THREE

STILL DAYDREAMING

XXXVI

Six more years of our Italian life passed. Time hadn't marched. Instead it was insidious, sliding by so silently we hardly noticed. On a trip to the shrine at Delphi in Greece I had asked the Oracle about how long I would remain in Rome. She didn't answer. But I needn't have been concerned about predictions: time alone made the decision when my contract was finally extended for six months beyond the mandatory retirement age of sixty-two.

We thought a long time about remaining in Europe but most of our friends had departed for new assignments far away. Kathryn and Steve were building a house on an island near Seattle. My mother was aging in Vancouver where she had lived for many years after my father died. She was near her childhood home and my relatives, but I hadn't seen her often enough. We weren't Europeans who could easily visit their home countries to keep in touch. After balancing the equation we made our decision: it was time to leave Rome and Europe rather than buy a *pied à terre* in the south of France or Spain as had many European friends. We flew to Seattle to find a home for our retirement. When we returned I worked to finish projects and began to turn work over to the man who was to replace me.

Some months later our rental contract expired. Movers came to pack up our lives again. We gave the plants on the terrace to friends. It was a sad day to see our olive tree lowered on ropes down to the ground and a waiting van. We moved to a temporary apartment on the Aventine Hill to house-sit. It was two blocks from the hotel where we had stayed on our first arrival in Rome thirteen years previously. Our lives had come full circle.

The year inevitably came to an end, along with the century and the millennium. To welcome the new millennium and mourn our departure, we had a celebratory dinner on the thirty-first of December with Mark and Sophia, who were to leave soon for Santiago, Chile. We dined on delights from Volpetti:

an enormous platter of Italian cheeses: *pecorino, caciocavallo, parmigiano,* and *gorgonzola.* They were ringed by cured meat: *salami, bresaola, prosciutto,* and *coppa.* Enough to feed us for a week. Adding to the selection, we started to empty the pantry by bringing out two old cans of *cassoulet,* remainders from a trip to France. After the gut-busting meal, we walked up to the orange garden at the top of the Aventine Hill. There we joined the crowd drinking champagne and watching fireworks shooting up over St. Peter's, a splendid way to mark so many transitions.

New Year's Day was warm and sunny. We stood on the steps leading up to the Campidoglio listening to a police band play snappy marches and watching a marathon. Spectators dressed in togas handed out bottled water to the runners as they rushed by. We ate our New Year's lunch outdoors surrounded by women in their furs, despite the warmth, chatting away on their *telefonini* while sharing their meal with husbands or lovers. We were subdued, rummaging through our memories and knowing that the movers would soon come again, this time to put a final end to our Roman holiday. Marcus Aurelius said: "Either thou dost continue in this life and that is it . . . or thou dost retire. . . . Be therefore of good comfort." Despite this advice, I wasn't at all in good cheer while considering what to do with the rest of my life.

• • •

For our last venture into the countryside we drove to Tuscania for a final look at history, and to Tarquinia, where we had found a workshop with a large selection of garden pots in all sizes. Tuscania, one of our favorites, is an easy drive east from the Via Aurelia, the coastal road, through olive groves and past a long section of Roman aqueduct still standing in lonely isolation in a field of wheat and poppies. The town has been in existence since at least the seventh century BC, mythically founded by Aeneas's son, Ascanius, in reality by the Etruscans as everywhere else in this part of the world. It sits on the Roman Via Clodia, a newish road built around AD 43. The city, not much different from many in the area, is still encircled with high walls of red-gold stone. But unexpectedly, the two main churches are far outside these walls, having been built long before the population shrank by half due to the Black Death in the fourteenth century. The plague necessitated that smaller defensive walls be built closer to the surviving inhabitants.

It was the two marooned eighth-century churches partly made of fragments from Etruscan and Roman times that always lured us to the town. These primitive monuments reflect the complexities of Italian history, like so many of the churches that drew us to contemplation of our past, present, and future. One, Santa Maria Maggiore, built over a pagan temple, has an extraordinary medieval Madonna and Child placed over the main entrance. The Madonna looks middle-aged, with a long chin, nothing like the Renaissance painters depicted her. Her feet hang into empty space free from the physical world. The Child's exophthalmic eyes with pinhole pupils pop out of his head. She is holding him but he also seems to be tied to her with a narrow rope, a practice we were told was common in medieval times. Despite this, the primitive carving gives the impression that he is about to slide off Mary's lap. The rest of the façade is made of a conglomeration of saints, and bits and pieces from Roman and maybe Etruscan times. Adding to the jumble is a Green Man—a face with vines growing out of the mouth, a pagan symbol of rebirth. Jackdaws circle the bell tower in front of the church making their chuffing sound, a noise that I always associate with cold winter days in cold hill towns. Inside the church, there are photos of the terrible damage inflicted by an earthquake in 1971. Above the triumphal arch we were greeted by a graphic and un-Etruscan Renaissance fresco of the Last Judgment, with the righteous zipping off to heaven and sinners being consigned to hell.

The other church, San Pietro, rests high on the site of the ancient Etruscan acropolis, farther from town. Flanked by two freestanding medieval towers on one side and the ancient bishop's palace across a greensward, the deserted church presents an even more lonely aspect, so far from the community it once served. The noisy jackdaws are always abundant here, too, as if they are drawn to emptiness or desolation. Empty it was on this last visit, except for a wizened caretaker, hunched and dressed in black, who collected an insignificant amount for the entrance fee. The damp and cold interior has a mosaic Cosmati-designed floor, a large circle burned into the floor where one of the bells was said to be cast, and Etruscan sarcophagi tucked away in a side aisle. Stone seats used by the medieval worshippers for community meetings beckon the visitor to rest.

Before leaving we descended the worn stairs to the crypt where Franco Zeffirelli filmed part of the Oscar-winning movie *Romeo and Juliet*. The crypt's ceiling is supported by a forest of pillars, each one a different style. Medieval workers must have dragged them to the site from fallen Roman temples, caring not for aesthetic harmony. Now the results of their labors are reduced to a background for films.

Just outside the complex we looked through the sculptures in a workshop specializing in reproductions of Etruscan statues and models of their tombs, all made in the local volcanic tufa. There stood a perfect memento: a triangular piece about two feet high carved with doors and steps leading to the unknown, so reminiscent of the tombs carved into the living rock high up on nearby cliffs. It now resides in our garden growing a coat of moss and dwarf ferns—maybe not so dissimilar to those that grew in the Etruscan hillsides in ancient times. I see it as a reflection of the permanence of human longing for a future afterlife.

After, we drove on to the terra-cotta workshop across from the cemetery in Tarquinia, the home of the painted underground tombs we had visited so many times. The owners tied up their barking and lunging Doberman and invited us into the area where they designed and manufactured the pots. As we watched, the red clay was pounded by hand into molds. After drying, the clay would be fired at 1,000 degrees Centigrade, causing the minerals to fuse into frost-resistant garden décor. We bought several large lemon pots so loved by Italians, who set them beside garden paths or on terraces where they last for more than a century. The pots brighten up the scene at all seasons with lemons' glossy green leaves, fragrant white flowers, and yellow fruit. Our pots have a less Italian life.

They now hold Japanese maples after the lemon trees we hopefully planted died in the cool and rainy Northwest climate.

As our last day approached I tossed some coins into the Trevi Fountain to ensure a return to Rome. We had parties with friends. A colleague gave me a small gold pendant depicting Medusa, another of the ancient Roman symbols for protection. Members of my staff chipped in and presented me with a painting of the fountain, a constant reminder of its ability to influence a return to Rome. True to form, our prior landlord came to my office with gifts so we would remember him, and then, after a screaming argument which I lost (again), he stuck us with several hundred dollars of bills for items never mentioned in the rental contract. Yes, we still remember him. As if we could ever forget.

The movers, with their heavy rolls of paper, finished packing our pots and a few other items while we sat on the sofa thinking of all the adventures we had, good and bad. For every misstep over the years there had been many more unforgettably marvelous moments. So many places still to visit, so many dishes and wines still awaited us, so many episodes of history we had not yet learned. But it is impossible to know all of Italy with its overabundance of everything. We were fortunate to have the opportunities we had and to let the country enrich our lives.

The last items that went into the crate were a reliquary and an old model sailboat with battered sails, chipped paint on the hull, and little flags flying on its mast. The boat was Glenn's, a reminder of his sailing adventures. An antique carved wood reliquary, also showing its age with the gilding flaking off, was my souvenir in memory of all the churches visited. It was a bust of an obscure saint, Anastasia, who may or may not have actually existed. She had a little window in her chest for a bone or hank of hair. We only knew about her because she was honored in an old church at the base of the Palatine Hill, not far from the apartment where we were now staying for the last month.

When the movers finished and our suitcases were packed, Glenn and I walked up to the orange garden at the top of the hill for a last look. It was only a month previously we had watched the fireworks bursting over Saint Peter's Basilica bringing in the new millennium. Easygoing Glenn was looking forward to gardening on our large lot, puttering with home maintenance, taking some cooking lessons, and enjoying not having to put up with the occasional annoyances of his Roman domestic life. I was already moping over losing my job, my continent, and my friends—my *dolce vita*. How would I make friends—no one was interested when we moved to DC. Why would they be now? What would I do? Relieving Glenn of household chores would take up time—but then what? I had hundreds of unread books on a list but sitting all the time wasn't good. Should I take up the cooking again when I knew Glenn didn't want to relinquish his domain? Try to find a job? Annoy Kathryn with unwanted advice? I felt as though my brain was atrophying already.

We flew "home," arriving in February, the depressed season of Seattle's bipolar weather. Our household goods showed up unharmed. We found a place for everything in a house much larger than our apartment, although small by American standards. When we unpacked I found a souvenir from a visit to the Holy Land, an ancient Roman glass bottle fragment purchased from an antique dealer. It was filled with ash. When I picked it up the ash fell out along with a small bone. The bone found its niche when we opened Saint Anastasia's back door and gently placed it in her bosom so it shows through the little glass window in front.

Glenn, able to adjust to nearly anything, happily perused Italian cookbooks, perfecting his skills in between working in the garden and fixing up our house, just as he planned. But reverse culture shock struck me again. My business suits, fancy scarfs, shoe collection, and briefcase began to molder with disuse. I looked at the clock first thing every morning. If it said six, it was three in the afternoon in Rome. By this time long lunches were concluding with *digestivi*. I sat and looked out the window thinking the same life thoughts I had before leaving Rome, still caught between past and future. In between, I traveled to Vancouver to see my mother, whose health suddenly declined. It was as if she was waiting for us to return before she gave up. Two weeks after her ninety-fifth birthday and only five months after we had returned, she died. Efforts to reconcile with our new life became more difficult.

Not long after, the phone rang early one morning: Would I come back to Rome for five months, with a short detour in Nairobi, to help plan an office reorganization? YES! Glenn encouraged me, knowing that it would provide a transition to help me adjust. I was back again in Rome, but as he already knew, it couldn't be the same. I was now a traveler rather than an expatriate—an outsider, although one who could still enjoy a little of the sweet life. Glenn flew over to visit a few times. We went to an exhibition of early Italian photographs at the Palazzo Poli, the backdrop for the Trevi Fountain. Someone had left a drapery pulled aside and a window open on the second floor. The sound of water attracted my attention. I walked to the window and looked out. I was above the fountain with Neptune; the gushing waters surrounded by tourists were below me. I knew that no matter how many coins I threw in the basin, my Italian intermezzo was complete.

To soothe my wounded soul, Glenn took me on a cruise from Bali to Oman—the lust to travel continuing unabated. And it helped. The pleasant days slid by with no need to do anything but watch the flying fish and take prearranged tours when we docked in a port. Maybe being a tourist wasn't so bad after all.

I was finished with Rome but WFP and I continued to connect with some consultant work accomplished long distance. Then an offer came for travel to Haiti, the Dominican Republic, and Nicaragua. Out came a suitcase and I was on my way again. A few other offers arrived, but it was truly time to embrace retirement and another type of travel, one where a case of Italian wine, a pot, or a painting couldn't easily be thrown in the car trunk to be carried home.

XXXVII

Since we left Italy no moss has gathered on either of us. Many model boats from other parts of the world have joined the old sailboat we brought home from Rome. Mercury has been good to me—a traveling life has taken me in *tutti le direzione*: from Port-au-Prince to Petropavlovsk, Madang to Mumbai, Ubud to Ushuaia, and Zanzibar to Zermatt relatively unscathed. In between trips, volunteering in the arts and civic organizations gives me many rewards and new friends. The Internet keeps me up to date with events in Italy and our many friends now scattered far away. I still check Rome's weather every morning and I return to the city almost every year.

There is a quote often attributed to Mark Twain: "Throw off the bowlines, sail away from the safe harbor. Catch the trade winds in your sails, explore, dream, discover." Wise advice. I often reflect on my fortune to grow from a tourist who has a brief chance to look at other cultures from a distance, to a traveler who has the time to step back, look, and consider, to an expatriate with the rarely granted opportunity to live a sweet life, the *dolce vita*, in Italy. The United Nations granted me opportunities to meet many dedicated UN workers and to travel far afield.

No matter where I have laid my head, my heart remains in Italy with its abiding connection to the past—a connection that pulls me back ever again to revel in the country's ancient glories and landscapes. When we return we see that Rome maintains a steady state—some sights crumble but new ones are discovered and old ones repaired. Some of the investigations into political corruption and the Mafia begun on our first stay are still in the headlines, but the papers also have stories about new music and art. Porta Portese is now mostly filled with junk from China, the Russian refugees have been replaced with those from Africa and the Middle East, but the Via Condotti still has its marvels of Italian design and craftsmanship. The old count has passed on to his reward but other friends remain. The Testaccio market has been moved to a new and more sanitary location. The subway has been expanded slightly, but many other improvements built for the millennium celebrations have deteriorated in the endless cycle of decay and renewal that make Rome what it is. My Italian is deteriorating too. When I last ordered a glass of prosecco, pronouncing it pro-sek-ko, the barman looked at me without comprehension. Then a light went on: "Ah—pro-SAY-ko," he said before pouring me a generous glass of bubbly for free.

The government regularly totters but everyone carries on, talking with their hands, words being insufficient to carry the full meaning. The mayor of Rome is criticized for the dirt and trash, but the Roman fountains still sparkle. The ground floor of our first apartment building is now covered in graffiti, but the monumental buildings in EUR have been restored with signage describing their architectural history. Cypresses and umbrella pines still shade the ancient monuments. Restaurants continue to await our pleasure, although the longtime waiters who always remembered our favorite dishes have retired.

No city could ever hold more attraction for me. As long as I travel, my road will always lead back to Rome and outward to the rest of Italy.

Sometimes when I open up a suitcase after a voyage I remember the contents from my first visit to Europe, now long ago. Our luggage was lost. The divorce was proceeding when the missing case turned up. I opened it and found a rotting cheese, bought in Amsterdam and then forgotten, perfuming my underwear. It was a metaphor for the marriage. Now what falls out of my luggage are pleasant mementos. My most treasured is an Italian etching. Set in a silvery frame, an archaic figure holding a staff gazes out over a landscape furnished with a bent and contorted olive tree, two cypresses, and a grove of umbrella pines. A bay surrounded by hills is in the distance. He must be a traveler, like me, contemplating what is beyond those hills. I'm hoping to acquire a lot more happy mementos like the picture before God ultimately pulls me off the baggage carousel of life.

When the west wind blows over the waters of Puget Sound in front of our home, I can hear train whistles from the track below. Sometimes it's the slow Amtrak train to Chicago or to Vancouver, Canada. More often, it is the rumble of long freight trains going who knows where, carrying wheat, apples, cars, and everything else. Freighters coming from Asia glide by on the waters. In summer, cruise ships on their way to Alaska pass by in the late afternoon. They return at four in the morning a week later with their lights lit up like the ship Fellini longed to be on in *Amarcord*. In the quiet of the night I can hear the faint chugging sound of a tugboat engine as it pulls a barge. In early fall mornings the foghorn makes its mournful sound over the blanket of moisture covering the water. Sometimes I can hear new Boeing jets on their test runs flying low near our home. They are not yet dressed in the livery of Korean, United, Turkish, British, or Ethiopian Airlines. Recently, though, we saw one for Alitalia, already decorated with the Italian colors of green, white and red.

These sounds amplify my eternal restlessness and my quest to see more of the world. Marcus Aurelius said that time was like a river's swift currents, made up of events that are soon carried away and replaced by others. What better description of travel with its too-swift passing of sights and people who are then supplanted by those from the next town or country?

I don't want Mercury to have to work too hard. But the globe is still spinning and I haven't yet reached my angle of repose. Ever more *Lonely Planet* and other guidebooks fill up our bookshelves while we decide where to go next. Being naturally phototropic, sunny spots like the Galápagos or a cruise with stops in Suriname and French Guyana are on the list. But should we wait until fall to return to Italy—my heart's true home? I'm looking at flight schedules right now.

The author and her husband on a return trip to Rome in 2014.

ACKNOWLEDGMENTS

Special thanks to my wonderful editor, Tricia Parker. And without the dedication of many helpers I would not have been able to tell this story. In particular, my daughter, Kathryn Schipper, who spent hours reading and rereading before making suggestions. My writers' group—Ginny Buzzell, Teresa Hayden, and Bev Austin—gave invaluable assistance. Readers Carol Schwennesen, Dorothy Johnson, Page Gorud, and Dora Furniss, among many others, also had lots of good ideas.

Thank you all so very much.